Embodying Sociology: Retrospect, Progress and Prospects

A selection of previous *Sociological Review* Monographs

Theorizing Museums*
ed. Sharon Macdonald and Gordon Fyfe
Consumption Matters*
eds Stephen Edgell, Kevin Hetherington and Alan Warde
Ideas of Difference*
eds Kevin Hetherington and Rolland Munro
The Laws of the Markets*
ed. Michael Callon
Actor Network Theory and After*
eds John Law and John Hassard
Whose Europe? The Turn Towards Democracy*
eds Dennis Smith and Sue Wright
Renewing Class Analysis*
eds Rosemary Cromptom, Fiona Devine, Mike Savage and John Scott
Reading Bourdieu on Society and Culture*
ed. Bridget Fowler
The Consumption of Mass*
ed. Nick Lee and Rolland Munro
The Age of Anxiety: Conspiracy Theory and the Human Sciences*
eds Jane Parish and Martin Parker
Utopia and Organization*
ed. Martin Parker
Emotions and Sociology*
ed. Jack Barbalet
Masculinity and Men's Lifestyle Magazines*
ed. Bethan Benwell
Nature Performed: Environment, Culture and Performance*
eds Bronislaw Szerszynski, Wallace Heim and Claire Waterton
After Habermas: New Perspectives on the Public Sphere*
eds Nick Crossley and John Michael Roberts
Feminism After Bourdieu*
eds Lisa Adkins and Beverley Skeggs
Contemporary Organization Theory*
eds Campbell Jones and Rolland Munro
A New Sociology of Work*
eds Lynne Pettinger, Jane Parry, Rebecca Taylor and Miriam Glucksmann
Against Automobility*
eds Steffen Böhm, Campbell Jones, Chris Land and Matthew Paterson
Sports Mega-Events: Social Scientific Analyses of a Global Phenomenon*
eds John Horne and Wolfram Manzenreiter

*Available from Marston Book Services, PO Box 270, Abingdon, Oxon OX14 4YW

The Sociological Review Monographs

Since 1958 *The Sociological Review* has established a tradition of publishing Monographs on issues of general sociological interest. The Monograph is an edited book length collection of research papers which is published and distributed in association with Blackwell Publishing. We are keen to receive innovative collections of work in sociology and related disciplines with a particular emphasis on exploring empirical materials and theoretical frameworks which are currently under-developed. If you wish to discuss ideas for a Monograph then please contact the Monographs Editor, Rolland Munro, at *The Sociological Review*, Keele University, Newcastle-under-Lyme, North Staffordshire, ST5 5BG.

Embodying Sociology: Retrospect, Progress and Prospects

Edited by Chris Shilling

Blackwell Publishing/The Sociological Review

BLACKWELL PUBLISHING
350 Main Street, Malden, MA 02148-5020, USA
9600 Garsington Road, Oxford OX4 2DQ, UK
550 Swanston Street, Carlton, Victoria 3053, Australia

Every effort has been made to trace copyright holders. The authors apologise for any errors or omissions and would be grateful to be notified of any corrections that should be incorporated in the next edition or reprint of this volume.

First published in 2007 by Blackwell Publishing Ltd

Library of Congress Cataloging-in-Publication Data

Embodying sociology : retrospect, progress, and prospects / edited by Chris Shilling. – 1st ed.
p. cm. – (Sociological review monographs)
Includes bibliographical references and index.
ISBN-13: 978-1-4051-6794-9 (pbk.)
ISBN-10: 1-4051-6794-7 (pbk.)
1. Body, Human–Social aspects. I. Shilling, Chris.

HM636.E43 2007
306.4–dc22

2006100540

A catalogue record for this title is available from the British Library

Set by SNP Best-set Typesetter Ltd, Hong Kong

Printed and bound in the United Kingdom by Page Brothers, Norwich

The publisher's policy is to use permanent paper from mills that operate a sustainable forestry policy, and which has been manufactured from pulp processed using acid-free and elementary chlorine-free practices. Furthermore, the publisher ensures that the text paper and cover board used have met acceptable environmental accreditation standards.

For further information on Blackwell Publishing, visit our website:
http://www.blackwellpublishing.com

Contents

Sociology and the body: classical traditions and new agendas 1
Chris Shilling

Culture, technologies and bodies: the technological Utopia of living forever 19
Bryan S. Turner

Somatic elements in social conflict 37
Donald N. Levine

Reclaiming women's bodies: Colonialist trope or critical epistemology? 50
Kathy Davis

Fieldwork embodied 65
Judith Okely

Researching embodiment by way of 'body techniques' 80
Nick Crossley

Breathing like a soldier: culture incarnate 95
Brian Lande

Listening to the dancer's body 109
Anna Aalten

Embodied knowledge in glassblowing: the experience of meaning and the struggle towards proficiency 126
Erin O'Connor

Vulnerable/dangerous bodies? The trials and tribulations of sleep 142
Simon J. Williams

Notes on Contributors 156

Name Index 159

Subject Index 164

Sociology and the body: classical traditions and new agendas

Chris Shilling

Abstract

Reflecting developments in consumer culture, the politics of social movements, public health policy, and medical technologies, the body has since the early 1980s become one of the most popular and contested areas of academic study. The following discussion introduces this monograph by positioning the body as a subject within contemporary sociology, accounting for the discipline's historical ambivalence towards embodiment in terms of sociology's foundations, and tracing the factors behind the 'rise of the body' across the social sciences and humanities. Having examined the background to the subject, I then explore how this volume makes three main contributions towards the ongoing embodiment of the discipline. The chapters that follow explicate and build *sociologically* upon the legacy of sociological, feminist and anthropological approaches towards embodiment. They also apply these approaches to issues such as conflict, health, cultural differences and technology that have become increasingly important in contemporary society. Finally, they demonstrate the empirical utility of taking embodiment seriously via a series of case-studies that focus on *body pedagogics*. In so doing, they outline a new approach towards the body, able to combine a concern with social power, cultural (re)production, lived experience and physical change.

Key words: The rise of the body, classical sociology, unstable bodies, body pedagogics.

Introduction

Throughout the history of sociology, particular subjects and issues have risen and fallen as matters of disciplinary interest in line with developments in industrial and 'post-industrial' societies, the varying strengths of national traditions of thought, the rise of social movements representing groups previously marginalized within society, and the vagaries of intellectual fashion. Over the last few decades, however, there has also been a widely acknowledged fragmentation of the discipline, and an increasing amnesia with respect to the sociological tradition (Shilling & Mellor, 2001). In this context, the contemporary preoccupation with all things bodily might appear to represent the latest fad among sociologists more interested in the transient features of consumer culture than in the problems of social and moral order that traditionally preoccupied the most influential figures within the discipline. There are several reasons, though, why such an interpretation of the rise of the body within sociology would be mistaken.

To begin with, the explosion of publications on the body that occurred from the early 1980s was not confined to sociology but spread across much of the social sciences and humanities. It seemed that this focus was not only a manifestation of academics coming to grips with a 'new' subject, but reflected issues that were fundamental to a variety of disciplines (e.g. Featherstone, 1982; Hirst & Woolley, 1982; Turner, 1984; Suleiman, 1986; Bynum, 1987; Lakoff, 1987; Feder, Naddaff & Tazi, 1989). Second, instead of simply becoming another subdisciplinary area of sociology, 'embodiment' was used to interrogate some of the longstanding nature/culture, action/structure, and subject/object dualisms that the discipline had wrestled with since its beginnings. 'The body' was also increasingly addressed as an essential issue in general theoretical works stretching across such areas as feminism, pragmatism, and realism (eg, Butler, 1990; Young, 1990; Joas, 1996; Archer, 2000). Third, while the body had not necessarily featured as a major subject in the writings of the founding figures of the discipline, there were a number of attempts to excavate the 'hidden heritage' or 'absent-presence' of classical writings on the subject which revealed how the organic foundations of our human being, social identities and relationships had an important, if sometimes implicit, place in the discipline's foundations (eg, Turner, 1991; Shilling, 1993). Finally, the rise of the body in sociology should be seen in the context of those scientific advances in *in vitro* fertilization, transplant surgery, genetic engineering and stem cell research that have the potential to alter our view of the 'species being' of the discipline's human subject matter. In dealing with these issues, sociological analyses of embodiment were exploring developments which might necessitate revisions in some of the fundamental presuppositions and parameters of the discipline.

Thus, far from residing on the outer fringes of the sociological imagination, or seeking merely to add yet another exotic subject to sociology's taste for cultural novelty and diversity, recent sociological concern with embodiment manifests a continuity with certain aspects of the discipline's roots and is part of far wider academic trends. Contemporary writings on the subject were not, however, in a position simply to recover neglected but comprehensive sociological perspectives on embodiment. There was a reason why existing sociological work could be described as having treated the organic nature of human beings as an absent-presence.

Flesh on the sociological terrain

Issues involving embodiment were not missing from the theories, narratives and methodological concerns associated with the foundations of the discipline, but sociology's major subject matter focused on the development of, and the structures and processes pertaining to, *industrial society*. As such it did not have as its central focus the anthropological concern with the relationship between nature and culture in which the ritual enculturation and classification of the body imparted boundaries, identities and sacred meanings to the tribal collectivity and the individual. Furthermore, in addressing itself to the longstanding and hugely influential Hobbesian 'problem of order' (of how social life could exist without degenerating into a constant 'war of all against all') sociology sought to carve out for itself a disciplinary identity that was clearly distinct from that of its competitors.

Comte's concern to establish sociology as 'social physics', for example, sought to build on yet also be more advanced than 'the simpler departments of science' (concerned with chemical, physical and biological phenomenon) in its aim of disclosing the natural laws of human progress (Levine, 1995). Durkheim's efforts to establish sociology as a reputable science established the discipline's proper subject matter as 'social facts' that were radically different from the subject matter of psychology or biology (Durkheim, 1982 [1895]). Simmel also identified the distinctive subject matter of sociology as existing above the level of the individual, and focused on the form and content of *social interaction*. Simmel's work was characterized by an enduring concern with 'the problem of personality', but for him it was the geometry, solidity and durability of sociations or interactions that imparted to society its complexity and consistency (Simmel, 1971 [1908a,b]). Even when the discipline focused unambiguously on individuals, it made a central distinction between action that was voluntaristic and socially meaningful, and action that was driven by habit or the affects and was more animalistic in its nature, and claimed for itself an interest in the former (for example, Weber, 1968). Again, this enabled sociology to be differentiated from existing disciplines that excluded social phenomena from their core conceptual apparatus and explanatory frameworks.

Sociology's determination to carve out its foundations from the bedrock of society, rather than from the materials that furnished other sciences, steered the subject away from attributing too much explicit attention to embodiment. Nevertheless this emphasis on social phenomena did not rule out a concern with the bodily being of social actors or with the corporeal consequences of social structures. Thus, Comte emphasized that humans are both intelligent and inherently emotional and active, and suggested that the impulse to act comes from the heart (Aron, 1965: 88). It is when embodied emotion and intellect support each other in promoting social feelings and acts that we can witness the emergence of society and a moral culture (Comte, 1853). Furthermore, for all his concern to establish sociology as a distinctive discipline and a subject that rested at the pinnacle of human knowledge, Comte was regarded as one of the leading theorists of biology in nineteenth century France and this was reflected in the biological analogies that pervaded his sociology (Heilbron, 1995: 246). His key concepts of crisis, organization, consensus and organic system all came from biological and medical models, while he viewed civilization as being like the human body, capable of spontaneously repairing itself (Pickering, 1993: 208).

Durkheim also addressed explicitly the embodied character of social actors in his writings on religion and the *homo duplex* nature of human beings. For Durkheim, society is built upon the basis of an enduring tension between our individual and social existence, and our nature as both egoistic and moral beings. Humans possess an individual body being, constituted by drives, appetites and sensory impressions which are 'necessarily egoistic', yet also possess the capacity to transcend themselves and develop on the basis of *social* categories and emotions (Durkheim, 1995 [1912]: 151). The body also provides the means to bridge these individual and social dimensions as it is possessed of 'a sacred principle that erupts onto the surface in particular circumstances' (manifest via forms of marking, decoration and dress), producing a bodily symbolism that helps create a shared moral whole by enabling individuals to recognize others as participants in a common culture (ibid.: 125). When combined with social occasions in which people meet together in the presence of phenomenon they regard as sacred – and experience a collective, transcending effervescence – this results during 'normal' periods of societal maturation in the individual egoistic pole of *homo duplex* becoming subordinated increasingly to its social and moral characteristics (Shilling, 2004).

Simmel's primary focus was on social interaction rather than social and moral collectivities, but he also developed a *homo duplex* model of the individual. Embodied subjects are characterized for Simmel by a distinction between individualized mental forms and pre-social contents and impulses, on the one hand, and social emotions and reciprocated mental forms, on the other, yet the body is once more possessed of socially generative properties that make it a basis for society. Bodily drives, dispositions and purposes involving erotic, religious and aggressive impulses, and motives of gain, attack, defence and instruction *propel* individuals towards others, into being with others, for others, or against others, and constitute an essential stage in the initial assembly of social forms (Simmel, 1971 [1908b]). Furthermore, the evolution of our physical, psychological and cognitive structures has equipped humans with an energy and creativity that acts as a source of social change; the 'flux', 'stream' and drive characteristic of embodied life ensures there is a constant 'reaching beyond' of the current boundaries and limits to its expression (Simmel, 1971 [1908c,d], 1971 [1918a]).

Weber might at first glance seem to be the sociologist least interested in the embodiment of social actors, given his comments about the animalistic character of action driven by affect or habit, but his 1904–05 *The Protestant Ethic and the Spirit of Capitalism* provides us with a sophisticated sociological analysis of how a religious ethic of discipline towards the body constitutes a foundation for a rational, modern work ethic. Similarly, his writings on politics as a vocation seek to demonstrate how morally informed actions are based upon a fusion of rational and emotional commitments involving the very core of the embodied actor as a whole (Weber, 1991 [1919a]).

If classical sociology did not bequeath to us ready-made theories of the body, and constructed foundations that sought at least formally to separate 'the social' from the subject matter of other disciplines, we can see from these few examples that its concerns did extend to a consideration of the bodily bases of the 'positive polity', and of moral orders, social forms and social actions. These considerations also informed critical sociological appraisals of how rapid economic growth, the advance of rationalization and the intensification of the money economy, and the disenchantment of the world, posed major threats (as well as offering opportunities) to the bodily well-being of present and future generations. In elaborating on these critiques, it is worth starting here with the writings of Karl Marx. Despite his ambivalent relationship to sociology, Marx was influential in shaping the concerns of the discipline and is the best known critic of the effects of capitalism on our bodily 'species-being'.[1]

For Marx, humans are natural beings possessed of fixed needs, which must be met if they are to survive, but also have the capacity to add to and partly transcend this natural state. Humans do this by becoming social beings who fulfill their natural needs in a variety of culturally specific ways and who also develop new needs unrestricted to the bare maintenance of life. As Marx (1973 [1939]: 92) argues, 'Hunger is hunger, but the hunger gratified by cooked meat eaten with a knife and fork is a different hunger from that which bolts down raw meat with the aid of hand, nail and tooth'. Even 'the senses of social man are different from those of non-social man' as they are available for cultivation and become thoroughly historical phenomena (Marx, 1975 [1844]: 353). This socialization of need and nature does not, however, make irrelevant relatively fixed needs forged by long-term processes of human evolution, and Marx uses these needs as one basis on which to evaluate socio-economic systems (Creaven, 2000). An individual deprived of, or condemned to struggle for, life's necessities is thrown back upon their natural, essentially animal existence. Indeed, it is precisely because capitalism is characterized by a division of labour that robs work of creativity, generates hunger and disease, and warps the sensory development of even the most privileged (for whom to experience is to *possess*) that Marx condemns it as a system that alienates embodied subjects from their own species capacities and their fellow embodied beings.

Durkheim (1970 [1897]) was explicit in his rejection of Marxism, but his studies of suicide and the division of labour deal critically with the bodily and emotional consequences of people's dislocation from appropriately integrative collectives, ritualized belief systems and moral frameworks (Durkheim, 1952 [1897] 1984 [1893]). Simmel's writings on culture, the metropolis and the money economy trace the transformation of the affect structure brought about by the modern world, and examine the difficulty faced by individuals seeking to channel their creative energies and personal values into activities that will result in the development of a coherent and morally satisfying embodied self (eg, Simmel, 1971 [1903]; 1971 [1918a]; 1990 [1907]). Weber was also deeply pessimistic about the onward march of rationality in the modern world, suggesting that the Puritan ethic of body discipline had become something of a cultural template for the West which had contributed to the disenchantment of experience, the spread of a morally corrosive relativism, and the shrinkage of enobling relationships to the spheres of friendship and eroticism (eg, Weber,

1991 [1904/1905]; 1991 [1919b]; 1991 [1915]). Thus, while Marx and Engels may have conveyed to us a more directly visceral sense of bodily exhaustion, depletion, breakdown and disability in their analyses of waged labour and surveys of the Factory Acts and the conditions of the working class, there is no doubting the bodily dimensions and significance of more conventional classical sociological criticisms of modernity. More generally, analyses of such issues as the effervescent binding together of communities, the occasionally all-consuming power of egoistic appetites, the regimes of body discipline employed by Puritans seeking to avoid the sins of sensual pleasure, and the devitalizing impact of a rationalized society in which people's bodily energies have become constricted and restrained by ossified social and cultural forms, demonstrate that sociology identified the body as *multi-dimensional* factor in the creation, reproduction and transformation of social phenomenon (Shilling, 2005a).

Despite this concern with the body, general interpretations of sociology tended to marginalize the significance of embodiment to social life. Talcott Parsons, for example, did more than any other figure in the history of the discipline to identify a 'sociological tradition' and to frame the major problems that shaped sociology during the twentieth century. Despite his enormously useful and bodily relevant writings on such issues as sickness, health, and the continuing influence of the Protestant ethic on the worldly instrumental individualism that pervaded American life, Parsons's influence as an interpretor of the sociological tradition meant that embodiment faded as an issue of sociological importance. In analysing the writings of Durkheim, Weber and others, for example, Parsons (1968 [1937]: 319, 449) downplayed the significance of such notions as collective effervescence. In his general theory of action, moreover, Parsons is concerned predominantly with the subjective understandings of the actor and the extent to which norms enter into that understanding, while action no longer occurs as a result of bodily passions or dispositions but as choices motivated by social norms (Parsons, 1968 [1937]: 47, 1991 [1951]: 541–2, 547–8). Parsons's work is by no means irrelevant to the project of embodying sociology (Shilling, 2002; Levine, this volume), but the waning of his influence from the 1960s helped prepare the ground for the reemergence of alternative and more bodily informed readings of the sociological tradition. This was also the context in which Goffman's focus on the physical dimensions of interaction and self-identity, C. Wright Mills's concern with emotion work, Marcuse's concern with the manipulation of emotions, and a host of other body-relevant writings attracted increasing attention. More directly, a number of other factors paved the way for the recent academic fascination with the subject.

The contemporary 'rise of the body'

Several of these factors have been well rehearsed, but it is worth mentioning them here in order to provide a fuller sense of the terrain on which the body became such a popular issue within contemporary sociology. They also help explain why it is that 'the body' has become such a contested concept in recent years, with its meaning, ontology and significance becoming hotly disputed issues. First, *analysts of consumer culture* identified appearance, body shape and physical control as having become increasingly central to people's sense of self-identity. This was associated with a shift in the culture of advanced capitalist societies during the second half of the twentieth century, in which conspicuous consumption replaced ascetic denial as the normative counterpart of hard work in the sphere of production (Featherstone, 1982). This topographical approach to the body as appearance and performance was associated with a decline in the traditional Christian approach to the flesh as a container of sin and a rise in the treatment of embodiment as both a project and a form of physical capital (Bourdieu, 1978; Shilling, 1993).

Second, and emerging partly as a reaction against this emphasis on consumption and external appearance, there emerged from the 1960s onwards a heterogeneous collection of groups and movements concerned with the cultivation of *meaningful bodily experience*, on the one hand, and a more *ecologically balanced* mode of living in relation to the external environment on the other. Elements of this may have appeared ephemeral, such as the counter-cultural experimentation with drugs. Nevertheless, this concern with living a life that was not dominated by the 'one-dimensionality' of white-collar or factory work and mass culture (Marcuse, 1964) also came to draw on methods of somatic improvement involving diet, yoga and a whole host of bodily practices and disciplines often associated with elements of Oriental spirituality such as Zen, Taoism or Tantra (and designed to heighten body awareness, interrupt damaging habits and improve well-being) which can be traced back hundreds of years (Eichberg, 1998; Shusterman, 1997: 43; Levine, 2006). This heightened concern with the 'internal environment' of bodily experience was complemented by the growth of ecological and green movements that focused on the damage advanced industrial society was doing to our external environment.

Third, the rise of 'second wave' *feminism* emphasized via a critical interrogation of the sex/gender divide that there was nothing natural about women's corporeality which justified their public subordination. The body uncovered by feminists was a biologically sexed body which should have few social consequences but which had been categorized and treated within patriarchal society in a manner that limited women's life chances. Because of the 'male stream' history of writing on the subject, feminists did not initially seek to place the body at the centre of social thought. As Grosz (1994: 4) points out, philosophers had traditionally associated men with freedom and the mind and women with 'unreason associated with the body' and this was hardly an incentive to return full-scale to this analytical terrain. Despite such ambivalence, however, feminists contributed much towards the popularity of body studies. Studies of the female body in law, of the construction of 'compulsory heterosexuality', and the erasure of female sexuality in male culture provided rich lines of empirical and theoretical inquiry (eg, Irigary, 1986 [1977]; Kristeva, 1986; Eisenstein, 1988; Mackinnon, 1989). Feminists placed on the agenda the project of 'reexploring, reexamining, notions of female corporeality' (Grosz, 1994: 14), have interrogated the body within ethics and standpoint epistemologies, and have constructed imaginative metaphysical conceptions of the female body as 'fluidity'. In a related vein, issues and controversies related to transgenderism and transsexuality (focused on sociologically by Garfinkel's ethnomethodological study of 'Agnes') provided an added dimension to the contingent and variable relationships that exist between the body and sexual identity (Stryker & Whittle, 2006).

A growing awareness of changing modes of governmentality constituted the fourth factor behind the rising popularity of the body as an object of study. Instrumental here were Foucault's analyses of how the creation of the modern subject was accompanied by a shift in the target, object and scope of governmental disciplinary regimes during which the fleshy body gave way to the mindful body as a focus of concern, preoccupation with matters of death was replaced by an interest in controlling details of life, and the control of anonymous individuals was replaced by attempts to manage differentiated populations (eg, Foucault, 1979a, 1979b, 1981). The eighteenth century witnessed a large increase in discourses on sexuality, for example, which linked the sex of individual bodies to the management of national populations, while the twentieth century was characterized by a continued shift away from negative forms of bodily repression towards positive forms of exhortation in which embodied subjects were encouraged to structure their lives in particular ways. This particular concern cast its spotlight on the problems governments faced in dealing with large (if uneven) growths in world population, in managing the spread of HIV/AIDS, and in policing flows of migrants and refugees.

Technological advances which contributed to a growing uncertainty about the 'reality' of the body and a radical doubt as to whether there was anything 'natural' about human embodiment constitute the fifth concern that raised the profile of this subject. Advances in such areas as transplant surgery (including face transplants), *in vitro* fertilization and stem-cell research increased the extent to which bodies could be controlled, but also instituted a weakening of the boundaries between science, technology and bodies that prompted some to reconceptualize humans as cyborgs. These same developments appear to have thrown into radical doubt our knowledge of what the embodied subject is. The principle of individuality accepted by Enlightenment thought depended on identifying what was unique to a person across the variables of date and location, yet the potential malleability of the body threatens such constancies. The Human Genome Project, for example, heralded the start of an era in which all aspects of embodiment are theoretically open to alteration. In this context, it is hardly surprising that post-modernist writings have abandoned the modernist project of knowing what the body is, analysing it instead in terms of a 'blank screen', a 'sign receiving system' or even, in the work of Deleuze and Guattari, an elusive 'body without organs' (Kroker & Kroker, 1988; Goodchild, 1996). Alternatively, these same developments have an affinity with the insistence that actor network theory places on relationality and connectivity when it comes to analysing the body: embodiment is recognized as significant but analysed only in terms of its ties to and interdependence with other phenomena.

The sixth major analytic concern, that continues both to increase the popularity of the subject and tie the growing interest in the body to other intellectual agendas, involves those academics who treat embodiment as a conceptual resource which can assist them in advancing their particular subject. In the case of sociology, theorists used the body to avoid the over-socialized conception of the individual associated with Parsons's (1991 [1951]: 541–2, 547–8) focus on values (which portrayed the body as merely a sub-system of the action system), and the unrealistic assumptions of rational choice theory (which holds that actors cognitively establish goals before acting, and views the body as a permanently available instrument of action immune to frailty, chance and epiphany). Analyses of 'creativity' (Joas, 1996) and 'human being' (Archer, 1995), for example, sought to provide concepts of the body which are resistant to it being analytically collapsed into any unidimensional view of social action or structurally determinist analysis of society. In these cases, the body constitutes an overlooked element of reality whose capacities have important implications for disciplinary analysis.

These social and cultural developments and analytic concerns have done much to stimulate and maintain the rise of interest in the body since the 1980s but they approached and defined the subject in very different ways. The body was a surface phenomenon which had become a malleable marker of identity and status subject to the vagaries of fashion for theorists of consumer culture. It was a vehicle for the cultivation of particular types of lived experience and a more balanced and sustainable relationship with the external environment for 'body therapists' and ecologists. It was a sexed object used to justify and reproduce women's subjugation for feminists. It was an object rendered passive by changing modes of control for Foucauldian analysts of governmentality. The body was changed into an uncertain and even rapidly disappearing remnant of pre-technological culture for those interested in the suturing of meat and machines that occurred with the development of cyborgs. Finally, it became a positive conceptual category for those concerned with addressing theoretical problems in their own discipline. Within each of these analyses, the spotlight rests on certain aspects of the body, leaving others obscured.

These disparate concerns are reflected in the enormous number of studies to have appeared on the subject since the 1980s. The sheer quantity of this work has been regarded as evidence of the healthy establishment of a new field of study. Writings on the body have challenged the assumption that 'society operates on us intellectually and consensually rather than directly upon our bodies' (O'Neill, 1985: 48), have established new sub-disciplinary areas of study, and have made general contributions to social and cultural theory. Nevertheless, 'the body' remains one of the most contested concepts in the social sciences: its analysis has produced an intellectual battleground over which the respective claims of post-structuralism and post-modernism, phenomenology, feminism, socio-biology, sociology and cultural studies have fought (eg, Howson & Inglis,

2001). Tied to competing agendas and against the huge diversity of body studies, varying aspects of embodiment are foregrounded, allowing others to fade into the background. This has the effect of making the body recede and slide from view, while undergoing a series of metamorphoses that render it unrecognizable from one incarnation to the next. Furthermore, the body seems for many to have become a mere metaphor through which particular concerns can be pursued. In this context, it is increasingly difficult to define the body or even say what is being examined within the field. In two of the best known studies on the subject, for example, Turner (1984: 8) concludes that the body may appear to be solid, yet is 'the most elusive, illusory . . . metaphorical . . . and ever distant thing', while Butler (1993: ix) is nothing if not candid when admitting that in 'trying to consider the materiality of the body', she 'kept losing track of the subject.'

Sociology has of course long thrived on the debate and contestation that arises from different perspectives and paradigms on the same subject, but there is a major problem with this degree of uncertainty about the embodied character of social actors. As we have seen, while classical sociologists such as Durkheim and Simmel may have worked within different traditions of thought, their writings on the body not only provided us with a sense of how people helped *generate* social phenomena, as well as being *shaped by* society, but also served as a basis on which they made judgements about the impact of particular developments, societies and even eras on the capacities, health, personalities and well-being of social actors. This concern to reinstate a clearer sense of what the body is and what it can do, so that it becomes possible to see how it is being changed by social and technological developments and to scrutinize the impact of these changes on those subject to them, has begun to inform recent writings on the subject that link embodiment to prominent traditions in sociology and social thought and to ethical issues relevant to the contemporary era. That brings us to the contents of this volume.

Moving forward

In providing a background and context for the contributions to this volume, I have organized my discussion around three themes: the ambivalent relationship that has existed historically between sociology and the body, the considerable if often implicit body-relevant writings that exist within the sociological tradition, and how the major factors informing the contemporary rise of 'body studies' contributed not only to a huge variety of theories and perspectives but also to a concept that was so thoroughly contested that it faded from view behind the competing agendas that had informed its popularity in the first place. The chapters that follow make important contributions to the analysis of each of these areas.

In terms of addressing the uncertainty around and apparent elusiveness of the body, the discussions that follow share a sensitivity to the capacity of embodied subjects to be shaped by their social environment, while also recognizing the social consequentiality of the body's materiality. The uses to which such insights are put vary considerably but they provide each of the contributors here with a basis on which they are able to examine how embodiment mediates the interplay between such issues as structure and agency, nature and culture, conflict and consensus, experience and knowledge, and practice and performance. Even speculations about a possible future characterized by massively enhanced life-expectancies (see Turner's chapter) are peopled by embodied subjects confronting issues such as alienation, anomie and the development of a coherent character, that have long preoccupied sociological discussion. Similarly, analyses of professional cultures and the processes involved in acquiring new skills, techniques and capacities (see the chapters by Aalten, O'Connor, Lande, Okely and also Crossley) illustrate how embodied subjects are not simply 'hailed' to assume subject positions, or controlled robotically by some 'discursive matrix' which compels them to conduct pre-determined performances, but undergo complicated apprenticeships in which 'success' or 'failure' is resultant upon the capacities and limitations of each embodied subject.

In terms of excavating and supplementing body-relevant work in the sociological tradition, and applying it to issues of contemporary importance, the first few chapters in this collection come from scholars whose work has done much to place the body on the agenda of sociology. Bryan Turner situates his discussion within fundamental debates about the animal/human, nature/culture, and culture/technology distinctions that lie at the intersection of sociology and anthropology. At the heart of both these disciplines lies the assumption that the bodily subject's capacity to be enculturated demonstrates that human actions are not determined by animal instincts but can be intentional, meaningful and ethical, and are intimately related to the agentic creation of ritual orders and social systems underpinned by moral orders. Turner then scrutinizes these assumptions on the basis of current genetic explanations and the potentially revolutionary technological changes to the body brought about by the promise of such advances as stem-cell research and therapeutic cloning, and suggests that the body threatens in the current era to be turned into a fleshy equivalent of Weber's 'iron cage'. A language of determinism increasingly pervades scientific suggestions that we are genetically predisposed to behave and think in certain ways, while medical advances hold out the promise of a life that is so prolonged that it threatens those religious and ethical cultures that are based upon the finitude of mortal life. In these circumstances, the body would not become irrelevant to social life or to people's capacities to act, but it would change the material basis on which humans experienced existential dilemmas in general and the problem of developing a coherent personality and a meaningful relationship with the world.

Donald Levine's chapter explores the marginality of embodiment in traditional conflict theory, examines how conflict involves complex links between the body and the external environment, and displays a keen concern for lived experience in identifying those factors that generate or dampen conflictual dispositions, actions and interactions. Levine also explicates the significance of these insights for a general theory of conflict and a Parsonian theory of action. In so doing, he not only provides a means of improving our understanding of conflict but also demonstrates the significance of the body for theories that have long been central to the sociological tradition. Parsons' writings have too often been dismissed as anachronistic, but Levine provides us with compelling reasons for appreciating the contemporary relevance of his work.

Drawing our attention to the importance of feminist work in this area, Kathy Davis revisits the ambivalent relationship that feminist *theory* has had with the body. In this context, she then seeks to bring theory and embodied practice together by focusing on women's self-help and health movements and engaging with Haraway's critique of the medical gaze adopted by health activists. Davis is sensitive to the balancing act faced by feminist scholars who write about the body as a basis for agency, experience and knowledge in a culture permeated by scientific discourses that have historically been associated with negative, controlling and oppressive practices directed towards women's corporeality. Nevertheless, through a balanced appraisal of this work she insists that feminist theory can learn from feminist health activists in terms of its ontological view of what the body is, in reconceptualizing embodied experience as something that is irreducible to dominant discourses, and in reconceptualizing women's epistemic agency by acknowledging that there exists some space in which women are able to undertake intentional action informed by what it means to inhabit a particular body with its own needs and capacities.

If sociology has had an affinity with anthropology in its view of the embodied subject's capacity for enculturation, so too has it at times shared with anthropology a recognition of the importance of fieldwork. This is especially evident in that work carried out by the Chicago School of Sociology in America which includes what I think can be referred to as one of the classics of embodied sociology, Nels Anderson's (1961 [1923]) *The Hobo*. It is anthropology, though, that has conducted the most sustained and detailed investigations into the bodily practices and identities of those groups that have tended to escape the sociological gaze. As Judith Okely's chapter notes, the sociology of the body has tended to adopt a Western focus, yet it is sometimes through a consideration of non-Western bodily forms and practices that the utility of analysing embodiment is most clearly apparent. The main focus of Okely's chapter, though, derives from her observation that the body of the anthropologist is often missing from published accounts, despite being so vital to the knowledge gained from fieldwork. Based on interviews with a number of prominent anthropologists, this discussion provides us with a fascinating analysis of how the bodily appearances, actions and interactions of anthropologists affect the reactions of the host group, are integral to the risks and dangers of fieldwork, and shape experiences of grappling with new work skills, body language and ritual practices involving such activities as dance. In providing us with a detailed illustration and more corporeally informed development of what Ottenberg (1990) refers to as 'headnotes' (insights that are not written down but which come from remembered observations, mnemonic triggers of total bodily experience, and puzzles felt in the bones and flesh of the fieldworker), this is an important contribution to the issue of what properly developed embodied sociological research might look like.

Okely provides a bridge between theoretical and empirical issues that have become of increasing concern to sociological work on the body in recent years. The common complaint has been that the number of sophisticated theoretical works on embodiment has yet to be matched by sufficient substantive investigations of the significance of the body to people's daily lives (eg, Nettleton & Watson, 1998). Nick Crossley's chapter takes this debate forward and offers some solutions to it by identifying Marcel Mauss's programmatic analysis of body techniques as a key means whereby embodiment can be opened up to empirical sociological research. Originally trained as a philosopher, Mauss was one of the key figures in the establishment of the journal *Anne' Sociologique* in which many of the fundamental ideas of social anthropology were first explored. Mauss's analysis of body techniques can be seen as an exploration of the corporeal foundations of his highly influential analysis of gift relationships – which revealed the principles of reciprocity underpinning exchanges between groups and individuals – and reveals both the social variability and the social, psychological and biological components that constitute particular bodily capacities and skills. In seeking to develop Mauss's analysis, by discussing in more detail the 'mindful' elements of body techniques and the inter-corporeal contexts in which they are deployed and developed, Crossley argues that a focus on body techniques can allow sociologists to explore how purpose, normativity and physicality are combined within the structure of the embodied subject. Such a focus on body techniques allows us, he suggests, to undertake historical research into their diffusion within and between cultures, as well as combining quantitative and qualitative research in exploring how they are distributed within and between groups and in ascertaining how such techniques are acquired.

The idea that social norms and social actions inhere within the deepest fibres of our bodily being says much about the importance of embodiment for sociology, and the other chapters in this volume can also be seen as engaging with issues raised by Mauss. While Mauss describes different body techniques and writes about the social, psychological and biological components of these techniques, however, he has little to say about the details of how they are actually *taught* or the *experiences* that people go through when acquiring (or failing to acquire) new skills and capacities. It is in this context that this monograph contributes towards the study not just of body techniques but of body pedagogies or *body pedagogics*. Body pedagogics may be defined as referring to the central pedagogic *means* through which a culture seeks to transmit its main corporeal techniques, skills and dispositions, the embodied *experiences* associated with acquiring or failing to acquire these attributes, and the actual embodied *changes* resulting from this process. This notion of body pedagogics inevitably simplifies the myriad processes, complexities and variabilities involved in the transmission and development of cultures, but it nevertheless provides us with an extremely useful ideal-typical and corporeally sensitive way of accessing some of the central elements involved in cultural reproduction and change. By exploring the power relations and normative content that inform institutionalized and non-institutionalized body pedagogics, and the relationship that these have with both the experiences of those embodied subjects seeking to learn new body techniques and the outcomes of these processes, it is possible to combine a concern with social control, lived experience and the corporeal foundations associated with social reproduction and social change (Shilling, 2005b; Shilling and Mellor, forthcoming).

Brian Lande's empirical investigation of body pedagogics is based on eighteen months he spent in the US Army Reserved Officer Training Corp. Following Levine, Lande's analysis demonstrates the partiality of sociological accounts of conflict that have overlooked the importance of the body. Lande's focus is specifically on the military and on the pedagogic methods employed to cultivate the capacities recruits require for becoming a soldier. By exploring the place of voice, demonstration, touch and forceful manipulation, this fascinating example of what Wacquant (2004) refers to as 'observant participation' provides us with a rich account of how the army stimulate in cadets a corporeal understanding of the breathing techniques that it considers necessary to run long distances, fire a rifle and project authority on the drill ground. For states to engage in armed conflict requires not just a disciplined military personnel but also one schooled in specific body skills suited to the conduct of such conflict and Lande's work is a valuable contribution to our understanding of what is involved in this training.

Anna Aalten's account of ballet culture may appear at first glance to have little in common with Lande's chapter on the army but both demonstrate how apparently dissimilar professionals are subjected to a body pedagogy which teaches them to distinguish pain from injury and to disassociate themselves (at least in part) from their bodily feelings. Aalten's research involved ethnographic study and extensive interviews stretching over seven years, and she traces how the culture of ballet revolves around techniques that 'defy the principles of human design' in seeking to create the 'disembodied sylph that is the ideal in ballet.' The bodies of ballerinas frequently 'speak up' and protest against the demands they face, but the identities of these professionals are so tied up with their chosen vocation that they readily absorb the implicit pedagogy of harsh physical discipline that pervades ballet. Bodies are not infinitely malleable, however, and the consequences of this culture have resulted in recurrent injuries and the spread of eating disorders.

Modes of pedagogic transmission such as those found in ballet and the military may constitute a disciplinary regime for those subject to them, but they achieve results in terms of bodily transformations that equip their members with a vastly heightened performative capacity compared with most individuals not involved in such disciplines. As well as involving the experience of discomfort and pain, moreover, it is important to recognize the sense of accomplishment, empowerment and even partial transcendence experienced by those who survive and prosper within such pedagogic regimes. Both Aalten and Lande provide a sense of this, but it is Erin O'Connor who focuses most directly on the lived experience of actually seeking to acquire a new set of skills. Based upon her time spent learning glassblowing in New York, O'Connor's chapter seeks to convey through its content and style what it is like to acquire practical knowledge. In so doing, she conveys a textured and layered sense of the importance of practical mimesis for corporeal comprehension, and of some of the key distinctions that exist between the attempted execution of skilled tasks by a novice and an expert. While the former tend to proceed in distinct, successive steps, the latter has a corporeal comprehension of the place of the part in relation to the whole and, as Polanyi (1962) notes, is more able to 'dwell' in tools that become extensions of the body. The flow of a bodily conscious style of writing employed by O'Connor conveys a vivid sense of the frustrations, crises and small victories experienced by someone becoming apprenticed in a skill who has understood that the acquisition of techniques depends not only on watching and mimicking but also on having understood enough with one's body to enable one to *see* what is actually occurring.

I emphasized at the start of this introduction that for all the body-relevant writings and resources that exist in the sociological tradition, there remains work to be done in developing a comprehensive sociological approach towards the body and society. If sociology has much to bring to bear on 'body studies', in other words, focusing on embodiment can in turn help to broaden the scope and depth of the discipline. This is evident in Simon Williams' chapter on sleep, a topic that has traditionally remained outside of the sociological imagination. In focusing on this issue, Williams provides us with a sense of the techniques, rituals and customs we employ in preparing for sleep (highlighting in the tradition of Goffman things that we take for granted in our daily lives but are not discursively aware of), but also demonstrates, though a focus on the vulnerabilities, risks and dangers associated with sleep, the importance of this subject for an embodied sociology. The increasing spread of work and leisure into times traditionally reserved for sleep, the scientific and medical intervention in the management of sleep, and the inequalities dividing those able to sleep in comfort and safety from those who sleep in doorways or under bridges and/or in danger of assault from others are just a few of the issues Williams explores that justify this conclusion.

Sociological studies of embodiment have been one of the most vibrant areas of interest in the discipline over the last few decades. Connecting the concerns of classical sociologists to new advances in social theory, anthropology, feminism, social research and the study of body pedagogics, this volume takes the sociological study of the body in exciting new directions and opens up new horizons for the sociological imagination.

Note

1 Given that Marx sought to anchor a vision of transcendent freedom (based on his view of future communist society) in this-wordly, capitalist realities, it is not surprising that his view of human

nature has been the subject of debate and criticism for its apparent inconsistencies (Levine, 1995: 221–2; see also, for example, Coser, 1971; Geras, 1983; McLellen, 1985).

References

Anderson, N. (1961 [1923]) *The Hobo*. Chicago: The University of Chicago Press.
Archer, M. (1995) *Realist Social Theory*. Cambridge: Cambridge University Press.
Archer, M. (2000) *Being Human: The Problem of Agency*. Cambridge: Cambridge University Press.
Aron, R. (1965) *Main Currents in Sociological Thought, Vol.1*. London: Weidenfeld & Nicholson.
Bourdieu, P. (1978) 'Sport and social class', *Social Science Information*, 17: 819–840.
Butler, J. (1990) *Gender Trouble*. London: Routledge.
Butler, J. (1993) *Bodies That Matter*. London: Routledge.
Bynum, C. (1987) *Holy Feast and Holy Fast*. Berkeley: University of California Press.
Comte, A. (1853) *The Positive Philosophy of Auguste Comte, Vol.II*. Translated by H. Martineau. London: John Chapman.
Coser, L. (1971) Masters of Sociological Thought. New York: Harcourt, Brace Jovanovich.
Creaven, S. (2000) *Marxism and Realism*. London: Routledge.
Crossley, N. (2006) *Reflexive Embodiment in Contemporary Societies*. Buckingham: Open University Press.
Durkheim, E. (1952 [1897]) *Suicide*. London: Routledge.
Durkheim, E. (1970 [1897]) 'Review of Antonio Labriola, Essay sur la conception historique de l'histoire' in E. Durkheim *La Science Sociale et L'action*. Paris: Presses Universitaires de France.
Durkheim, E. (1982 [1895]) *The Rules of Sociological Method*. London: Macmillan.
Durkheim, E. (1984 [1893]) *The Division of Labour in Society*. London: Macmillan.
Durkheim, E. (1995 [1912]) *The Elementary Forms of Religious Life*. New York: Free Press.
Eichberg, H. (1998) *Body Cultures: Essays on Sport, Space and Identity*. London: Routledge.
Eisenstein, Z. (1988) *The Female Body and the Law*. Berkeley, CA.: University of California Press.
Featherstone, M. (1982) 'The body in consumer culture', *Theory, Culture & Society*, 1: 18–33.
Feder, M., Naddaff, R. & Tazi, N. (1989) *Fragments for a History of the Human Body*. 3 Vols. New York: Zone.
Feldenkrais, M. (1977) *Awareness Through Movement*. New York: Harper Collins.
Foucault, M. (1979a) *Discipline and Punish*. Harmondsworth: Penguin.
Foucault, M. (1979b) 'Governmentality', *Ideology and Consciousness*, 6: 5–22.
Foucault, M. (1981) *The History of Sexuality, Vol.1. An Introduction*. Harmondsworth: Penguin.
Geras, N. (1983) *Marx & Human Nature*. London: Verso.
Goodchild, P. (1996) *Deleuze and Guattari*. London: Sage.
Grosz, E. (1994) *Volatile Bodies*. London: Routledge.
Heilbron, J. (1995) *The Rise of Social Theory*. Minneapolis: University of Minnesota Press.
Hirst, P. & Woolley, P. (1982) *Social Relations and Human Attributes*. London: Tavistock.
Howson, A. & Inglis, D. (2001) 'The body in sociology: tensions inside and outside sociological Thought', *Sociological Review*, 49(3): 297–317.
Irigary, L. (1986 [1977]) *This Sex Which Is Not One*. New York: Cornell University Press.
Joas, H. (1996) *The Creativity of Action*. Cambridge: Polity.
Kristeva, J. (1986) *The Kristeva Reader*. Edited by T. Moi. New York: Columbia University Press.
Kroker, A. & Kroker, M. (1988) *Body Invaders*. New Haven, Conn: Yale University Press.
Lakoff, G. (1987) *Women, Fire and Dangerous Things*. Chicago: University of Chicago Press.
Levine, D.N. (1995) Visions of the Sociological Tradition. Chicago: University of Chicago Press.
Levine, D.N. (2006) *Powers of the Mind: The Reinvention of Liberal Learning*. Chicago: University of Chicago Press.
Mackinnon, C. (1989) *Towards a Feminist Theory of the State*. Cambridge, MA.: Harvard University Press.
McLellen, G. (1985) 'Marx's concept of human nature', *New Left Review*, 149: 121–124.

Marcuse, H. (1964) *One Dimensional Man*. London: Abacus.
Marx, K. (1973 [1939]) *Grundrisse*. Harmonsworth: Penguin Books / New Left Review.
Marx, K. (1975 [1844]) 'The economic and philosophic manuscripts of 1844', in *Karl Marx: Early Writings*. Harmondsworth: Penguin.
Nettleton, S. & Watson, J. (1998) *The Body in Everyday Life*. London: Routledge.
O'Neill, J. (1985) *Five Bodies. The Human Shape of Modern Society*. Ithica, NY: Cornell University Press.
Ottenberg, S. (1990) 'Thirty years of Fieldnotes: Changing Relationships to the Text' in R. Sanjek (ed.) *Fieldnotes: The Makings of Anthropology* London: Cornell University Press.
Parsons, T. (1968 [1937]) *The Structure of Social Action*, 2 Vols. New York: The Free Press.
Parsons, T. (1991 [1951]) *The Social System*. London: Routledge.
Pickering, M. (1993) *Auguste Comte: An Intellectual Biography, Vol.1*. Cambridge: Cambridge University Press.
Polanyi, M. (1962) *Personal Knowledge: Towards a Post-Critical Philosophy*. Chicago: University of Chicago Press.
Shilling, C. (1993, 2nd edition 2003) *The Body and Society Theory*. London: Sage.
Shilling, C. (2002) 'Culture, the "sick role" and the consumption of health', *British Journal of Sociology*, 53 (4): 621–638.
Shilling, C. (2004) 'Embodiment, emotions and the foundations of social order: Durkheim's enduring Contribution', in J.C. Alexander & P. Smith (eds), *The Cambridge Companion to Durkheim*. Cambridge: Cambridge University Press.
Shilling, C. (2005a) *The Body in Culture, Technology & Society*. London: Sage.
Shilling, C. (2005b) 'Body Pedagogics. A Programme and Paradigm for Research', paper presented to the School of Sport & Exercise Sciences, University of Loughborough.
Shilling, C. & Mellor, P.A. (2001) *The Sociological Ambition*. London: Sage.
Shilling, C. & Mellor, P.A. (forthcoming) 'Cultures of embodied experience: Technology, religion and body pedagogics', *The Sociological Review*.
Shusterman, R. (1997) 'Somaesthetics and the body/media issue', *Body & Society*, 3(3): 33–49.
Simmel, G. (1971 [1903]) 'The metropolis', in D. Levine (ed.), *Georg Simmel on Individuality and Social Forms*. Chicago: University of Chicago Press.
Simmel, G. (1971 [1908a]) 'The problem of sociology', in D. Levine (ed.), *Georg Simmel on Individuality and Social Forms*. Chicago: University of Chicago Press.
Simmel, G. (1971 [1908b]) 'How is society possible', in D. Levine (ed.), *Georg Simmel on Individuality and Social Forms*. Chicago: University of Chicago Press.
Simmel, G. (1971 [1908c]) 'Subjective culture', in D. Levine (ed.), *Georg Simmel on Individuality and Social Forms*. Chicago: University of Chicago Press.
Simmel, G. (1971 [1908d]) 'Social forms and inner needs', in D. Levine (ed.), *Georg Simmel on Individuality and Social Forms*. Chicago: University of Chicago Press.
Simmel, G. (1971 [1918a]) 'The transcendent character of life', in D. Levine (ed.), *Georg Simmel on Individuality and Social Forms*. Chicago: University of Chicago Press.
Simmel, G. (1971 [1918b]) 'The conflict in modern culture', in D. Levine (ed.), *Georg Simmel on Individuality and Social Forms*. Chicago: University of Chicago Press.
Simmel, G. (1990 [1907]) *The Philosophy of Money*. Edited and with an introduction by T. Bottomore and D. Frisby. London: Routledge.
Stryker, S. & Whittle, S. (2006) (eds), *The Transgender Studies Reader*. London: Routledge.
Suleiman, S. (1986) (ed.), *The Female Body in Western Culture*. Cambridge, MA.: Harvard University Press.
Turner, B.S. (1984) *The Body and Society*. Oxford: Blackwells.
Turner, B.S. (1991) 'Recent developments in the theory of the body', in M. Featherstone, M. Hepworth & B.S. Turner (eds), The Body. Social Process and Cultural Theory. London: Sage.
Wacquant, L. (2004) *Body & Soul. Notes of an Apprentice Boxer*. Oxford: Oxford University Press.
Weber, M. (1968) *Economy and Society. 2 Volumes*. Berkeley: University of California Press.
Weber, M. (1991 [1904/1905]) *The Protestant Ethic and the Spirit of Capitalism*. London: Harper Collins.

Weber, M. (1991 [1915]) 'Religious rejections of the world and their directions', in H. Gerth and C.W. Mills (eds), *From Max Weber*. London: Routledge.
Weber, M. (1991 [1919a]) 'Politics as a vocation', in H. Gerth and C.W. Mills (eds), *From Max Weber*. London: Routledge.
Weber, M. (1991 [1919b]) 'Science as a vocation', in H. Gerth and C.W. Mills (eds), *From Max Weber*. London: Routledge.
Young, I.M. (1990) *Throwing Like a Girl and other Essays in Feminist Philosophy and Social Theory*. Bloomington: Indiana University Press.

Culture, technologies and bodies: the technological Utopia of living forever

Bryan S. Turner

Abstract

There are two parts to my discussion of the sociology of the body. I first examine, via an account of the development of anthropology and sociology, how technology and culture have historically been analysed as mediations between the scarcity of natural resources and the vulnerable human body. Technology has been crucial in providing societies with some control or dominion over nature, including therefore control over the human body, yet is often thought to involve hubris against the gods and a threat to human life. Culture, in contrast, has more usually been seen as nurturing nature, providing humans with a symbolic means of mediating and domesticating their external physical environment. Whereas culture nurtures nature, technology can so easily destroy it. In the second part of my article, I demonstrate how these conceptual distinctions have assumed new dimensions in the contemporary era and analyse these by focusing on the implications of medical technologies for longevity (for example, therapeutic stem-cell research, regenerative medicine, and new reproductive technologies). Medical technology holds out the promise of prolongevity as a new mirage of health, offering life-enhancement or the secular promise of eternal life.

Key words: technology, culture, anthropology, longevity, ethics

Introduction: Body, culture and technology

The classificatory division between animal and human has had an important role in human societies for millennia. In the Abrahamic religions, this division has been fundamental. Adam, in naming the animals in the Garden of Eden, shows his mastery and separation from them. In Hinduism and Buddhism, the doctrine of karma implies an ontological hierarchy rather than a categorical division. If we eat animals but not humans, then we have a separation rather than a hierarchy of merit. While we are separated from animals in religious terms, we nevertheless as mammals share a common life as living organisms. Hence there is an ambiguity, both moral and conceptual, surrounding our embodiment.

The debate about the human body in the philosophy of the social sciences can therefore be regarded as an implicit or disguised discussion about the actual animality of humans. If human beings could reasonably be considered as wholly and unquestionably members of an animal kingdom, then sociology could be subsumed under zoology. Instead this disguised or implicit issue of animality surfaces primarily in anthropology as a discussion of the division between culture and nature, and in a minor key as a division between technology and nature. Outside of zoology, the human body as a topic in sociology and cultural anthropology emerged firstly as a more or less neutral site upon which language and religion were erected as topics of analysis. Secondly, the body as a topic has an implicit existence in the technological mediation between society and nature.

This debate about humanity and animality is of course connected to issues regarding the relative weight of nature and nurture in the explanation of human behaviour that have dominated philosophy and social sciences in the western world for centuries. It has appeared in various guises – Aristotle's political philosophy, Christian theology, medical sciences, evolutionary biology, Darwinism and evolutionary psychology.

This nature/nurture problem cannot be easily solved for several reasons. It is an arena within which the divisions between idealism and positivism become particularly acute. The issue also creates deep ethical problems about the question of moral responsibility. If human behaviour is primarily determined by nature, then we cannot hold people morally responsible for their actions, and there is no justification for punishing people who commit crimes (if we believe their behaviour is for example genetically determined). There are no crimes in the animal world; there is only a struggle for survival. Naturalistic explanations tend therefore to involve both determinism and reductionism. Cultural explanations, drawing on the legacy of German idealism, tend to be hermeneutic and idiographic, being concerned with the meaning of human actions rather than with their causes. Hermeneutics tends to be more optimistic than positivism, in the sense that it is assumed that human behaviour can be changed by education, training and correction. The contemporary popularity of genetic explanations suggests that modern societies are pessimistic about the chances of changing 'human nature' simply through educational means alone. The implication of much contemporary genetic theory and research is that people can be more efficiently controlled through drugs, genetic counselling or medical surveillance. Most governments are reluctant to recognize the practice of eugenics, at least overtly, but eugenic management is implicit in contemporary applications of stem-cell research. The Enlightenment view of human behaviour as rational, once liberated from its arbitrary, authoritarian constraints, is in retreat.

While cultural anthropology and sociology have by contrast fashioned the ideas of culture and technology to distinguish between the animal and the human, in both disciplines the body has had a somewhat ambiguous status. In this contribution to the sociology of the body, I want to consider historically certain approaches to technology as the mediation between the natural scarcity of resources and the vulnerability of the human body, and at the same time to consider the difficulties of establishing a satisfactory analytical relationship between culture and technology. In the history of human groups, technology has been crucial in helping human beings establish some control over or domination of nature. Since the human body can be regarded as part of nature, technological change involves control over the natural world, and hence over the body. Insofar as technology can 'improve' the body, for example through the humble pair of spectacles that I need to read this page, technology is often thought to involve hubris with respect to the gods and in more recent history involves a threat to human life itself. The Frankenstein theme summarizes (male) hegemony over nature and its threat to human (as opposed to sheer) survival. Whereas culture gently nurtures nature, for example through moral cultivation, technology threatens to destroy it by arrogantly modifying, improving or replacing it. These tensions between the rationality and irrationality of technological innovation with respect to culture and the body have come to a defining moment in recent scientific developments such as therapeutic stem-cell research, regenerative medicine, and new reproductive technologies. In particular, I want to consider the promise of 'living forever' through the application of therapeutic cloning and stem-cell research as a classic illustration of technological changes to the human body. This promise of living forever can be treated as a secular version of the religious promise of eternal life. Contemporary applications of medical science to human longevity open up the possibility of transforming the character of human embodiment. Does this mean that scientific technology will radically transform human nature, creating what Francis Fukuyama (2002) has called a post-human existence?

The emergence of culture in anthropology

Let us first consider the issue of culture. This division has been crucial to social anthropology which conceptually elaborated the idea of 'Culture' as the arena of symbols and meaning, and hence anthropology saw 'Man' as a symbol-producing creature. This way of thinking about the nature/culture or nature/nurture division was very clear in the work of an influential cohort of American anthropologists such as Franz Boas (1858–1942), Alfred Kroeber (1876–1960) and Clyde Kluckhohn (1905–1960). All three men, who did their ethnographic fieldwork on native American cultures, made culture the central topic of anthropology and placed language at the crux of all cultural activity. Boas was particularly important because his approach to anthropology was hostile to evolutionary arguments and claimed that 'race' had no scientific merit. By emphasizing the cultural significance of language, they also created a significant conceptual gap between 'physical anthropology' and their own work. Boas's analysis of culture was especially important to anthropological contributions to human rights, because his approach shaped the response of the American Anthropological Association in 1947 to the Declaration on Human Rights, arguing that all peoples and social groups have a right 'to realize their capacity for culture'. This intellectual orientation to language and culture and their suspicion about racial categories had the consequence of marginalizing the study of the body. More precisely, it had the consequence of marginalizing the study of the phenomenology of the body, emphasizing instead the idea of the body as a system of cultural classification. Culture became important in anthropology as a conceptual means of avoiding or denying the relevance of biologically defined 'race' in the explanation of human behaviour. Whereas 'race' implied fixed attributes and capacities, 'culture' facilitated a view of human nature as plastic and dynamic. Race separated humans into fixed, separate and potentially hostile ontological communities. In the biological gap between racially separated groups, there was no equivalent to translation, and thus no possibility of genuine communication. By contrast, culture kept open the possibility of mutual understanding through recognition and comprehension.

American anthropology had considerable influence over the development of the social sciences. Kluckhohn invented the notions of 'culture area' and 'cultural configuration', but it was in a joint essay by Kroeber and Parsons that the relationship between cultural anthropology and sociology was clearly formulated. They argued that culture refers to 'transmitted and created content and patterns of values, ideas, and other symbolic-meaningful systems as factors in the shaping of human behaviour and the artefacts produced through behavior' and by contrast they defined the 'social system' in terms of the 'specifically relational system of interaction among the individuals and collectivities' (Kroeber and Parsons, 1958: 582–3). Although in this period of his intellectual development of the theory of social systems, Parsons was influenced by the theory of homeostasis in biological systems, the embodiment of the social actor did not play an important part in his conception of social action, and hence it did not feature in an understanding of 'the relational system of interaction'. The body of the actor was lost to American sociological theory, and it appeared in cultural anthropology as a slate upon which culture could inscribe meaning.

Cultural anthropology developed as a science of symbolic communication, which was critical of evolutionary theory and rejected race as a biological category. The anthropological criticism of reductionism was that symbolic life could not be reduced to biology. In his evaluation of the legacy of Clyde Kluckhohn, Parsons argued that early American anthropology had tried to avoid a Darwinistic treatment of human societies and more specifically had sought to reject 'the pressures towards biopsychological reductionism' (Parsons, 1973: 46). Kluckhohn did not want to reject biology entirely and came instead to stress the plasticity of the human organism and its openness to cultural influences. In emphasizing culture, Kluckhohn had rejected instinct theory which saw human behaviour as determined by genetically specific needs. Humans are not (simply) animals because they live in a symbolic universe that constructs reality in terms of a system of meanings. Sociology is that discipline which studies social interaction between individuals and groups, within which values, ideas and symbols are transmitted.

We can understand the rise of cultural anthropology in America as a reaction against social Darwinism and against theories of race, contrary to the Christian view of the Old Testament, claiming that the different races of humanity had separate and distinct origins. While such theories rejected the view that human beings have common ancestors, cultural anthropology asserted, amongst other things, that the Navaho, Kwakiutl, Arapaho and American whites were not distinctively different as human beings; they simply had different cultural adaptations to their natural environment.

Technology and Nature

In effecting a distinction between man and animal, the other major option for the social sciences has been in terms of technology. This option, as I want to argue, opens up some important and rather dramatic alternatives to culture as a symbolic universe. Whereas culture to some extent either leaves nature intact or bypasses it in creating a 'sacred canopy' (Berger, 1967), technology of necessity transforms nature through direct intervention and manipulation. Culture appropriates nature by re-definition, that is by social construction and classification. Technology appropriates nature by alienation, that is by reconstituting it as an object. But in the alienation of nature, 'Man' opens up the possibility of working on the body, of transforming human ontology. Culture transforms nature through what Émile Durkheim and Marcel Mauss (1963) called 'primitive classification', whereas technology changes nature by denaturalization.

In its simplest form, human beings are defined as tool-making and tool-bearing creatures, who, according to Karl Marx, constantly change their own natures as they change the environment within which they live. To define human beings in terms of their technological adaptation to the environment raises some profound questions about what counts as humanity. It could be said that changes in culture – such as linguistic changes or the emergence of a new religion – do not involve a change in human ontology, whereas changes in modern technology – such as the development of stem-cell research – raise questions about the possibility of human continuity. Bio-technological change raises in principle the question as to whether humanity could become a new order of being, that is whether a post-human society is possible.

Of course, defining 'technology' raises as many questions as defining 'culture'. In the social sciences, technology has had several distinctive definitions and has been addressed by a number of diverse traditions. There is the idea of technology as a collection of machines that are useful in changing nature and helping human beings to dominate it. There is the related idea of a technological civilization, and finally there is the idea in contemporary sociology from Michel Foucault of techniques or practices for developing the self. These three forms of technology all have a problematic relationship to the body, because they involve in various ways control over nature (the body) and over the self (consciousness). Because technology presumes to control and change nature, it presents human beings with the prospects of utopian surmounting of the limitations of our natural animality, and therefore opens up the ever-present prospect of disaster. Much of science fiction has been concerned with a future world in which the current limitations of the human body have been transcended but with catastrophic consequences.

Whereas culture has been interpreted as beneficial to humanity and as a principal mode of defining us differently from the world of animals, technology is generally regarded as having an ambiguous relationship to humanity. In Greek mythology, technology appears in many narratives that involve the themes of theft or envy. Man acquired a major piece of technology, namely fire, by theft from the gods. In the story of Icarus, Daedalus built wings in order to escape from the Labyrinth but his son, disregarding his father's warnings, flew too close to the sun and when the wax holding his wings together melted, Icarus plunged to his death in the ocean. Technology helps humans to overcome the natural limitations of their bodies, but at the same time it threatens to destroy their natural harmony with nature.

The themes of embodiment, utopia and catastrophe have been persistent aspects of western philosophical speculation about technology. The catastrophic theme of the body and technology has been in recent social philosophy advanced by the work of Paul Virilio who has developed a 'war model' of the modern city and human society in which social change is driven not by production techniques but by the mechanics of war. He has invented a new science of 'dromology' to study the impact of speed on society. The political occupation of territory depends on efficient movement and circulation. There is a logical relationship between technology and accidents. For example, society has to develop the train in order to have a train crash, and as technology improves the potential of machines, then the size of catastrophe also grows. The question facing modern society is what the biological catastrophe would look like in a post-human age, and can we survive the speed of modern space technology (Virilio, 1999). The main counter argument to technological dystopia has been consistently argued by Donna Haraway, who sought to deconstruct the absolute authority of science to distinguish between animality and humanity but argued that, rather than abandoning science, feminism had to provide better accounts of reality. In 'Manifesto for Cyborgs' (1985), she argued that the cyborg helps to blur the distinction between nature and culture, between the living and the inert. The cyborg promises future freedoms.

Instrumentalities

The basic meaning or at least the commonsense meaning of technology has involved instrumentalities, tools and machines. The principal meaning of technology in the early seventeenth century referred to a systematic discourse on art or the arts. By 1859 it referred to the practical arts collectively, giving rise eventually to the notion of a technologist. Marx's view of technology was primarily in terms of physical capital and his complaints against what has subsequently come to be described as 'technological determinism' are well known. Marxist sociology is important in establishing the argument that technology has to be understood as always mediated by social relationships. It cannot exercise simple causal determinism outside the context of social relations. In short the stirrup does not produce feudalism or, as Marx said in *Capital* Volume 3, 'capital' is not simply a thing but rather a set of definite social relations of production, belonging to a definite historical period of society which is manifested in a thing, thereby giving this thing a specific social character.

Like most great thinkers, Marx often contradicted himself and in his popular writing slipped into technological determinism, as when commenting upon India. Writing in the *New York Daily Tribune*, for example, Marx said that British railways and newspapers had exploded the stationary nature of the Asiatic mode of production by creating private property, an emerging class system and efficient technologies of communication and transport. The railway thus produced modern India.

The enduring value of Marxist thought is, however, to understand humanity in terms of its labour on nature via the creation of technology. Marx argued that 'in his work upon the objective world man really proves himself as a *species being*. By means of it nature appears as *his* work and his reality' (Marx, 1963: 128). This production is not simply intellectually constructed but is actively created through technical practices. Marx's social theory of labour and nature offered humans either the prospect of utopia in a classless society without private property or a catastrophe in capitalism whereby the human body would be subjected to technology, becoming merely an addendum to the machine. For the young Marx, nature was simply the 'inorganic body' of humanity.

In twentieth-century social theory, perhaps the most obvious example of technological determinism was in the work of Marshall McLuhan. A much neglected social theorist, McLuhan was initially influenced by Wyndham Lewis's manifesto *Blast* of 1911. He established the Centre for Culture and Technology in Toronto to study the social effects of new technologies. Because his works were popular, they were often dismissed by sociologists such as Daniel Bell for (allegedly) trivializing the issues facing a 'post-industrial society'. In 1974 Bell wrote *The Coming of Post-Industrial Society* in which he argued that knowledge-based industry would replace manufacturing industries. In so doing, he opened up a new debate about the impact of information technology on economic production and the social structure, and ultimately on the transformation of the body.

It was, however, McLuhan's catch phrases – the medium is the message, the Gutenberg era and the global village – that offered an imaginative understanding of the implications of print and electronic media as modes of communication. His media theory and the notion of the global village captured the social impact of important technological changes, especially their implications for universities and education in general. Text-based knowledge required pedagogic techniques that were becoming obsolete in the electronic era of global communication. Technologies, he argued, are extensions of the body – the book is an extension of the eye and the information media, of the nervous system. While the body played an interesting, if somewhat minor, part in McLuhan's theory, technologies can be said to supplement by extension the limited capabilities of the natural body.

McLuhan foresaw that these new media would change the linear conception of time that went with print media, introducing new metaphors of space and time that did not depend on assumptions about linearity. The metaphor of the web in modern communications perfectly captures the fact that modern knowledge is not linear, and cannot be learnt by pedagogic methods that presuppose an apprenticeship that starts at some agreed beginning. Although McLuhan's work in the 1960s was ahead of its time, three criticisms of his theory remain. First, his historical views constituted an extreme example of technological determinism. The stirrup created feudalism; the computer, the modern age. Secondly, McLuhan's technological determinism meant that he nowhere considered the ownership and control of the means of communication – issues that have become central to the contemporary period in which the digital divide has created a new system of social stratification. Finally, McLuhan's vision of the global village was essentially utopian; it did not allow for struggles between elites, and he failed to understand the centrality of media to global military power.

The incomplete animal

If McLuhan's media sociology was without fail optimistic, then most theories of media and technology in the twentieth century have been pessimistic. Martin Heidegger's critical analysis of technology in the modern world has been the most influential vision of the negative consequences of a technological civilization. Heidegger's famous commentary on *The Question concerning Technology* (1977) was originally a lecture given in 1953 to the Bavarian Academy of Fine Arts in Munich and published in 1954 in *Vorträge und Aufsatze* (Safranski, 1998: 393). Like so much of his philosophy, Heidegger is concerned to get to the etymological roots of words in order to get a better understanding of what things are. In *What is Philosophy?* (1963), for example, he argued that deconstructing the meaning of ancient Greek philosophy brings the thinker into contact with 'the thing itself'. *Techne* then was originally a form of understanding that is a skilled and thorough knowing about the world that disclosed or revealed the world.

This *techne* as a form of revealing has in the modern world been replaced by technology as a form of control that offers human beings a picture of the world in which they hold dominion or mastery. Nature becomes merely an object of human subjectivity and will. Whereas traditional techniques allowed nature to emerge, modern technology challenges and controls nature. Thus, technological thinking is nihilistic. Heidegger gave very concrete and specific targets for his criticisms of modern nihilism: hydroelectric plants on the Rhine, consumerism, technology as an end in itself, and the development of efficiency without thought for its end. At a personal level, Heidegger claimed always to use a pen, refusing to adopt the typewriter because it came between the author and the text.

Heidegger was not, however, simply a critic of modern technology; he was not a German Luddite. A bridge over a river does not necessarily challenge nature, whereas a hydro plant redirects a river, thereby dominating it. His main anxiety was not about technology as an assembly of instrumentalities but rather that we should not adopt a technological mentality in order to solve technical problems. We should not become trapped by technological forms of thinking – otherwise we would be wholly unable to respond to modern society appropriately.

Heidegger was in this criticism of modern society heavily influenced by Nietzsche (Dreyfus, 1993). In his *Nietzsche* (1987) Heidegger drew attention to the 'biologism' of Nietzsche's thought in which the capacity to create knowledge as a system of technical skills is essential for survival. He went on to accept Nietzsche's nihilistic condemnation of the world and also followed Nietzsche's judgement that in the modern world God is dead. However, Heidegger argued ironically that it is precisely this loss of the holy as an objective reality that has made modern 'religious experience' possible. It is only with the loss of this objective reality that the subjective experience of the individual gains prominence. In short, Heidegger condemned modern forms of individualistic subjectivity. We can place Heidegger's emphasis on the unmediated relationship between body, thought and locality within a broader trend in German thought that contrasted technical civilizations with Life. Heidegger shared with romantic philosophers such as Ludwig Klages a sense of the 'darkening' of the world, the standardization of humanity, the destruction of the earth, and the erosion of spiritual life. However, while Klages remained an antirationalist and a 'Pan-struck biosophist deep in the primordial mystery of things which is forever closed to a "disinterested" reason', Heidegger struggled to recall a 'forgotten truth' which reclaimed the union between *logos* and *physis*, that is between beings and Being (Wiedmann, 1995: 186–7).

If we say that Heidegger treated *techne* as one aspect of something much larger, namely a technological civilization, then we can see that Heidegger's critical reflections on technology are similar to Max Weber's writing on 'rationalization processes' and 'disenchantment', the Frankfurt Schools critique of modernity in the dialectic of Enlightenment and Norbert Elias's reflections on 'the civilizing process' (Elias, 2000). These German debates were originally placed in the context of the contrast between 'culture' (values, art, and religion) and 'civilization' (technology, industry, and the economy). But the contrast was, if only implicitly, a contrast between American civilization, a profit-driven society at the cutting edge of technology, and European culture, which celebrated the distinction flowing from education, spirituality, and taste. By the time

Heidegger gave his technology lecture, Europe was entering the Cold War and the fear of an Atomic War was dominant in western politics. Aldous Huxley's *Brave New World* was a best-seller in Germany in the 1950s and thus Heidegger's concerns about the negative consequences of technology were certainly shared by his audience.

Heidegger's approach depended on Nietzsche's notion of human beings as a 'not yet complete animal', that is because human beings are poorly developed in terms of their instinctual equipment, they need to develop cultural institutions as a 'sacred canopy' (Berger, 1967) to protect themselves from their somewhat hostile environment. This view of human incompleteness became the basis of Arnold Gehlen's philosophical anthropology and following Gehlen's work Peter Berger and Thomas Luckmann established their influential view of the human construction of social reality (Berger and Luckmann, 1966). This development of the sociology of the body out of Gehlen via Berger and Luckmann is relatively well known (Turner, 2001). The most interesting elaboration of this theme in Nietzsche has been in the work of Giorgio Agamben (1998) in *Homo Sacer* and more recently in *The Open* (Agamben, 2004). Starting with Aristotle, Agamben notes that, while philosophy and theology attempt to separate man and animal, man is an animal (*zoe*) who cannot be separated from a form of life (*bios*). Man is subject to exclusion as animal and to inclusion as humanity. Political sovereignty is exercised over the border between animality and humanity.

Agamben pursues this argument about what he calls 'bare life' through a study of Heidegger. Whereas Heidegger depicts the animal as 'poor in this world', man is a 'world-forming creature'. This distinction appears to be wholly in line with the arguments of Nietzsche and Gehlen. Heidegger's originality possibly lies in the fact that man suffers most, not from anxiety, but from boredom. Animals cannot be bored because they cannot have self-reflexive consciousness about their position in the world; their instincts perfectly match their worldliness. Humans through their boredom experience a sense of alienation, that is being bored. The religious world emerges out of this vacuum of being bored (Raposa, 1999).

Agamben attempts to avoid Heideggerian pessimism with man as the creature that is bored with life through, for example, a discussion of sexual fulfilment in Titian's painting of the 'Nymph and Shepherd' in which humans can discover each other beyond the separation of animal and humanity. However, Agamben's philosophy remains ultimately pessimistic because in modern politics the marginalization of humans to the border of 'bare life' is precisely illustrated by the zone of indeterminate existence in such institutions as the Guantanamo bay prison.

Technology of the self

A further meaning of technology which we need to consider is derived from the work of Michel Foucault, who developed the idea of the training of the self through discipline as a technology of the self. We can for example give a Foucauldian framework to McLuhan's analysis of the media by asking what forms of 'technologies of the self' are produced by different media of knowledge and information technologies? If globalization involves the destruction of linear time and space by information technology, we can expect new forms of training and education to shape 'personality' into these revolutionary technological conditions.

In *The Idea of the Self*, Jerrold Seigel (2005) has argued that any theory of the self will have to embrace three components. To be a reflective self, we need self-consciousness; that is to say, we must be able to reflect upon our identities, our social actions and our relationships with others. Language and memory are both necessary for such forms of consciousness. Selfhood must have this capacity for continuous self monitoring. Secondly, the self is not, of course, a free-floating consciousness, because the phenomenological self is defined by embodiment. Recognition of the self depends not simply on memory and consciousness but also on the peculiar physical characteristics and physical mannerisms of the individual. This aspect of the discourse of the self involves the body and bodily practices, and recent sociology has insisted that the self involves an embodied subjectivity towards the world. In the sociology of Pierre Bourdieu, the individual is expressed through a particular configuration of dispositions and taste that constitute the habitus of an individual. Bourdieu's notions of practice and habitus are derived ultimately from Aristotle's virtue ethics in which training produces a particular type of character that is manifest in their virtues, and so the dispositions of the self are a product of the habitus within which they are embodied. The final dimension of this model of the self is the notion of the self as the historical product of society. From the perspective of sociology, the self is always situated within a dense network of social relationships. Although the western possessive self has often been represented in the isolated and amoral figure of Robinson Crusoe, sociology has interpreted the self as inextricably and always a social being. While different theories of the self tend to emphasize particular aspects of the self – reflection, embodiment and social relationships – these theories of the self have necessarily to address directly or indirectly all three aspects.

Seigel's theory is primarily concerned with the analytical dimensions of the self, but we can suitably give these three dimensions a historical dimension. The reflective self was predominantly associated with the eighteenth and nineteenth centuries as a consequence of the Enlightenment after Immanuel Kant's philosophical challenge to throw off traditional, that is religious, constraints on the autonomy of the individual self. The Romantic reaction to the rationalism of the Enlightenment placed greater emphasis on individuality, subjectivity and embodiment. With the rise of industrial society and the emergence of sociology as a science, the self was no longer emphatically divorced from the social. Of course, the idea of the social came to be criticized by Hannah Arendt as a sign of modern totalitarianism. Modernization paved the way for sociology as an academic discipline in which there emerged the view that the individual is merely a product of social forces. This sociological view of the passive self which dominated the middle of the twentieth century was articulated in sociological theories of mass society, the managerial revolution, and the other-directed self. The classical debate around this vision of managerial man was expressed in William H. Whyte's *The Organization Man* (1956).

The individual became reflexive that is passive rather than actively reflective. However, the corporeal self has become the dominant paradigm of contemporary society, because the scientific revolutions in information science, microbiology and genetics have created a language of genetic determinism in which the self is determined genetically. The 'homosexual gene', 'the criminal gene' and the 'divorce gene' now preclude any recognition of individual reflexivity and moral responsibility. The individual self is now thought to be driven by whatever genes they have contingently and fortuitously inherited from parents and ancestors. In a 'somatic society' the body becomes the site of political debate and social anxieties (Turner, 1992: 13).

This sociological tradition can be related to Heidegger's condemnation of modern subjectivity, a condemnation which was shared by Foucault. Modern secular society has become dominated by the subjectivity of the self which we can interpret as a consequence of an 'expressive revolution' (Parsons, 1974). Subjective individualism in popular culture is expressed through the importance of choice in lifestyles and values. The new 'quest cultures' have been critically evaluated as manifestations of expressive individualism. This American religious revolution involved a shift from the cognitive-instrumental values of early capitalism to an affective-expressive culture. Individuals are free to reinvent and refashion themselves constantly and self-consciously. The expressive revolution signified in the student rebellions of the 1960s a new cultural movement that was a significant departure from the asceticism that Weber had described in *The Protestant Ethic and the Spirit of Capitalism* (1930). The expressive revolution celebrated hedonism, self-expression and hostility to conventional norms and social institutions. This discourse of personal freedom from the 1960s has been challenged by a return to the discourse of biology which is grounded in determinism rather than a notion of subjective freedom. The body in this technological discourse has become an 'iron cage' rather than a site of pleasure and personal fulfilment. It involves a language of genetic causation that is very different from the celebration of the hedonistic body that characterized the post-war period, emerging critically in the 1968 Events (Turner, 2006). The free flowing youthful body of post-war consumerism has been joined by a new social imagery – the geriatric, technically enhanced, dependent body.

Technology and biological life: living forever

The sociology of the body has entered an interesting phase in its development, where the revolution in biology is changing the ways in which we understand 'life'. Hence the tradition that connects Nietzsche, Heidegger and Agamben appears to be the most significant framework for understanding the crisis of modern society. Somatic society is constructed around a set of urgent questions relating to bio-technology and the future of biological life. The traditional anthropological arguments about culture are now constantly challenged by the findings of genetic research. In public discourse, it is often claimed that there is a gene to explain some aspect of human behaviour – such as a divorce gene to show why some people are prone to divorce or a God-gene to show why some people are more prone to spiritual experiences than others. These popular notions are often rejected by genetic scientists who claim that the causal connection between genes and human behaviour is more complex than popular debate suggests and can rarely be reduced to the effect of a single gene. The new genetics have made important scientific strides in explaining the prevalence of certain specific diseases such as Huntington's Disease, but it has been unable to achieve similar results in the explanation of complex human behaviour such as criminality.

In some respects this discussion of the relevance of biology to understanding human behaviour is an old debate, going back for example to positivist criminology. The new bio-technologies, however, such as stem-cell research and therapeutic cloning, raise a new generation of ethical questions that go well beyond the issues surrounding organ transplants and new reproductive technology. The creation of so-called biological chimeras such as the 'geep' (a combination of goat and sheep) raise the possibility that, if these chimeras are in some sense new creatures, then human science is creating a brave new world. These developments have significant consequences for religious doctrines such as creationism. They also mean that the human body is no longer conceptualized as an organism but has to be understood as a system of information that can be expressed as a map, for example in the human genome programme.

In traditional societies, the relationship between resources (especially the food supply) and life expectancy was, more or less, regulated by a Malthusian logic. Classical economics was associated with the demographic theories of Thomas Malthus who in *Essay on the principle of population as it affects the future improvement of society* in 1798 argued that, given the sexual drive, the need for food, and the declining yield of the soil, the increase in population would inevitable supersede the food supply (Malthus, 1926). Population increase could either be controlled by positive means (such as famine, disease, and war) or by preventive means (such as vice, chastity, and late marriage). Any attempt to improve the living conditions of the working class could not be sustained in the long term, because such reforms would increase the population, thereby reducing living standards by reducing the food supply.

History does not appear to have entirely supported the logic of this Malthussian pessimism. For example in Britain, the invention of contraception in the 1820s, the expansion of the food supply through colonial expansion, and technical improvements in agricultural cultivation and production controlled reproduction and expanded resources. With improvements in nutrition, food supply and distribution, water quality, public sanitation, and housing, the death rate fell and the increase in population was supported by these technical improvements in agriculture. Eventually the birth rate also declined as life expectancy rose with the successful treatment of childhood illness such as whooping cough. However, the possibility of significantly extending the expectation of life in the affluent societies of the northern hemisphere through the application of medical research on stem-cells has clear Malthusian implications for the world as a whole.

It is unclear what causes ageing. Medical interest in ageing goes back at least to writers such as Luigi Cornaro (1464–1566) who in his *Discourses on the Temperate Life* of 1558 argued that his own longevity was a consequence of temperance, exercise and a good diet. The body's finite supply of vital spirits could be husbanded by temperate practices of diet and exercise. The idea that ageing is inevitable has been the basic presupposition of gerontology ever since. If ageing is an inevitable process of cellular degeneration, then the question (do we have a right to live forever?) does not arise, apart from fanciful speculation. It is obviously the case that life expectancy increased dramatically in the late nineteenth and twentieth centuries, but in the second half of the twentieth century it had reached a plateau. If we take men in the United Kingdom, the expectation of life at birth in 1901 was only 45.5 years, but by 1991 this was 73.2 years. However subsequent demographic data indicate only a modest increase from 75.4 in 2001 to a projected 77.6 by 2020.

In conventional gerontology, 'living forever' might in practical terms mean living a full life and achieving the average expectation of longevity. More recently however, there has been considerable speculation as to whether medical science could reverse this ageing process. Between the 1960s and 1980s the view put forward by biologists was that normal cells had what was known as 'replicative senescence', that is normal tissues can only divide a finite number of times before entering a stage of quiescence. Cells were observed *in vitro* in a process of natural senescence, but eventually experiments *in vivo* established a distinction between normal and pathological cells in terms of cellular division. Paradoxically pathological cells appeared to have no such necessary limitation on replication, and therefore a process of 'immortalization' was the distinctive feature of a pathological cell line. Biologists concluded therefore by extrapolation that finite cell division meant that the ageing of whole organisms was inevitable. These laboratory findings supported the view that human life had an intrinsic and predetermined limit, and that it was only through pathological developments that some cells might out survive the otherwise inescapable senescence of cellular life. Ageing was both normal and necessary.

This conventional framework of ageing was eventually disrupted by the discovery that human embryonic cells were capable of continuous division in culture and showed no sign of any inevitable replicative crisis or limitation. Certain non-pathological cells (or stem cells) were capable of indefinite division, and hence were 'immortalized'. The cultivation of these cells as an experimental form of life has challenged existing assumptions about the distinctions between the normal and the pathological, and between life and death. Stem-cell research begins to redefine the arena within which the body has reserves of renewable tissue, suggesting that the limits of biological growth are not immutable or inflexible. The body has a surplus of stem cells capable of survival beyond the death of the organism. With these developments in micro-bio-gerontology, the capacity of regenerative medicine to expand the limits of life becomes a plausible prospect of medicine, creating new economic opportunities in the application of life sciences. This new interpretation of replication locates ageing as a shifting threshold between biological surplus and waste, or between obsolescence and renewal.

Because World Bank economists have seen the ageing of the developed world as a significant threat to continuing global economic growth, there is considerable interest in the commercial possibilities of stem-cell research as a feature of regenerative medicine. Companies operating in the Caribbean and south-east Asia are already offering regenerative medicine as part of holiday packages, designed to alleviate the negative consequences of degenerative diseases such as multiple sclerosis or diabetes. The idea of regenerative tourism might become an addendum to sexual tourism in the world of advanced bio-capitalism.

The human consequences of these changes will be rapid and radical, but little thought has been given to the social and political consequences of extended longevity. Although it is mere sociological speculation, one can assume that a new pattern of ageing would produce a number of major socio-economic problems. Growing world inequality between the rejuvenated or immortalized North and the naturally ageing senescent South would further inflame the resentment of deprived social groups against the wealthy aged populations. The labour market would be unable to cope with the increasing number of human survivors, and there would be similar crises in housing markets. The food supply would not be able to respond effectively to the resulting population expansion, producing increasing economic dependency on genetically modified food. Environmental pollution, global warming, and further depletion of natural resources would follow, with declining species diversity. Intergenerational, ethnic and class conflicts over resources would increase, including conflicts over jobs, retirement benefits, pensions and housing. The rapid transformation of family structures would continue as the elderly survived in greater numbers, presumably taking on new partners and reproducing in new households through unlimited serial monogamy. Geriatric holidays in such places as northern Thailand would further intensify the sexual exploitation of young, poor women. There would be a rapid expansion of gated communities for the elderly, for example from Japan, Sweden and Britain, in such destinations as Penang and Portimao. As young black migrants stream northwards out of Africa in search of jobs, elderly retired survivors will stream southwards in search of cheap housing and warm climates.

The theological notion of an after-life would probably disappear, since most survivors would literally experience eternal life or at least indefinite life on earth. However, if we assume that, while genomic sciences could reduce mortality, it would, at least in the short term, increase morbidity as chronic illness and geriatric diseases increased. Living forever would mean in practice living forever in discomfort, in a morbid condition. There would therefore be increasing psychological problems including depression, ennui and despair as surviving populations discovered new levels of boredom through the endless repetition of the same, resulting periodically in bouts of collective boredom, hysteria, and suicide.

The prospect of indefinite life would thus raise an acute Malthusian crisis and make Cornaro's vision of a healthful long life, a living nightmare. These transformations imply an interesting change from early to late modernity. In the early stages of capitalism, the social role of medical science was to improve health care, thereby making the working class healthy. The application of medical science was to produce an efficient labour force, but late capitalism does not need a large labour force at full employment, because technology has made labour more efficient. In the new biotechnological environment, disease is no longer a negative force in the economy but on the contrary an aspect of the factors of production.

This new biological technology goes to the core of Nietzsche's views on morality and the 'overman'. Can biology replace morality by allowing us to live forever, regardless of our behaviour in this world? If medicine can offer a certain cure for such conditions as venereal disease, lung cancer and obesity, would I change my behaviour towards my sexual partners, would I abandon my preference for cigars and chocolate cakes in favour of asceticism? The new medical technologies imply that human beings could in principle live forever. If the new biological sciences make possible the idea of living forever, then we can have a life beyond ethics. The Christian idea of an afterlife and the Buddhist quest for release from the karma-rebirth cycle would become problematic obscure beliefs. It is difficult to see how the ethical determinism of Buddhist doctrine could for example survive the genetic determinism of modern medical sciences. Technology thereby cuts the relationship between ethics and the bodily regulation of life. If we can live forever through medical technologies, why bother with ethics?

Conclusion

The utopian aspect of scientific technology declined in the twentieth century as the prospects of nuclear disaster and environmental pollution became dominant aspects of public debate. Rene Dubos (1974: 147) who coined the expression the 'mirage of health' has argued that 'technological innovations commonly have disastrous secondary effects, many of which are probably unpredictable'. This public unease with scientific advance has been reflected in opposition to genetically modified food and in growing awareness of the hitherto unforeseen consequences of global warming. This lack of confidence and trust in science possibly explains the academic success of the concept of risk society as a general explanation of our dilemma (Beck, 1992). In this discussion of technology and the body, I have tried to suggest that current stem-cell research has potentially far greater consequences for society and the status of the human.

Such research is difficult to regulate and its medical results appear to be beneficial for the individual. Stem-cell research perfectly illustrates an interesting problem in the idea of rationality. It is rational for me as an individual to want to live forever, even if this means that I shall spend much of my life bedeviled by geriatric disease as I wait for future cures for my contemporary morbidity. One example would be the prevalence of type two diabetes in old age. We could imagine a situation where stem-cell research has cured various forms of heart disease, Parkinson's disease and high blood pressure, but it has found no cure for diabetes. We are living longer but with mounting problems from our (as yet) incurable diabetes. While it may be rational for me as an individual to live forever, this desire to exist whatever the personal costs creates huge problems for the society in which I live.

The prospects of living forever are at present remote, and the moral arguments against such a goal are considerable. It is here also that Heidegger's notion of boredom might become useful. Prolonged life with no purpose will result in a profound boredom when we are trying to kill time, or passing the time by diversions. Heidegger believed however that at the end of this process there was the possibility that one could find an emptiness that would release one from boredom. This development is, with modern technology, an unlikely outcome. If medical technology can in principle make it possible, at least for the affluent West, to live forever, technology will corrode ethics, because there will be little motivation to follow an ethical diet, that is a government of the body. At least religious culture will be undermined by the prospect of an eternal secular life, even if that secular existence is one of boredom and discomfort. At this point, humanity will have progressed well beyond the conventional division between culture and technology, and the division between animality and humans will become meaningless.

References

Agamben, G. (1998) *Homo Sacer. Sovereign Power and Bare Life*, Stanford: Stanford University Press.

Agamben, G. (2004) *The Open: man and animal*, Stanford, CA: Stanford University Press.

Beck, U. (1992) *Risk Society*. Cambridge: Polity.

Berger, P.L. (1967) *The Sacred Canopy* Garden City, NY: Doubleday.

Berger, P.L. & Luckmann, T. (1966) *The Social Construction of Reality*, Garden City, NY: Doubleday.

Dreyfus, H.L. (1993) 'Heidegger on the connection between nihilism, art, technology and politics' in Charles B. Guignon (ed.) *The Cambridge Companion to Heidegger*, Cambridge: Cambridge University Press, pp. 289–316.

Dubos, R. (1974) *Beast or Angel? choices that make us human* New York: Charles Scribners

Elias, N. (2000) *The Civilizing Process*, Oxford: Blackwell.

Fukuyama, F. (2002) *Our Posthuman Future. Consequences of the Biotechnology Revolution*, New York: Farrar, Straus and Giroux.

Haraway, D.J. (1985) 'Manifesto for Cyborgs: science, technology and socialist feminism in the 1980s' *Socialist Review* 80: 65–108.

Heidegger, M. (1963) *What is philosophy?* Worcester: Vision.
Heidegger, M. (1977) *The Question Concerning Technology and Other Essays*, New York: Harper & Row.
Heidegger, M. (1987) *Nietzsche,* New York: Harper.
Kluckhohn, C. (1962) *Culture and Behavior*, New York: Free Press.
Kroeber, A. and Parsons, T. (1958) 'The concepts of culture and of social system' *American Sociological Review* 23(5): 582–583.
Malthus, T. (1926) *Essay on the principle of population as it affects the future improvement of society*, London: Macmillan.
Marx, K. (1963) *Early Writings,* London: C.A.Watts.
Parsons, T. (1973) 'Clyde Kluckhohn and the Integration of Social Science' in Walter W. Taylor, John L. Fischer and Evon Z. Vogt (eds) *Culture and Life. Essays in Memory of Clyde Kluckhohn* Carbondale and Edwardsville: Southern Illinois University Press, pp. 30–57.
Parsons, T. (1974) 'Religion in Postindustrial America: the problem of secularization' *Social Research* 41(2): 193–225.
Raposa, M.L. (1999) *Boredom and the Religious Imagination*, Charlottesville: University Press of Virginia.
Safranski, R. (1998) *Martin Heidegger. Between Good and Evil*, Cambridge, Mass.: Harvard University Press.
Seigel, J. (2005) *The Idea of the Self*, Cambridge: Cambridge University Press.
Turner, B.S. (1992) *Regulating Bodies. Essays in Medical Sociology*, London and New York: Routledge.
Turner, B.S. (2001) 'Peter Berger' in A. Elliott and B.S. Turner (eds) *Profiles in Contemporary Social Theory*, London: Sage, pp. 107–116.
Turner, B.S. (2006) 'The 1968 Student Revolts: the expressive revolution and generational politics' in A.Q. Sica and S. Turner (eds) *The Disobedient Generation. Social Theorists in the Sixties*, Chicago: Chicago University Press, pp. 272–284.
Virilio, P. (1999) *Polar Inertia* London: Sage.
Weber, M. (1930) *The Protestant Ethic and the Spirit of Capitalism,* London: Allen & Unwin.
Whyte, W.H. (1956) *The Organization Man, New* York: Simon & Schuster.
Wiedmann, A.K. (1995) *The German Quest for Primal Origins in Art, Culture and Politics 1900–1933*, Lampeter: the Edward Mellen Press.

Somatic elements in social conflict*

Donald N. Levine

Abstract

Although social conflict has obvious ties with physical combat, the literature on social conflict ignores its corporeal substratum. Reviewing that literature yields a paradigm of sources of conflict comprising six major variables: hostility level, reactivity, rigidity, moral righteousness, weak conflict-aversive values, and ineffective dampening factors. Each of those variables has some representation in the body. Realizing this enables us to ask what kinds of conflict-relevant meanings emanate from processes within the human body itself, and what supra-organismic variables imbue bodily conduct with meanings that relate to conflict. That analysis in turn opens up a new dimension of the general theory of action by way of amending Parsons-Lidzes's concept of the behavioural system. The chapter suggests calling this the *actional organism* – the subsystem of action where the organism's input of energies and the inputs from sources of meanings meet and interpenetrate.

Key words: action, aggression, conflict, somatics, organism

Introduction

Social conflict presents a topic where the wish to bring bodies into sociological analysis should meet no resistance. Although conflict theory can be dryly abstract, its close connections to the realities of physical combat, by metaphor when not literally, makes it easy to link representations of social conflict with the interaction of physical bodies. Think of conflict and you quickly bump up against bodies – yelling and screaming, pushing and shoving, punching and wrestling, stabbing and shooting. Even in purely verbal conflict the body swerves quickly into view: reddened faces, clenched jaws, tensed muscles, and quickened breath. Even when conflicts of interests or ideas are negotiated in a non-combative mode, differences in bodily posture and demeanor readily appear. And bodily changes manifest even when the parties to conflict are not in direct physical proximity.

Yet for the past century the literature on social conflict has ignored its corporeal substratum. Post-war classics – Coser (1956), Coleman (1957), Boulding (1962/1988), and Schelling (1960) – do not mention the body. Randall Collins's (1975) comprehensive *Conflict Sociology* has nary a reference to the bodily dimensions of his subject, nor does Louis Kriesberg's (1973) compendious analysis of conflicts, destructive and constructive. Instead of bemoaning such neglect, suppose we turn the point around and view that neglect as understandable, if not warranted, given the paucity of theoretical resources on how to formulate such linkages. Suppose then that we address the problematic of social conflict and the body with an eye for openings through which we might insert fresh lines of substantive work.

As point of departure for such an effort I shall reference the contributions of Talcott Parsons. This will seem odd to those who consider Parsons irrelevant to such concerns on grounds that his stressing the normative dimension of action precluded engagement with the body in society. As with many other dismissive glosses on Parsons, this one is hard to square with a review of what he actually produced. In publications spanning more than thirty-five years, Parsons considered the organismic dimension of human action in a number of places. These encompass subjects related to age and sex, including seminal papers on the incest taboo and youth subcultures; contributions to the theory of socialization; analyses of the cultural framing of life and death; an influential discussion of the parameters of medical practice; classic papers on aggression and reactions to social strains; writings on the human body itself – with attention to such phenomena as proper clothing, treatment of bodily injuries, and norms regarding physicians' access to patients' bodies; and intermittent efforts to weave the corporeal dimension into the general theory of action, culminating in his testamentary 'Paradigm of the Human Condition' in 1978.

In spite of these substantive contributions, in his general theory of action Parsons did not focus on the organismic dimension anywhere near to the extent that he did when analysing the psychological, social, and cultural dimensions of action. To be sure, on occasion he signalled his awareness of the theoretical lacuna between the physiological body, as one of the external environments of action, and the orientations of actors. Given his commitment to the Weberian concept of action, which conceives action as subjectively meaningful conduct, Parsons had some sense of the difficulty involved in leaping from purely biological process to a process imbued with meanings. He attempted to address that problem with intermittent, almost perfunctory, glosses on what he called the *behavioural organism*. This concept made it possible to represent aspects of action that involved the body but contrasted with the merely 'vegetative' aspects of the organism's functioning. The conception of the behavioural organism came to include certain organ systems and physiological processes, especially those involved in mental functioning. Although the usual connotations of 'behaviour' excluded meaning, Parsons used the term behaviour to mean that these processes represent capacities that manifested certain kinds of meaning. He located that dimension in what he was calling the adaptive subsystem of the general universe of action, and treated it in terms of the general quality of intelligence. Lidz and Lidz (1976) developed this notion further, emphasizing the separation from a purely organismic processes by calling it the *behavioural system* and incorporating thereunder work by Jean Piaget that analysed complexes of intelligent operations as universal capacities.

Three decades later it appears that this piece of action theory has been left where Lidz and Lidz left it (Bare, 2005). In the meantime, explorations in other disciplines, related especially to education, have greatly extended the notion of behavioural capacity. The notion of intelligence has been expanded well beyond its earlier restricted sphere, to include a number of different functions including audiovisual powers, interpersonal skills, emotional capacities, and language abilities.[1] Although the Lidzes' intervention threw new light on the topic, it rested on a questionable Cartesian split between body/mind and neglected the fact that humans possess, after all, only one nervous system. What is more, the body itself has come to be theorized as the seat of a number of powers of its own, involving kinesthetic perceptual abilities and movement skills, and has come to be understood as participating intimately in all of the other powers just enumerated. The latter field has been investigated and documented by work in the field known as somatics. In the words of one of the most brilliant pioneer somatic investigators, Moshe Feldenkrais, 'the most abstract thought has emotional-vegetative and sensory-motor components; the whole nervous system participates in every act' (Feldenkrais, 1949, 26).

Following Piaget, Lidz and Lidz articulated the constituents of the behavioural system as 'capacities to act which are intrinsic to human adaptation,' likening them to the notion of grammar in transformational linguistics; that is, grammar as denoting the ability of competent speakers to form sentences under any conditions (1976, 197). Adopting this notion provisionally, I propose to understand the behavioural system as signifying *the repertoire of human capacities that consist of physical abilities and dispositions together with the somatic components of 'non-physical' behaviours*. Accordingly, this would include physical capacities that are involved in the execution of conflicts and the ability to control conflict. I shall return to the general issue of how to integrate the body-conflict nexus into the general theory of action after I have reviewed afresh the general theory of conflict.

A paradigm of social conflict

To investigate conflictual phenomena thoroughly requires that we differentiate among types of conflict with respect to a variety of salient dimensions. These include the media of conflict (verbal/physical), intensity (violent/nonviolent), systemic location (internal/external), type of conflictual party (family, community, nation), and type of outcome (constructive/destructive). On the other hand, supposing that something is to be gained by considering conflict at a more abstract level I shall outline a paradigm of generic conflict.

As a form of social interaction, conflict has properties that can be investigated without reference to the orientations of individual actors. Even so, its basic dynamics derive from actions of parties that can be represented as acts of individual subjects, as follows:

1. A makes a bid for conflict by aggressing against B (verbally or physically).
2. B responds through counter-attack of some sort. Thereafter,
3. A and B continue to engage in conflict, establishing
   a) a static equilibrium in which conflict becomes a constitutive element of the relationship, or
   b) a dynamic equilibrium in which both parties continue an escalating spiral, until one of them
      i) defeats the other, or
      ii) tires or has a change of heart about the conflict, or
      iii) responds to an outside force that dampens or resolves the conflict.

From this paradigm, it follows that the elements involved in the generation of conflict will be the factors that dispose party A to aggress, party B to counter-attack, and the two parties to continue waging their conflict.

What factors account for those dispositions toward aggressive action? From the literature on conflict I have culled six factors that abet the process (as well as two countervailing variables that dampen these dispositions).

1. *Hostility level.* In his pioneering treatise on the subject, *Conflict and Defense: A General Theory* (1962), Kenneth Boulding related the disposition to engage in conflict to an initial base of dispositions to aggress against others.
2. *Reactivity.* James Coleman (1957) noted the tendency for conflict to escalate when a provoked party reacts in ways that antagonize the initiating party further, until the escalating process takes on a life of its own. Boulding designated the tendency for parties to react in this way as a reactivity coefficient.
3. *Positional rigidity.* Boulding also viewed a factor that lessens the disposition for conflict to be a willingness to accept other satisfactory utilities as a substitute for one that another party craved equally. In a popular textbook on the subject, Roger Fisher and William Urry (1981) depict this as a capacity to alter 'positions' regarding means to secure a particular 'interest.'
4. *Moral righteousness.* Hostile energy is intensified when conjoined with a sense of moral valorization. Georg Simmel analysed how conflict becomes intensified when objectified out of purely personal reactions into combat for a cause. Bettelheim and Janowitz (1950) identified a number of emotional dynamics in which out-groups were hated for qualities that the in-group members found unacceptable.

5. *Weakness of conflict-aversive values.* a) Some cultures glorify combat and the virtues of the warrior. b) Conversely, Freud stressed the importance of internalized controls over the expression of social aggression: the superego process employs aggressive energy to inhibit or repress the activation of hostile impulses, the ego-ideal instantiates cultural ideals of harmony and peace. Durkheim similarly identified conscience and 'effervescence' in groups as brakes on conflict.
6. *Weakness of external dampening factors.* Parsons (1951) and Coleman (1957) among others delineated a range of social structural factors crucial to the existence of conflict. The absence or weakness of such factors facilitates the escalation of conflict. Conversely, the presence of such factors serves to dampen conflict. These factors include, for example, the activation of policing processes; the invocation of shared transcending values; the availability of mechanisms of cooptation, and customs that favor the resort to mediation.

In what follows, I inquire into how these factors that generate or dampen conflictual actions relate to features of the physical body. Following Weber's authoritative definition of 'action' as behaviour to which some sort of meaning is attached, I ask: what kinds of conflict-relevant meaning might emanate from processes within the human body itself, and what supra-organismic variables imbue bodily conduct with meanings that relate to conflict?[2] I suggest renaming the site of these linkages as the *actional organism*–the subsystem of action where the organism's input of energies and the inputs from sources of meanings meet and interpenetrate.

Somatic elements that promote conflict

1. The body and aggressive impulsivity

When social science does appropriate knowledge about bodies into its discourse on conflict it often relies on assumptions about an inherent human disposition toward aggression. On the eve of World War I William James did so by asserting that 'our ancestors have bred pugnacity into our bone and marrow, and thousands of years of peace won't breed it out of us' ([1910] 1974, 314). In his landmark formulations on political realism, political scientist Hans Morgenthau argued that the social world results from forces inherent in human nature, which render it 'inherently a world of opposing interests and of conflict among them' (1960, 4). Ethologist Konrad Lorenz (1966) depicted aggression as an essential part of the life-preserving organization of instincts, arguing that for numerous species conflict provides clear adaptive advantages: balancing the ecological distributions, selecting the fittest specimens through fights among rivals, mediating ranking orders needed for complex organizations, even instigating ceremonies that promote social bonding. Another ethologist, Nikolaas Tinbergen, likewise posits a universal instinctual proclivity to intraspecific conflict and finds human aggressiveness marked by a socially disruptive quality: 'Man is the only species that is a mass murderer, the only misfit in his own society' (1968, 180).[3] More recently, Richard Wrangham and Dale Peterson (1996) summarize evidence from ethological studies to conclude that the human animal, and the male of the species preeminently, has inborn propensities to attack and kill others that exceed adaptive needs.

Despite vicissitudes of instinct theories, psychoanalytic psychology has tended to assume an innate reservoir of egoistic and aggressive impulses that, amplified by externalization and projection, flood into interpersonal conflicts. Freud thought violent conflict endemic to humans, both to resolve conflicts of interest and to express an 'active instinct for hatred and destruction.' He bemoaned the destructiveness of modern warfare but held little hope that cultured aversions to war could overcome the aggressive dispositions so deeply rooted in man's biological makeup ([1932] 1939). Freud's theory posited a self-destructive 'death instinct' which gets diverted from the self toward others, thereby producing a constant fund of conflictual energies. Most psychoanalysts rejected Freud's assumption of a death instinct and some substituted a destructive instinct for the polar opposite of the sexual instinct.

Freud and his followers view the human organism as a perpetually renewed source of instinctual energies that well up and produce inner discomfort until they get released. Psychic and somatic symptoms reflect failures in the personality's ability to release those instinctual tensions, which eventually find outlet through indirect channels. In one way or another human aggression represents a constantly flowing impulse that emanates from the human body such that humans can never escape the proclivity to harm if not destroy either themselves or others. Although Lorenz took a more positive view of conflict, he too espoused a mechanistic-hydraulic view of aggression. Lorenz likens aggression to a gas constantly being pumped into a container or to a liquid in a reservoir dischargeable through a spring-loaded valve at the bottom. In Lorenz's conception, energies specific for an instinctive act accumulate continuously in neural centers for that behaviour, leading animals and humans to hunt for stimuli in order to trigger the release of those energies.

For those who view conflictual action in this perspective, the propensity to act out aggressive impulses is limited by one or both of two other basic drives. For Freudian psychology, the aggressive instinct is balanced by Eros, the drive to form harmonious relationships with others. For Tinbergen, it is limited by fear of the countervailing force of enemies. To some extent, Hobbes can be seen as combining both combative and pacific drives. The perpetual and restless desire of power after power to which all men are inclined would lead inexorably to constant civil strife were it not for the activation of an even stronger natural inclination: the wish to avoid violent death. Humans are also motivated by a wish to live comfortably by means of conveniences, which only a regime of peace can procure. So the impulse to aggress against others gets subordinated to a wish for peaceful coexistence, a condition procured by establishing a sovereign political authority.

The logic of Hobbes's argument can be modified to cover a variety of social arrangements designed to control conflict: the body is the home of divergent impulses including aggressiveness, but aggression can get inhibited by other propensities that support institutions designed to prevent conflict. This image of the body is not unlike what we find in writers like Nietzsche and Sorel. The latter visualize a natural human disposition to be fierce and combative, a disposition that (for them, unhappily) gets swamped by fear and desires for convenience, thereby deflecting martial impulses into innocuous channels.

What none of these theories offers, however, is a way of connecting those dispositions with the constitutive systems of bodily organisms, a way that the relatively new discipline of somatics may help to illumine. Such analyses would proceed, for example, from considering hormonal levels of aggressivity through neuronal responses that mobilize aggressive physical or verbal impulses. Acting out such impulses involves their translation into complex neuro-muscular-skeletal responses. The behavioural capacity to enact those responses, and thereby direct aggressive energies toward some social object, brings hormonal levels into the orbit of human action. Hormonally grounded aggressivity is the portion of the actional organism that energizes a trained capacity to attack and injure others.

2. The body and conflictual reactivity

In his analysis of the dynamics of social conflict, Boulding points to a second variable that figures in the equation regarding escalation of conflict. He refers to these as 'reaction processes,' processes in which a movement by one party provokes a movement by the other which in turn changes the field of the first, and so on. He proposes to designate this variable as a reaction coefficient: 'the amount by which the equilibrium level of hostility of the one increases per unit increase in the hostility of the other' (1962, 26). Whatever the degree of initiating aggressive impulses, the actuation of conflict depends essentially on some level of reactivity on the part of the attacked party. It depends further on the rate of change of the reaction coefficient as hostility from the other increases. As Boulding emphasizes, the reaction of a party depends on the images it holds, both of itself and of the other. The reaction coefficients are likely to be high if a party feels itself to be misunderstood.

With this variable, we enter the domain of the self and its vulnerabilities. The more a self is threatened, the more likely that party is to resort to ego-defensive measures. The more fragile or insecure the self, the more likely the party is to perceive itself as being misunderstood and to perceive slights where none exist or at least to exaggerate their import. It is here that a more recent school of thought within the psychoanalytic tradition makes an important contribution. This stems from the work of figures like Winnicott, Kohut, and Bowlby, who view the need for attachment to social objects as a more fundamental instinct than the disposition toward aggression. In this perspective, aggression is not a primary drive, but a response to threats to attachment. Its manifestation in physical violence is then viewed as a product of disintegration or fears of disintegration, in which counter-phobic responses reenact dissociated traumatic events that seem intolerable for individuals in groups (Smith, 1993; Scheff and Retzinger, 1991). Neurophysiological processes, in this view, bring bodily functions into the orbit of aggressivity through hard-wired anxiety.

3. The body and mental rigidity

In discussing what he calls static models of conflict, Boulding analyses conflict in terms of interests rather than passions. In this context, he defines conflict as 'a situation of competition in which the parties are *aware* of the incompatibility of potential future positions and in which each party *wishes* to occupy a position that is incompatible with the wishes of the other' (1962, 5). The extent to which parties are committed to gaining specific positions rather than exploring ways of satisfying their needs forms a disposition towards conflict. The ability to do otherwise – to focus on *interests* rather than *positions* (Fisher and Urry, 1981) – depends on how rigid the competing parties are in pursuing their objectives by specific means.

Here again, the repertoire of available actional responses depends on a bodily infrastructure. Many workers in the field of somatics have demonstrated that the tightness of sets of muscles is related to the inability to be open and flexible – cognitively, emotionally, and behaviourally. Whereas high reactivity to threats reflects how weak and vulnerable the self is, rigidity of habits indicates how strongly defended the self is.

John Dewey's teachings about human nature considered the matter of rigid habits a central issue in human experience. It was Dewey's lessons with renowned somatic teacher F. M. Alexander, who focused attention on the proper relaxed use of the body, that he said enabled him to hold a philosophical position calmly and to change it if new evidence came up warranting a change. Dewey contrasted this disposition with that of academic thinkers who adopt a position early on and then go on to use their intellects to defend it indefinitely (Jones, 1979, 97).

4. The body and moral righteousness

Simmel early on identified the dynamic whereby conflicts become intensified the more they are separated from the personality of the parties to the conflict. His chief examples in that regard were conflicts carried out through legal procedures and conflicts on behalf of social causes. One can generalize Simmel's point by saying that conflicts become intensified whenever they become informed by normative directives. Although Simmel's cases were chosen to show how shifting the locus of conflict away from the personalities of the engaged parties works to heighten the intensity of a conflict, this may be seen just as well when applied intrapsychically. This is to say that once conflicts enlist the support of the superego, they will be driven by the same emotional energies that constitute the punitive forces of the ordinary superego. The statement by one presidential political campaigner – at first I just wanted to defeat my opponent, now I want to save the country from him – nicely illustrates the dynamic at work here. Both moral indignation and bigoted antagonisms of the sort analysed by Bettelheim and Janowitz (1950) represent striking exemplars of this syndrome.

Moral righteousness can be said to involve an infusion of bodily energies akin to the aggressive or counterphobic instincts that drive the initiation of conflicts. One can almost visualize the way in which aggressive impulses intensify as the adrenaline flows and the blood boils on behalf of righteous indignation. This will escalate the conflict, although not necessarily make it more lethal. The infusion of so much agitation into the conflictual process might, as well-trained warriors and martial artists know, interfere with the optimal execution of a task and the actual execution of combat.

5a. The body and conflict-supportive values

The activation of conflict depends not only on those elements that dispose parties to engage in conflict: high levels of aggressive impulsivity, reactivity, rigidity, and proclivity for moral indignation. It depends just as much on factors that work to inhibit the outbreak or continuance of conflictual interaction. These are primarily of two sorts, general values regarding conflict and the operation of social controls.

Cultural values can work either to instigate conflict or to suppress it. Conflict-supportive values appear in cultures where masculine aggressivity is particularly esteemed and promoted. This appears where the symbolism of warriorhood holds an esteemed place, as in archaic Greece and ancient Rome. In the cultures of Japan and Ethiopia, the values of warriorhood were so esteemed that they came to permeate the culture as a whole (Levine, 2002). The same is true of elements of Islamic tradition that idealize violence against those perceived as infidels or legitimate objects of external jihad. Masculine aggressivity is also valorized where considerations of proper recognition of the self are paramount, most famously in Mediterranean 'honor and shame societies' (Giordano, 2005). Cultures that embrace masculine aggressivity provide socializing experiences that enhance combative bodily dispositions and abilities.

Somatic elements that reduce conflict

5b. The body and conflict-aversive values

On the other hand, cultural values of harmony and peaceableness have been developed in most cultures. Where such values are dominant, as in particular institutional sectors like monasteries, or in societies reported to possess entirely pacific cultures, impulses to engage in conflict tend to be nipped in the bud if not entirely repressed.

Contemporary somatics supports the view that human bodies are actually designed to function in a loving, empowered way. Fear and anger weaken the body and therefore the whole self. Actions driven by feelings of fear and anger tend to create, escalate, and perpetuate conflict. As Paul Linden puts it, 'Generally, disputes are carried out in a spirit of distrust, competitiveness, fear, and anger, which leads to escalation and the generation of new disputes. Conflict, as it is usually experienced, includes fear and anger. When people are afraid or angry, they lash out and try to hurt the people who make them feel afraid or angry' (Linden, 2003). To minimize such reactions, Linden prescribes a number of bodily practices, including a relaxed tongue and a soft belly, which he associates with the normative natural state for human bodies.

These views are supported by millennia of wisdom about the body cultivated in a number of Asian traditions. This hearkens back to ancient Hindu traditions starting with the *Bhagavad Gita*, which described a state of human fulfillment brought about by a practice that calms the mind and the passions. This practice of unification – of 'yoking,' or *yoga* – of the body with the soul, the individual self with the universal spirit, involves a complex of methods that are physical as well as moral and mental. They include *asana*, a discipline of holding postures, designed to exercise every muscle, nerve and gland in the body, and *pranayama*, exercises in the rhythmic control of the breath. In similar ways the art of aikido, developed two millennia later in Japan, incorporates notions of unifying the entire bodily system through proper posture and of unifying the body with the mind by focusing one's attention on the bodily center of gravity. In the words of its founder, aikido 'is the way of unifying the mind, body, and spirit' (Saotome, 1989, 33).

What does the image of the body conveyed by yoga and aikido imply about social conflict? When students of those disciplines stand or sit in the relaxed and centered postures cultivated in their practice, they experience calmness. From that experience they derive a conviction that there is no inherent, inexorable force driving human beings to aggress against one another. They also know that, compared to the state of calm enjoyment they experience, the act of committing aggression is unpleasant. When they sense an impulse to aggress proactively or reactively, they connect it with an immature or impure response, which can be overcome with training.

Yoga and aikido conceive the bodily harmony promoted by their teachings as a model of mature human functioning and accordingly view social conflict as a byproduct of inner discord. Yoga complements the state of inner harmony, which its physical and meditative disciplines aim at with various *yama*, or ethical disciplines, by cultivating harmony with others. Closely related to this is the principle of *abhaya*, freedom from fear: 'Violence arises out of fear, weakness, ignorance or restlessness. To curb it most what is needed is freedom from fear' (Iyengar, 1973, 32). Similar ideas were articulated by the founder of aikido, Morihei Ueshiba. Although Ueshiba created his discipline as a *budo*, a martial art, he came to insist that in his particular form of *budo* 'there are no enemies.' The only enemy consisted of the egoistic and aggressive strivings of the immature self, and the only victory worth pursuing was a victory over that immature self. For achieving this state, the powerful effects of a softened belly and an open heart have long been identified.

6. The body and social controls

Sociologists have analysed a variety of mechanisms of social control that work to mute or dampen conflictual processes. These include binding arbitration; voluntary mediation; cooptation of antagonists; deflecting attention to symbols of higher allegiance; and dramatizing threats that transcend the partisan interests of the conflicting parties. Such mechanisms operate at the psychological and social levels, and would seem to admit little playroom for corporeal variables. Even so, one can ask: what psychosomatic processes inform the ways in which actors respond to intervening agencies?

That question in fact opens an enormous complex of possibilities. One process has to do with the degree of openness to arbitrating or mediating parties. This is the obverse of rigidity which, we saw above, demonstrably has a somatic basis. This openness is sometimes experienced as a relaxation of the visceral organs. Another process has to do with openings with new conflict-transcending social objects like larger communities or cultural objects such as values that enjoin conciliation and harmony. In the body, these are experienced as located in what have been called a mind-heart nexus.

Implications for general theory

The foregoing investigation opens up new lines for work in the general theory of conflict. The paradigm of generic conflict processes offers a framework with which to assemble contributions from various, normally disconnected, research traditions. Current advances in psychoneurophysiology and comparative ethology, for example, promise to enrich our understanding of anger, anxiety, and aggression a good deal. A generic conflict paradigm also enables us to develop a much more differentiated schema for analysing the onset, dynamics, and resolution of social conflict. It adds to the repertoire of existing conceptual tools such notions as hormonal levels, rigidity, reactivity, moral indignation – notions that come from different disciplines and that carry different sets of associations and supporting evidence. With that, it provides a framework with which to begin to consider more precisely somatic elements that pertain to conflict.[4]

Returning to our point of departure, the material assembled above instantiates more general points that could provide a basis for revisiting the Parsonian legacy in a way that facilitates a more systematic analysis of the interfaces between the body and the other action systems of action. The conceptual link would be what I am calling the actional organism, defined, again, as 'the subsystem of action where the organism's input of energies and the inputs from sources of meanings meet and interpenetrate.'

In a sense, this could be taken to mean something like returning to a modified version of the old instinct theories. Those were discarded because they were taken to represent hard-wired dispositions that propelled types of conduct no matter what. Incorporating this subsystem into the framework of action theory permits a clearer and more precise specification of interconnections.

Thus, within the cybernetic hierarchy, the actional organism is energized from below by the processes of the organic and inorganic systems. It energizes and receives direction, then, from the organized motives of the personality system; the organization systems of status-roles in the social system; and the organized symbolic complexes of the cultural system. Concrete action stands to be understood more completely by incorporating this set of abstractions that might now be more clearly identified and investigated.

Notes

* Revised version of a paper presented at the 37th World Congress of the International Institute of Sociology, Stockholm, Sweden. July 6, 2005. For help in revising I thank Michael Bare, Daniel Kimmel, Paki Reid-Brossard, Dan Silver, and Mark Walsh.

1 Howard Gardner (1983, 1993) has been a leading figure in this development. For its manifestation in liberal education programs at the undergraduate level, see Levine (2006).

2 Chris Shilling's recent discourse on the topic (2005), not to mention classic formulations like those of Max Scheler (1928/1961) and Talcott Parsons (1951/1964), iterates that streams of causality or influence flow in both directions.

3 This condition, Tinbergen explains, comes from a combination of instinctual, cultural, and technological factors. Whereas in other species and earlier human periods the impulse to fight was balanced by the fear response, humans have contrived cultural conditions that dampen the impulse to flee from battle, while the technology of fighting at a distance eliminates the taming effect of personal contact in face-to-face encounters.

4 Future collaborative exploration by professionals in somatics and social psychology might well explore a hypothesis of organ specificity in this regard: the idea that even though all organismic responses are thought to involve the entire bodymind system, it may be possible to locate the physical seat of each in some part of the human body. Thus one might hypothesize that impulses of instinctual aggressivity are felt primarily in the visceral organs ('guts') and the shoulders; fear in the lungs and shoulders; rigidity in the throat, jaw, and neck ('stiff-necked'); moral anger in the head and the dorsal shoulders; receptiveness to masculine aggressive values in the upper chest.

References

Bare, M. (2005) 'Behavioural Organism, Behavioural System, and Body in the Social Theory of Talcott Parsons.' Unpublished M.A. thesis, Department of Sociology, University of Chicago.

Bettelheim, B. and Janowitz, M. (1950) *Dynamics of Prejudice: A Psychological and Sociological Study of Veterans*. New York: Harper.

Boulding, K.E. (1962/1988) *Conflict and Defense: A General Theory*. Lanham, Md.: Univ. Press of America.

Coleman, J.S. (1957) *Community Conflict*. New York: The Free Press.

Collins, R. (1975) *Conflict Sociology: Toward an Explanatory Science*. New York: Academic Press.

Coser, L. (1956) *The Functions of Social Conflict*. Glencoe, Ill.: Free Press.

Feldenkrais, M. (1949) *Body and Mature Behaviour*. Tel-Aviv: Alef.

Fisher, R. & Urry, W. (1981) *Getting to Yes: Negotiating Agreement without Giving In*. Boston: Houghton Mifflin.

Freud, S. (1932/1939) 'Letter to Albert Einstein.' In *Civilization, War and Death: Psycho-Analytical Epitomes*, No. 4, ed. John Rickman. London: Hogarth Press.

Fromm, E. (1973) *The Anatomy of Human Destructiveness*. New York, NY: Holt, Rinehart and Winston.
Gardner, H. (1983/1993) *Frames of Mind: The Theory of Multiple Intelligences*. New York: Basic.
Gilligan, J. (1996) *Violence: Reflections on a National Epidemic*. New York: Vintage.
Giordano, C. (2005) 'Mediterranean Honor and beyond. The social management of reputation in the public sphere.' *Sociologija Mintis ir Veiksmas*. 01/2005.
Iyengar, B.K. (1973) *Light on Yoga*. New York: Schocken Books.
James, W. (1910/1974) 'The Moral Equivalent of War', in *Essays on Faith and Morals*, ed. R.B. Perry, 311–28. New York: Longmans, Green.
Jones, F.P. (1979) *Body Awareness in Action*. New York: Schocken Books.
Kriesberg, L. (1973) *The Sociology of Social Conflicts*. Englewood Cliffs, N.J.: Prentice-Hall.
Levine, D.N. (1994) 'Social Conflict, Aggression, and the Body in Euro-American and Asian Social Thought.' *International Journal of Group Tensions* 24: 205–17.
Levine D.N. (2002) 'The Masculinity Ethic and the Spirit of Warriorhood in Ethiopian and Japanese Cultures', Paper presented at the World Congress of Sociology, July.
Levine, D.N. (2006) *Powers of the Mind: The Reinvention of Liberal Learning*. Chicago: University of Chicago Press.
Lidz, C.W. and Lidz, M.L. (1976) 'Piaget's Psychology of Intelligence and the Theory of Action.' Ch.8 in *Explorations in General Theory in Social Science*. New York: Macmillan.
Linden, P. (2003) *Reach Out: Body Awareness Training for Peacemaking–Five Easy Lessons* [online]. CCMS Publications. Available from World Wide Web: (www.being-in-movement.com).
Lorenz, K. (1966) *On Aggression*. New York: Harcourt, Brace and World.
Mead, M. (1937) *Cooperation and Conflict among Primitive Peoples*. New York, NY: McGraw-Hill.
Morgenthau, H. (1960) *Politics Among Nations*, 3rd edn. New York: Knopf.
Parsons, T. (1951/1964) *The Social System*. New York: Free Press.
Parsons, T. & Shils, E. (eds) (1951) *Toward a General Theory of Action*. Cambridge, MA: Harvard.
Saotome, M. (1989) *The Principles of Aikido*. Boston: Shambhala Publications, Inc.
Scheff, T.J. & Retzinger, S.M. (1991) *Emotions and Violence: Shame and Rage in Destructive Conflicts*. Lexington, MA: Lexington Books.
Scheler, M. (1928/1961) *Man's Place in Nature*. New York: Noonday Press.
Schelling, T.C. (1960) *The Strategy of Conflict*. Cambridge, Mass: Harvard University Press.
Shilling, C. (2005) *The Body in Culture, Technology, & Society*. London: Sage.
Smith, T.S. (1993) 'Violence as a Disintegration Product: Counterphobic Reenactments of Dissociated Traumatic Events in Individual and Group Life.' Institut International de Soziologie, Paris.
Tinbergen, N. (1968) 'On War and Peace in Animals and Man: An Ethologist's Approach to the Biology of Aggression', *Science* 160, 1411–18.
Wrangham, R. & Peterson, D. (1996) *Demonic Males: Apes and the Origins of Human Violence*. Boston: Houghton Mifflin.

Reclaiming women's bodies: Colonialist trope or critical epistemology?[1]

Kathy Davis

Abstract

In a path-breaking essay, 'The Virtual Speculum in the New World Order (1999),' Donna Haraway links *Our Bodies, Ourselves* (the book and the slogan) to a critique of the US women's health movement, claiming that both draw implicitly upon colonialist metaphors of discovery and acquisition of territory. Haraway's critique does not stand alone, but belongs to a broader discussion within poststructuralist feminist theory which has been concerned with denaturalizing the female body, with the rejection of 'experience' as basis for feminist knowledge projects, and with deconstructing women's position as autonomous epistemic agents. Given the popularity of this much-cited and often reprinted essay, as well as Haraway's enormous influence on feminist (body) theory, feminist epistemology and technoscience politics, I will use her essay to consider the gap between contemporary poststructuralist feminist theory and women's health activism. On the basis of alternative feminist theoretical (phenomenological) perspectives on women's bodies and embodiment, I conclude that Haraway's critique, while provocative, has little to offer as an epistemological foundation for feminist health activism.

Key words: Poststructuralist feminist body theory; phenomenology; women's health activism; embodied epistemology; 'natural' body, epistemic agency; Donna Haraway

Introduction

In a path-breaking essay, 'The Virtual Speculum in the New World Order' (1999), Donna Haraway, one of the most important contemporary feminist theorists on women's bodies and feminist politics of knowledge, provides a devastating critique of feminist self-help, which was popular in US women's health movement during the 1970s.[2]

> Armed with a gynaecological speculum, a mirror, a flashlight, and – most of all – each other, in a consciousness-raising group, women ritually opened their bodies to their own literal view. The speculum had become the symbol of the displacement of

> the female midwife by the specialist male physician and gynecologist. The mirror was the symbol forced on women as a signifier of our own bodies as spectacle-for-another in the guise of our own supposed narcissism. Vision itself seemed to be the empowering act of conquerors.
>
> More than a little amnesiac about how colonial travel narratives work, we peered inside our vaginas toward the distant cervix and said something like, 'Land ho!' We have discovered ourselves and claim the new territory for women.' In the context of the history of Western sexual politics – that is, in the context of the whole orthodox history of Western philosophy and technology – visually self-possessed sexual and generative organs made potent tropes for the reclaimed feminist self. We thought we had our eyes on the prize. I am caricaturing, of course, but with a purpose. Our Bodies, Ourselves was both a popular slogan and the title of a landmark publication in women's health movements (Haraway, 1999: 67).

Although the women's health movement, and gynaecological self-help are not – and never were – identical, Haraway views them as expressions of the same feminist politics of knowledge. The image of women recovering ownership of their own sexual and reproductive organs pervaded the US women's health movement. While Haraway acknowledges that her critique is something of a caricature, she, nevertheless, regards it as an important and, indeed, necessary intervention in feminist health politics.

Haraway argues that when feminist health activists draw upon metaphors of 'discovery' and 'recovery' when they look at their bodies through a speculum, they unwittingly adopt the same objectifying medical 'gaze' which has historically been central to the medical appropriation of women's bodies. Tongue in cheek, she compares feminist health activists to the well-known 1973 feminist cartoon of Wonder Woman, complete with steel bracelets and stiletto high heels, seizing a speculum from a stethoscope-wearing doctor in white, while announcing 'with my speculum, I am strong! I can fight!' (Haraway, 1999: 68).[3] According to Haraway, the belief that women might have access to their bodies or might come to know their bodies in ways that stand outside the purview of science and culture is mistaken. In actuality, these would-be feminist explorers are no different than the male doctors they are attacking. And, indeed, they may even be considerably worse. Her 'colonial travel narrative' evokes troubling images of white European male colonizers intent on conquering indigenous peoples in faraway places. She suggests that the 'speculum' employed by white, well-educated, feminist health activists in the seventies represented an epistemological practice which could never be empowering to 'African American women in poverty' (p. 72). It does not begin to address the dramatic differences in morbidity, mortality and access in health care within the US. In her view, the 'right speculum for the job' would allow feminist health activists to document these differences ('statistics for freedom projects'), thereby generating the painful, but necessary structures of accountability between differently located women, both in the US and worldwide (p. 72). In short, a new politics of knowledge is required for a 'truly comprehensive' feminist politics of health and of technoscience more generally (Haraway, 1999: 84).

Haraway's critique does not stand alone. It belongs to a broader discussion within poststructuralist feminist theory concerning the appropriate ingredients of a feminist politics of knowledge. Given the popularity of Haraway's much cited and often reprinted essay as well as her considerable influence on feminist (body) theory, feminist epistemology, and health politics, I will use it as a starting point to consider the gap between contemporary poststructuralist feminist theory on the body and women's health activism. In order to explain this gap, I will now examine some of the points of contention in more detail: namely, the significance of the 'natural' body (and the importance of 'denaturalizing' women's bodies), the value of experiential knowledge (and the necessity of 'deconstructing' experience as authentic source of knowledge), and the value of women's epistemic agency (and the problem of the autonomous individual). I will then suggest some alternative (phenomenological) approaches to women's bodies and health which can provide a more viable epistemological foundation for a practical feminist politics of embodiment.

Feminist body theory/Feminist body politics

Women's bodies and health have always been central to feminist politics. The women's health movement was – and continues to be – one of the most vibrant fields of feminist activism. Beginning in the early 1970s with reproductive issues like abortion rights, sterilization abuse, access to birth control and 'mother friendly' birthing arrangements, it has developed into a global movement which encompasses a much broader range of health issues of concern to women from different social, cultural, and geopolitical locations.

Despite the wide range of issues (everything from sexual violence to AIDS to the effects of racism, poverty, and sustainable environment on health), the international women's health movement rests upon the assumption that women's material bodies as well as their embodied experiences are central to the development of a critical knowledge and health politics which is empowering to women both individually and collectively.

In contrast, feminist theory has been more ambivalent about women's bodies and embodied experience. Beginning with the 'equality versus difference debate,' the female body has posed a problem for feminists (Gatens, 1999). Some feminists have responded to the disadvantages encountered by women in the public sphere by citing their capacity to bear children. In this view, the biological body is held responsible for women's subordinate position *vis á vis* men in society. Equality can only be achieved by overcoming – or transcending – the female body. For other feminists, the idea that the female body needed to be 'transcended' for the sake of sexual equality was completely unacceptable. It simply mirrored misogynist attitudes toward women's bodies. It was, therefore, argued that a much better feminist strategy would be to affirm or even celebrate the female body and, particularly, women's capacity for motherhood.

Deciding between equality or difference, transcendence or celebration, proved a mission impossible, however, so attention shifted to the dilemma itself. Contemporary feminist body theory began to focus on dismantling the dualistic thinking which linked women to their biological bodies in the first place (Bordo, 1987). Biology was regarded as a culprit, often used to justify women's inferiority and social subordination. Thus, the first intervention was to separate biological sex from socially and culturally constructed gender.

This theoretical intervention was important., It had an unintended consequence however, namely, a 'somatophobia' among feminist theorists (Spelman, 1988). The fear that any mention of the female body would open the doors to biological determinism meant that women's biological bodies were left untheorized. It also meant that many feminist theorists looked at feminist health activism with its focus on women's sexual organs, reproductive function, and the benefits of cervical self-help with grave suspicion. This activism seemed to be nothing more than a reflection of masculinist medicine's obsession with women as 'wombs on legs' (Birke, 1999: 12). The female body was the starting point for feminist health activism but, for feminist theory, it was a call to let the deconstruction begin.

In addition to getting rid of the biological body, feminist theorists were engaged in debunking claims of objectivity in science as little more than a masculinist fiction. Theorists like Evelyn Fox Keller (1985), Sandra Harding (1991), Patricia Hill Collins (2000), Dorothy Smith (1987; 1990) and many others situated sentient, embodied, experiential knowing as a resource for unmasking the universalist pretentions of science and for providing the basis for an alternative, critical epistemology, which would be grounded in the material realities of women's lives. Asserting the primacy of women's experience became the '*sine qua non* of any feminist project of liberation (Kruks, 2001: 132).'

The ascendancy of postmodernism and the 'linguistic turn,' however, made this project more complicated. Once regarded as the very bedrock of second-wave feminism, 'experience' came to be seen as an increasingly suspect concept (Scott, 1992). If all knowledge was regarded as culturally shaped, then neither women nor feminists had special access to the 'truth' (Haraway, 1991). While this critique was a needed corrective to simplified claims about the authenticity of experience and opened up space for reflexivity, it had the unintended consequence that the entire concept of experience was discarded. A seemingly unbridgeable rift emerged between feminist theorists, who regarded experience as nothing more than a discursive construction, and feminist health activists, who saw women's embodied experience as an important corrective to the hegemony of medical knowledge (Kuhlmann and Babitsch, 2002).

In the meantime, the 'body' had returned to postmodern feminist theory with a vengeance as more and more feminist theorists embraced Foucault (McNay, 1992; Bordo, 1993; Davis, 1997). The Foucauldian body, however, was not an experiencing, sentient, lived body. It was a discursive body, a cultural text, a surface upon which culture could be inscribed. The body became a site for understanding the workings of modern power or for 'reading' culture. As cultural text, the female body was no longer linked to biology, nor was it treated as the seat of authentic experience, but rather it was viewed as a cultural construct in need of deconstruction. While postmodern feminist theory contributed to a more sophisticated understanding of how power works through the female body, it also stood on somewhat uneasy footing with the question of women's agency. Despite its concern for possibilities of resistance and transformation in women's bodily practices, it proved to be more suited for delineating the collusions and compliances of women's body practices with dominant cultural discourses than for theorizing collective forms of feminist action in and through the body (Bordo, 1993).

It is clear that postmodern feminist body theory has raised many important theoretical issues. It is also clear, however, that it has left some issues undertheorized. And these are precisely the issues which are of utmost concern for feminist health activism. It is, therefore, not surprising that feminist body theory has had little to offer feminist health activism and, conversely, feminist health activism has had little effect on feminist body theory. It is my contention, however, that this state of affairs is not inevitable. Feminist theory could, in principle, have much to offer – and much to learn from – feminist health activism. Bridging the gap, however, would require at least three shifts in feminist body theory: a reconceptualization of the body, of embodied experience, and of epistemic agency.

Fleshing out the body

Postmodern feminist theories of the body have been successful in radically pulling the rug out from under biological discourses that naturalize the female body. As Kuhlmann and Babitsch (2002) note, however, in their excellent review of feminist body theory and its usefulness for women's health issues, 'we must face the question of what price we are willing to pay in exchange for the delimitation of naturalized categories' (p. 436). They argue that the price of making the body central to theoretical projects (dismantling essentialism, deconstructing dualisms, emphasizing fluidity) may be a disembodied body. Even theorists who claim that they are concerned with the materiality of the body (Butler, 1989, 1993), still lend little credence to the material reality of women's flesh-and-blood bodies, bodies which are recognizable to ordinary women as their own. There seems to be an absence of bodies in contemporary feminist body theory that can be touched, smelled, tasted, or perceived. There are no bodies with an 'inside' – reproductive organs, lungs and heart, glands and capillaries. Ultimately, the focus seems to be upon the surface of the body and on how culture becomes imprinted upon it.

While there can be no doubt that women in general and feminist health activists in particular need to be sensitive to the perils of essentialism and dualistic thinking, the silence of feminist theorists on the flesh-and-blood body, as well as on the possibilities that biology might have to offer for understanding women's bodies, is not without its costs. The vulnerabilities and limitations of the body, which invariably accompany illness, disease, disability or, quite simply, aging, are given short shrift in theories which concentrate on the body in endless flux. The body as ongoing performance implies a transformability that belies the bodily constraints with which most people must live at different periods in their lives. Postmodern feminist theory has little to offer in understanding what it means to live with a disability or a chronic illness or even the temporary discomforts of menstrual cramps and labour pains.

In her excellent study on disability, Susan Wendell suggests that postmodern feminist theory erases much of the everyday reality of living in/with/through a body with limitations and vulnerabilities, which are particularly salient for most women's embodied experience. Moreover, the one-sided insistence on the need to avoid dualisms underestimates the subjective appeal of the mind-body dualism for women in their everyday interactions with their bodies (Wendell, 1996: 169). Living with chronic illness, for example, would be impossible without a certain amount of splitting. The suffering that bodily vulnerability entails means that a certain amount of transcendence (ie, mind over matter) can be welcome and, indeed, necessary for an individual's well-being.[4] Indeed, as some critical disability scholars have argued, the most important task facing feminist theory on the body should be to think of embodiment in terms of its limitations rather than its unbridled capabilities (Breckenridge and Vogler, 2001). In a more just environment, everyone should be treated as 'temporarily able-bodied', resulting in a definitive break with restrictive notions of 'normalcy' and a reorganization of the lived environment with biological vulnerability in mind.

Birke (1999) also takes issue with the ubiquitous feminist theoretical rebuttal of biological determinism. While she also acknowledges the need to avoid essentialism and dualistic thinking, she suggests that this does not require rejecting biology altogether. And, indeed, she warns, feminists avoid the biological body at their own peril. As she puts it:

> . . . theories which deny the biological serve us ill, not least because it is through the biological body that we live in and engage with this world at all. But also, and significantly, our failure to engage adequately with biology (except to criticize it for determinism) fails those people (and non-humans) who are most readily defined by it, and also who may suffer because of it (Birke, 1999: 175).

Birke argues that the body is best viewed holistically, as a self-organizing and structured materiality and organismic integrity, which both enables and constrains an individual's engagement with the world around her.[5] Her aim is to retrieve the 'biological body' – the body that is not just 'skin deep,' nor disembowelled, but has organs, an inside as well as an outside (p. 2). She looks for ways to understand 'what goes on' physiologically in women's bodies, while avoiding the problems of determinism which have been elaborated *ad nauseam* by contemporary feminist body theory. Like other feminist body theorists, Birke does not view the body as a static entity, hermeneutically sealed off from the world. Bodies have their own developmental histories and capacities for transformation. Neither, however, is the body an assemblage of practices, a cultural text, or an 'imaginary.' In her view, the ubiquitous emphasis on the 'fluidities and fracturings' of the body may offer the promise of endless transformation, thereby making it attractive to feminist theorists. This same transformability of the body, however, also opens the flood-gates for a total manipulation of human and non-human nature, resonating with the literal dismemberment of bodies in modern medicine. Organ transplantations, hysterectomies, and plastic surgery all rest on a conceptualization of the body as 'a set of bits,' which can be removed or manipulated (Birke, 1999: 171). In contrast, Birke offers a theory of the biological body which includes change and organismic integrity, a body which enables but which also provides constraints that defy even the most advanced technological interventions.

In my view, Wendell and Birke provide a promising alternative to the disembodied body in feminist body theory. Both take up the project which feminist activists of the 1970s started – namely, a concern for women's embodied vulnerabilities and a desire to engage critically with medical knowledge. They show how it is possible to learn from biology without falling into biological determinism, thereby justifying a feminist epistemology which engages with the female body as an anatomical and physiological entity, without ignoring the body's capacity for change. They also tackle the biological conditions which enable and constrain an individual's interactions with the world around her without ignoring the role of culture in giving meaning to these conditions. And, last but not least, they assume that knowledge about women's bodies and how they work should not be left to biology, but should be an integral part of feminist inquiry.

Retrieving experience

Postmodern feminist theory has provided an important cautionary warning against treating experience as self-explanatory and the reminder that experience is always mediated by cultural discourses and institutional practices is well taken. A strong case has been made for developing feminist methodologies that can critically analyse patriarchal or masculinist assumptions in *all* domains of knowledge, including feminist knowledge. The postmodern feminist commitment, however, to the theoretical project of deconstructing cultural discourses has had the unintended consequence of eclipsing the analysis of experience as situated knowledge.

Many feminist scholars have reacted with uneasiness and even alarm at attempts to discredit women's experience, arguing that feminist theory risks 'throwing the baby out with the bathwater' (Varikas, 1995: 99), has been left stranded in disembodied 'high altitude thinking' (Kruks, 2001: 143), can no longer engage meaningfully with the experience-oriented texts of women who are trying to take control of their own representation (Stone-Mediatore, 1998: 118), and, last but not least, has seriously undermined the critical potential of experience for disrupting dominant knowledge paradigms (Alcoff, 2000: 46). Alcoff (2000) argues against the necessity of choosing between an unreflective conception of experience as authentic source of knowledge and the rejection of experience as hopelessly contaminated and of little use to feminist theory. In her view, this is a 'false dilemma', which simply replays the 'tired modernist debates between empiricism and idealism' (p. 45). There is no reason that feminist scholars should not insist upon experience as 'epistemologically indispensable' without having to assume that experience is also 'epistemologically self-sufficient.' Kruks (2001) suggests that rather than rejecting experience as a 'suspect concept,' as Scott has advocated, feminist scholars should be devoting their energies to finding ways to *theorize* it (p. 131). Women's experience provides an essential starting point for understanding the embodied and material effects of living under specific social and cultural conditions. The task at hand is to link individual women's subjective accounts of their experiences and how these affect their everyday practices, with an analysis of the cultural discourses, institutional arrangements, and geopolitical contexts in which these accounts are embedded and which give meaning to them.

For many feminist scholars, phenomenology provides a useful theoretical helpmeet for retrieving experience as a resource for feminist inquiry. Phenomenological perspectives treat women as embodied subjects who think, act, and know through their bodies. Their experiences are drawn upon as important resources for understanding what it feels like to have a particular body (pregnant, breasted), to experience a particular bodily sensation (menstrual cramps, labour pains), or to live through a specific event (childbirth). Discourse alone cannot explain the affective realm of embodiment, the 'sentient knowing' which is involved when individuals connect the physical, cognitive and cultural dimensions of their embodied lives at the site of their body. As Kruks (2001) puts it, the 'fact that experiences are also discursively constructed does not diminish the importance of treating them . . . as a 'point of origin,' or even a 'foundation from which to work' (p. 139).

There is a rich body of studies exploring the experience of feminine embodiment from a phenomenological perspective, covering topics like being breasted or 'throwing like a girl' (Young, 1990), pregnancy (Marshall, 1996), sexual harassment or masochism (Bartky, 1990), sexual trafficking or genital cutting (Kruks, 2001; Bartky, 2002). Experiences are articulated which have been marginalized, distorted, or pathologized by dominant discourses. By subjecting these experiences to phenomenological description, they are not so much revealed as made discursively available; ie, accessible for interpretation and debate. In this way, many body issues which had previously been part of tacit, taken-for-granted, or 'unnameable' experiences, can become part of an explicitly political or feminist agenda.

Martin (2001) provides a three-pronged methodology which brings together a phenomenological description of women's accounts of their experiences with a discourse analysis of cultural metaphors about women's bodies and a sociological analysis of how social location (including poverty, class, and 'race') shapes women's reproductive lives. She shows how medical metaphors treat menstruation as 'failed production' in which the endometrial lining 'disintegrates' or 'decays.' Menopause is treated as a 'breakdown in the hierarchical communication system' of the body, whereby the ovaries regress, decline, atrophy, shrink, and become totally without 'function.' While such pathologizing metaphors shape how US women perceive their bodies and bodily functions, their stories about their embodied experiences also display signs of resistance. One of Martin's most interesting findings – and one which provides Haraway's notion of situated knowledge with some empirical grounding – is that working class women are less inclined to adopt medical understandings about women's bodies, preferring instead to emphasize how their own body feels, looks, or smells; the inconvenience and discomfort that bodily functions like menstruation or labour entail; or the significance such functions have in terms of femininity (menstruation as a rite of passage). She calls this everyday resistance a 'phenomenological perspective' in contrast to a 'medical model,' which is divorced from women's experience. Martin's approach illustrates how an understanding of experience as discursively shaped does not preclude the detailed analysis of how women experience their bodies.

Moya (1997) has criticized the poststructuralist rejection of experience from the perspective of marginalized women of colour. In an argument for a more 'realist' feminist theory, she takes up Scott's claim that experiences are always discursively mediated and elaborates it to include the 'cognitive component' of this mediation through which women gain knowledge of the world. In her view, embodied experiences are not merely discursive constructions; they are always embedded in the concrete physical realities of an individual's particular social location. As such, they are an invaluable source of knowledge about the material effects of living in a specific place at a particular moment in history. She suggests that feminist theorists should not turn away from but, rather, turn toward women's bodies as a source of knowledge and starting point for feminist analysis. The physical realities of women's lives – including 'our skin colour, the land we grew up in, our sexual longings – profoundly inform the contours and contexts of knowledge and should be part of feminist epistemology as 'theory in the flesh' (Moya, 1997: 135).

Taken together, feminist scholars have productively drawn upon the insights of phenomenology to retrieve experiential knowledge as a central element for feminist epistemological projects. They have convincingly taken issue with poststructuralist critiques for providing impoverished understandings of knowledge, which reduce women's experience to discourse. The result is feminist theory that is both disembodied and dislocated. They show how women's embodied experiences are necessary for feminist critiques of dominant forms of knowledge – 'not merely as endpoints or data that require theoretical illumination, but as capable of shedding light on theory itself' (Alcoff, 2000: 56).

Women as epistemic agents

Postmodern feminist theory has been instrumental in decentring the autonomous subject as a seat of authentic and undistorted knowledge about the world. It has underlined the pervasive power of cultural discourses to shape how women experience their bodies as well as the body practices that they adopt. The ideologically loaded issues of freedom and choice have been problematized, whereby women's agency is showed to be often more about compliance than about subversion (Bordo, 1993).

The price, however, for this emphasis on the power of discourse to shape women's embodied experiences, is often a steep one. It can obstruct the possibility of understanding how ordinary women might actively gain, evaluate, and critically interpret knowledge about themselves, their lives, and the world around them. It may become difficult to imagine how they mobilize knowledge for their personal empowerment, let alone for collective feminist projects, as this knowledge is invariably embedded in oppressive cultural discourses and institutional arrangements. In short, postmodern feminist theory does not leave much space for understanding how ordinary women exercise epistemic agency.

Turning to Kruks (2001) once again, phenomenology can provide a corrective to some of the limitations of postmodern conceptions of agency. It focuses on the embodied, sentient subject whose lived experience provides a starting point for a critical (feminist) epistemological project. It also provides a view of a 'practical' subject who acts with a certain degree of intentionality, albeit never fully articulated, a subject who embarks upon projects which 'transform something into a further possibility' (p. 120). A phenomenological concept of agency makes it possible to see how women's experiences are connected to practical projects of individual empowerment. It also offers a starting point for thinking beyond the individual's experiences and enables us to imagine the suffering of others as well as the kinds of intentional projects upon which they embark. In Kruks' (2001) view, it is the recognition that others – however different their projects are – are also involved in intentional projects, which allows for reciprocity and the possibility of collective praxis (pp. 124–125).

Another approach to the problem of women's epistemic agency is provided by Dorothy Smith (1990). While she claims an affinity to Foucauldian notions of discourse, she employs a sociological perspective which takes specific texts as a starting point for analysing how individuals actually interpret these texts and how these texts organize their interpretive practices. For her, individuals are not simply entangled in discourses; they have to engage with them actively, in ways which involve planning courses of action, drawing upon past knowledge, making on the spot calculations, and imagining what the results of the action might be. Without agency, discourses simply could not work. Smith's notion of discursive agency opens up space for exploring how women knowledgeably, competently, and flexibly draw upon, interpret, and re-articulate cultural discourses as they negotiate their life circumstances.

Mohanty (2003), Lugones (2003), Stone-Mediatore (1998) and others have taken issue with postmodern feminist theory, arguing that it leaves no way to engage with the myriad ways that women resist. The activity of criticizing hegemonic discourses and developing imaginative alternatives requires that those who have been marginalized in the production of knowledge be situated as epistemic agents, who generate critical and alternative forms of knowledge as a basis for empowerment. These theorists share and, indeed, have introduced some of the concerns of postmodern feminist theory – for example, the problem of privileging the experiences of white, middle class feminism as universal for all women. This does not lead, however, to the conclusion that epistemic agency needs to be abandoned altogether. Indeed, Mohanty (2003) has argued that a concept of agency is necessary for understanding the ways that US and Third World women are constantly engaged in interpreting, reflecting upon, and renaming their experiences (pp. 106–123). These interpretations are not only a matter of recycling existing metaphors and rhetorical strategies, as just 'one discursive production among others' (Stone-Mediatore, 1998: 121). It is important to understand how individuals come to favour certain discourses over others – decisions which are shaped by situational, biographical or socio-political circumstances. Lugones (2003) is also critical of what she refers to as the 'highly attenuated understandings of agency in late modernity' (p. 6). Resistance is not intentional in the sense of a clear-cut choice among an array of desirable and less-than-desirable options. She argues that feminists need to become attentive to the subtle and variegated ways women act, even when – at first glance – it doesn't seem to be about resistance in the narrow sense of the word. Resistance can also be refusal or simply 'trying to survive.' One of the goals of feminism should be to discover the ways women might have for 'moving together and connecting' with one another (pp. 6–7).

In conclusion, postmodern feminist theory has focused on the power of discourse to shape women's practices. While agency is acknowledged in the abstract, little attention has been paid to women as producers of critical knowledge, as epistemic agents. This theory cannot account for why individual women might be motivated to employ oppositional discourses. Theorists like Kruks, Smith, Mohanty, Lugones, and others have shown, however, that it is possible to recognize the power of discourse, without discarding women's epistemic agency. By exploring discourses as actively mobilized by individuals as epistemic agents, they show how women can deliberately and strategically reinterpret their lives or actively pursue oppositional discourses. This involves an approach to agency that is not abstract but practical. Agency is always embedded in women's everyday interpretive activities. This means that feminist theory needs to explore how, why, and under what circumstances women actively use knowledge to pursue oppositional ends.

Embodied theories

This chapter opened with a fragment from an essay by the postmodern feminist theorist Donna Haraway, in which she makes a caricature of the politics of knowledge which underlies feminist health activism. Haraway's strategy – while good for a laugh or two – does not seriously engage with the politics of knowledge expressed in this activism and, more seriously, exacerbates rather than bridges the gap between feminist theory and feminist activism concerning women's bodies and health. Haraway's intention is, of course, less to discredit feminist health activism than to address a more fundamental political concern. She is worried that feminist health activism has not sufficiently addressed the health needs of poor women and women of colour in the US and, more generally, has been inadequate for coming to terms with global disparities in health and well-being. In her view, the dramatic global differences in health outcomes and the lack of care for even the most basic health needs require a very different feminist response than the politics of 'self help,' which was so empowering for white, middle-class, US feminists in the 1970s.

Haraway's concern for how differences in social location shape the politics of knowledge is well-taken and she is right in pointing out that any comprehensive feminist health politics would need to begin with an acknowledgment of and a serious engagement with these differences and disparities. Although women of colour have always played an active role within the women's health movement, Haraway does not draw upon their 'situated knowledge' or epistemic practices in developing a feminist politics of knowledge which reflects the specifics of their location.[6] Paradoxically it is Haraway herself, armed with the knowledge practices (statistics) of mainstream social science, who speaks for them, dismissing their experiences as inconsequential for feminist theory.

While I share Haraway's concern and believe that attention to social inequalities between women is of great relevance to the future of feminist health politics, it is my contention that this concern deserves a more serious – and less ironic – treatment than Haraway's essay provides. In other words, instead of producing a caricatural 'straw dog' to be rhetorically knocked down, it would make more sense to develop a critique of feminist health activism which is grounded in the situated knowledge practices of feminist activists 'on the ground.' As an antidote to Haraway's strategy, I have turned to other feminist scholars who, while engaged with the same issues which have preoccupied poststructuralist feminist theorists like Haraway, have come to very different conclusions. Feminist theory on the body does not need to distance itself from feminist health activism in order to develop a better feminist critique of science. It can instead take up and elaborate the epistemological project which this activism has already begun. Bridging the gap would, however, require at least three shifts in feminist body theory: a reconceptualization of the body, of embodied experience, and of epistemic agency.

The first shift would be a reconceptualization of the body. The body is more than a surface, a cultural 'text', or a site for the endless deconstruction of Cartesian dualisms. Bodies are anatomical, physiological, experiential, and culturally shaped entities. They age, suffer injury or illness, become disabled or infirm, and limit our activities. Feminist theory must acknowledge the vulnerabilities of women's bodies without having to resort to biological determinism or the notion of an 'essential female' body. While most women have a body which is coded female, the details of each woman's embodiment vary according to her specific social location. Bodies have their own idiosyncratic histories and are constantly interacting with their surroundings. And, finally, common bodily complaints or problems – whether eating disorders or high blood pressure – may change over time, becoming more or less relevant to understanding women's embodiment at a particular historical moment or in a particular geographic location. Women's bodies shape how they live in the world, just as how they live in the world is shaped through their bodies.

The second shift would be a reconceptualization of embodied experience. Feminist theory needs to find ways to address how differently located women perceive, feel about, and understand their bodily experiences. While it is important to acknowledge that experience is never a simple reflection of reality, it can, nevertheless, still be used as a starting point for understanding what it means to live in a particular body, at a specific moment in time, or in a particular social location. Their experiential accounts can be validated as an important source of knowledge without treating them as authentic or absolute. Women's experiences do not stand alone but can be juxtaposed with other forms of knowledge: medical findings, cultural understandings about women's bodies, or the experiential accounts of other women with similar and/or different experiences. It is the interaction between these forms of knowledge, which allows experience to become a helpmeet for women to engage critically with dominant forms of knowledge.

The third shift would involve a reconceptualization of women's epistemic agency. Agency is not simply a discursive effect, an artefact of shifting cultural discourses. It involves the practical and – to some extent – intentional activities of situated knowers, who interpret, reflect upon, and rework their experiences. Precisely because knowledge practices are always embedded in conditions which are both enabling and constraining, it is important to develop sociologically grounded analyses of how women in the concrete circumstances of their everyday lives develop critical knowledge as well as individually or collectively empowering courses of action.

Notes

1 This chapter draws upon my cross-cultural history on the global impact of the feminist classic on women's health, *Our Bodies, Ourselves* (Davis forthcoming).

2 Self-help groups were formed by primarily white, middle-class women who shared information and stories, educating themselves about their bodies, the medical establishment, and alternative treatments. Self-help incorporates a range of practices including self-exams (breast, cervical, vaginal, vulvar), alternative therapies (home treatments for vaginal infections, nutritional changes, herbal remedies, menstrual extraction), as well as a wide range of community support groups around issues like cancer, menopause, weight management, AIDS, incest, or substance abuse. See, Kapsalis (1997); Morgen (2002); Murphy (2004).

3 The speculum was a particularly potent symbol for the early women's health movement because of the nefarious role it had played within US gynecology where it was initially employed by J. Marion Simms, the 'Father of American Gynecology,' in his surgical experiments on unanethesitized slave women. The appeal of appropriating what had originally been an instrument of oppression to help women 'take back their bodies' was obvious. See, Kapsalis (1997).

4 See, also, Davis-Floyd (1994) for a different context, but similar argument. She shows how professional women engage in a splitting off of the body in their preference for C-sections, which

protect them from the troubling dissonance between their professional persona as career women and their embodied pregnant persona.

5 See, also, Fausto-Sterling (2005) for a similar approach which treats the biological body as a dynamic system that changes according to life circumstances and cultural conditions.

6 Women of colour, active in the women's health movement, have often been just as concerned with recovering women's bodies and validating women's experiences as the white activists have been who have born the brunt of Haraway's critique. See, for example, White (1990), Smith (1995), Springer (1999).

References

Alcoff, L.M. (2000) 'Phenomenology, Post-structuralism, and Feminist Theory on the Concept of Experience.' In L. Fisher and L. Embree (eds), *Feminist Phenomenology*. Dordrecht: Kluwer.

Bartky, S.L. (1990). *Femininity and Domination. Studies in the Phenomenology of Oppression*. New York: Routledge.

Bartky, S.L. (2002) *'Sympathy and Solidarity' and Other Essays*. Lanham, Rowman & Littlefield, 2002).

Birke, L. (1999) *Feminism and the Biological Body*. New Brunswick, N.J.: Rutgers University Press.

Bordo, S. (1987) *The Flight to Objectivity: Essays on Cartesianism and Culture*. Albany: SUNY Press.

Bordo, S. (1993) *Unbearable Weight. Feminism, Western Culture, and the Body*. Berkeley: California University Press.

Breckenridge, C.A. and Vogler, C. (2001) 'The Critical Limits of Embodiment: Disability's Criticism', *Public Culture* 13, 3 (2001): 349–357.

Butler, J. (1989) *Gender Trouble: Feminism and the Subversion of Identity*. New York: Routledge.

Butler, J. (1993) *Bodies That Matter: On the Discursive Limits of 'Sex.'* New York: Routledge.

Collins, P.H. (2000) *Black Feminist Thought. Knowledge, Consciousness, and the Politics of Empowerment*, 2nd edition. New York: Routledge.

Davis, K. (1997) 'Embody-ing Theory: Beyond Modernist and Postmodernist Readings of the Body.' In *Embodied Practices. Feminist Perspectives on the Body*, ed. Kathy Davis, 1–23. London: Sage.

Davis, K. (forthcoming) *The Making of Our Bodies, Ourselves. How feminist knowledge travels across borders.* Durham, N.C.: Duke University Press.

Davis-Floyd, R.E. (1994) 'Mind Over Body. The Pregnant Professional.' In *Many Mirrors: Body Image and Social Relations*, ed. Nicole Sault, 204–234, New Brunswick, N.J.: Rutgers University Press.

Fausto-Sterling, A. (2005) 'The Bare Bones of Sex: Part 1- Sex and Gender.' *Signs* 30, 2: 1491–1527.

Gatens, M. (1999) 'Power, Bodies and Difference.' In *Feminist Theory and the Body*, ed. Janet Price and Margrit Shildrick, 227–234. Edinburgh: Edinburgh University Press.

Haraway, D. (1991) 'Situated Knowledges: The Science Question in Feminism and the Privilege of Partial Perspective', In *Simians, Cyborgs, and Women* by Donna Haraway, 183–202. London: Free Association Books.

Haraway, D. (1999) 'The Virtual Speculum in the New World Order.' In *Revisioning Women, Health, and Healing*, ed. Adele E. Clarke and Virginia L. Olesen, 49–96. New York: Routledge.

Harding, S. (1991) *Whose Science? Whose Knowledge: Thinking from women's lives.* Milton Keynes: Open University Press.

Kapsalis, T. (1997) *Public Privates. Performing Gynecology From Both Ends of the Speculum.* Durham, N.C.: Duke University Press, 1997.

Keller, E.F. (1985) *Reflections on Gender and Science.* New Haven: Yale University Press.

Kruks, S. (2001) *Retrieving Experience. Subjectivity and Recognition in Feminist Politics*. Ithaca and London: Cornell University Press.

Kuhlmann, K. and Babitsch, B. (2002) 'Bodies, health, gender – bridging feminist theories and women's health.' *Women's Studies International Forum* 25, 4: 433–442.

Lugones, M. (2003) *Pilgimages/Peregrinajes. Theorizing Coalition against Multiple Oppressions*. Lanham, MD.: Rowman & Littlefield.

McNay, L. (1992) *Foucault and Feminism*. Cambridge: Polity.

Marshall, H. (1996) 'Our Bodies Ourselves. Why We Should Add Old Fashioned Empirical Phenomenology to the New Theories of the Body', *Women's Studies International Forum* 19, 3: 253–265.

Martin, E. (2001) *The Woman in the Body*. Boston: Beacon Press.

Mohanty, C. (2003) *Feminism Without Borders. Decolonizing Theory, Practicing Solidarity*. Durham, N.C.: Duke University Press.

Morgen, S. (2002) *Into Our Own Hands. The Women's Health Movement in the United States, 1969–1990*. New Brunswick, N.J.: Rutgers University Press.

Moya, P.M.L. (1997) 'Postmodernism, "Realism," and the Politics of Identity: Cherríe Moraga and Chicana Feminism.' in J. Alexander and C. Mohanty (eds), *Feminist Genealogies, Colonial Legacies, Democratic Futures* 125–150. New York: Routledge.

Murphy, M. (2004) 'Immodest witnessing: The epistemology of vaginal self-examination in the U.S. Feminist self-help movement.' *Feminist Studies* 30, 1: 115–147.

Scott, J.W. (1992) 'Experience.' in *Feminists Theorize the Political*, ed. Judith Butler and Joan W. Scott, 22–40. New York: Routledge.

Smith, D.E. (1990) *The Conceptual Practices of Power. A Feminist Sociology of Knowledge*. Boston: Northeastern University Press.

Smith, D.E (1987) *The Everyday World as Problematic. A feminist sociology*. Toronto: University of Toronto Press.

Smith, S.L. (1995) *Sick and tired of being sick and tired: Black women's health activism in America, 1890–1950*. Philadelphia: University of Pennsylvania Press.

Spelman, E. (1988) *Inessential Woman: Problems of Exclusion in Feminist Thought*. Boston: Beacon Press.

Springer, K. (1999) (ed.), *Still Lifting, Still Climbing: African American Women's Contemporary Activism*. New York: New York University Press.

Stone-Mediatore, S. (1998) 'Chandra Mohanty and the Revaluing of "Experience".' *Hypatia* 13, 2: 116–133.

Varikas, E. (1995) 'Gender, experience, and subjectivity: The Tilly-Scott disagreement.' *New Left Review* 211: 89–101.

Wendell, S. (1996) *The Rejected Body. Feminist Philosophical Reflections on Disability*. New York: Routledge.

White, E.C. (1990) (ed.), *The Black Women's Health Book. Speaking for Ourselves*. Seattle, WA: The Seal Press.

Young, I.M. (1990) *Throwing Like a Girl and other essays in feminist philosophy and social theory*. Bloomington: Indiana University Press.

Fieldwork embodied

Judith Okely

Abstract

Participation entails bodily engagement. Participant observation has been integral to anthropological fieldwork. Although cross-cultural ideas of the body have been elaborated theoretically in social anthropology, the Cartesian mind/body dichotomy has privileged the cerebral in the understanding of fieldwork practice and the bodily experience of the fieldworker has been under-scrutinized. In seeking to rectify this situation, this chapter draws on extensive dialogues with leading anthropologists about their fieldwork. Examples are selected from Africa, Iran, Afghanistan, India, Malaysia and Europe. The anthropologists' conscious and hitherto unarticulated bodily adaptations are disentangled, and research is examined as a process of physical labour, bodily interaction and sensory learning which constitutes a foundation for the production of written texts.

Key words: Participation, identity, imitation, movement, knowledge

Introduction

It is only recently that greater attention has been paid to the embodied nature of knowledge, but many key publications continue to focus on the body within Western modernity. The challenge of avoiding ethnocentrism may be even greater for anthropologists in the field who have internalized through bodily experience a taken-for-granted perspective on embodiment informed by Western norms and values. Moving and living beyond the familiar by engaging with other cultures, groups and societies, however, entails learning about difference in all aspects: economic, political, religious, ideological *and* bodily. As participant observation is integral to social anthropological fieldwork, and participation entails physical engagement, this means that the anthropologist needs to unlearn or at least be able to recognize the bodily knowledge from his/her lived past that informs interpretations in the field.

Anthropology is uniquely placed to explore the diversity of ways in which people live in and as their bodies across a variety of cultures inside and outside of the West. Indeed, cross-cultural ideas of the body have been theoretically and ethnographically elaborated in social anthropology (Mauss, 1936; Douglas, 1966; Blacking, 1977; Martin, 1987; Csordas, 1994, 2002). Furthermore, the discipline has moved beyond the tendency to present research as if it were conducted by a near invisible fieldworker lacking specificity. In the volume *Anthropology and Autobiography* (Okely and Callaway, 1992), for example, the gender, age, ethnicity and personality of the fieldworker have been considered worthy of inclusion. Despite this, the bodily experience of the fieldworker as research process and source of knowledge has been under scrutinized. There have been some dramatic exceptions, often through unexpected eroticized bodily encounters (Abramson, 1987; Kulick and Wilson, 1995), or even the rape of the fieldworker (Winkler, 1994; Moreno, 1995), but these do not change the general picture.

Drawing on extensive and transcribed dialogues with anthropologists about their field practice,[1] I begin to redress this omission by focusing here on their bodily experiences and the interconnection of these experiences with emergent knowledge. In what follows I examine the relationship between embodiment, knowledge and understanding by exploring the areas of gender/sex and race, movement, work, risk and death, and highlight the intimate links between particular 'modes of embodiment' (Mellor and Shilling, 1997) and the findings of anthropologists.

Arrivals as sexed and racialized others

The biological sex and perceived 'race' of the fieldworker were often the first bodily markers of identity for the people in whose group or society the anthropologists came to live. Clifford and Marcus have paid considerable attention to the outsider's 'arrival' scenes written in anthropologists' monographs (1986). But there is no consideration of the other side, namely the impact of the incomer anthropologist's arrival upon the hosts. This is an important omission, however, as the body of the anthropologist can be a marker for mystery and categorization through which the outsider incomer may be genderized and racialized as 'other'.

Signe Howell (1984), arriving among the Chewong in tropical forest Malaysia, found that people would scream whenever she approached them. Eventually they invited her to live with them. The crucial event, she discovered months later, was being seen bathing.

> *Howell*: Much later . . . I was told this, when I got to know them very well, and they became very friendly, and I'd learnt their language pretty well. One evening we were talking, and the woman I subsequently met, who became my 'mother', she was laughing . . . And I said 'Well what did you think about me when I first arrived?' And she said, 'We were frightened. And especially the women and the children'. And I knew they were frightened, because whenever they caught sight of me at a distance they would drop whatever they had and just turn around and scream – literally! They really

were. And so they laughed about that. But she said, 'We just didn't know really what you were . . . who you were, what you wanted'. They hadn't ever actually seen a white woman before. They had seen some white men. And then one day and then she told me– (they all laughed a lot telling me this) – how I had been bathing on my own, and a man had come past and he'd seen me. I hadn't seen him, or I can't remember, but anyway – he'd then gone to the nearby houses and he'd said, 'It! It is a woman! It has breasts!' And then they all felt so happy because at least then I was definable. Women are much less frightening than men – at least outsiders. You see, they're very frightened of outside men, for very good reason.

In this vivid example the female body of the fieldworker, considerably taller than the indigenous people, was eventually genderized as less threatening and enabled the anthropologist to gain easier acceptance.

Another example in Ghana reveals how the anthropologist was perceived initially as a bodily white 'other' but this was soon explained away. Louise de la Gorgendière (1993), as a white Canadian woman arriving in a Ghanaian village, was believed to be a confused ancestor who had been born in the wrong body.

de la Gorgendière: When I first went to the village the old lady that I interviewed said that she had only ever seen one other white person, in the village, and couldn't understand why I had come there. That other white person was a missionary who had been there in the 1940s. No other white person had ever come, and this was quite a miracle. What the people decided was that I was actually quite a confused individual. They thought I was an ancestor who had come back in a white person's body. They insisted on coming up with this same tale over and over again, during the course of my fieldwork. Even when we were in the shrine, people would pour libations, and they would tell the ancestors, 'One of our ancestors has returned here, in the body of a Akua Afriyie.' And they said to me, several times, 'You are one of our ancestors.' I said, 'Well, how do you explain my white body, and the fact that I'm Canadian?' And they said, 'Somehow your spirit got confused. But you've come . . . why else would you come to this village? How could you know our language? How could you know our customs? How can you remember all our names after only two weeks?' I said, 'I read books. I've studied the language.' And they said, 'Well, why *our* village? Of all the villages in Ghana, why *our* village?' That's typical of Asante. It's like talking about witchcraft, or the supernatural. You can explain scientifically why the tree falls down – but why did the tree fall down and kill that person? We would just say, 'Well, it's fate, or it's a coincidence.' They say, 'No. There's another reason behind that.' (cf. Evans-Pritchard, 1937).

In England, when I was conducting fieldwork among the Gypsies (Okely, 1983), my sexuality/gender was exploited to sanction a man criticized for his womanizing. My bodily state was seized upon and distorted by another Gadje (non-Gypsy) woman to divert attention away from her own well publicized sexual misbehaviour. When I told her that I had a stomach upset, she passed on a complete fabrication that I was pregnant. This successfully encouraged the Travellers to focus on my alleged sexual misbehaviour rather than that of my accuser. Next the Travellers used me as outsider to draw attention indirectly to the real past sexual misbehaviour of another Traveller. He had a reputation for womanizing and, when he ran off with another Traveller's wife some years previously, this resulted in a deadly feud. For their own purposes, the camp residents claimed I was now pregnant by this same Gypsy man whom they wished to censure for his past. I, as outsider non-Gypsy, was a convenient target to settle old internal Gypsy scores. Elsewhere I have elaborated how I managed to resolve this potentially dangerous accusation (Okely, 2005).

Helena Wulff was also made aware of her gendered and racialized identity first via her body. She had to adapt accordingly. Studying teenage girls in south London in the early 1980s (Wulff, 1988), she found that urban fieldwork was dangerous for a young woman. She and another young woman anthropologist were initially unprepared. She had to clothe her body correctly and learn how to walk, move and look in a different way from her past bodily experience.

> *Wulff*: When we went to the cinema, we had to take precautions. People were raped and murdered all around us. It was dangerous in the tube. . . . The area is now gentrified. We dressed casually in sneakers and jeans and tried to walk like a man so the cars wouldn't stop. I learned how to walk in the street so as to be safe . . . not too close to the cars. My landlady taught me that if there was a strange character approaching, you had to turn without appearing to be avoiding him. To avoid being mugged don't have a handbag. . . . I always put money in my shoe so I could take a taxi home . . . It was better that I was Swedish than being British.

Not only had Wulff to reconfigure her visible gendered identity but she was also confronted with her unchangeable white identity; something which she could not corporeally change. A key incident occurred when she was queuing for a Reggae concert in Brixton. She was naively and visibly holding her ticket. A black boy ran past and grabbed it. Her friends said he would never have taken it from a black girl. Although her black girl friends were angry she realized this was what it was like for them.

> *Wulff*: I was very upset in the tube I was thinking; 'I'm Swedish, Sweden has never been colonialist. It's not my fault but I'm white'. It was inverted racism. I looked down at my skin. I couldn't change it . . . It was an extremely educative experience to experience racism that was what it's like . . . humiliation – you can't do anything about it. I couldn't change the colour of my skin.

Thus the anthropologist learned painfully how 'race' as skin colour can essentialize identity.

The body moving, sitting and working

When anthropologists live alongside a different people, they may not only be first categorized by their sex/gender and 'race'. The simplest and seemingly taken-for-granted of their bodily movements, posture and actions are subject to new unpredictable scrutinies. The anthropologist may attempt to adjust, but sometimes their attempts serve to reveal how skilled or culturally loaded different uses of the body can be.

For several anthropologists the very act of walking through tropical forests was difficult as well as hazardous. For Brian Morris, who lived with hunter-gatherers in tropical forest India (1982), it was especially sobering to realize that at his prime he could not keep up with an elderly woman. His relatively youthful body was exposed as incompetent.

> *Morris*: On one occasion this woman would've been about 70 years of age. She was only five foot and very slender. I was finding it difficult to keep up with her. It was incongruous, this 34 year old, sort of in my prime, traipsing behind this little woman and she was jumping over logs and scrambling over streams and I was trying to keep up with her.

The labouring body: skills recognized

Many anthropologists learned through participation in physical labour. This did not mean that the fieldworker became competent at the required skills. It was frequently the very recognition of the anthropologists' incompetence that made them realize how special the labour was. As Morris' example shows, he could not walk as fast as an elderly woman, neither could he slash the undergrowth as effectively as young children:

> You had to bash this creeper with an adze. Now I used to work in a foundry so I was used to hard work. It nearly killed me, this job. This particular day I was faint. I was completely exhausted. And I looked around and these little kids were bashing away! There were lots of occasions like that where I thought, I'm just physically not up to this.

Milking cows

I asked to hand-milk cows after first meeting a woman farmer in Normandy. She was so astonished at my seeming subversion of her French image of an academic that she disappeared only to return with flash camera. She photographed me attempting to milk the cow. Thus the anthropologist's body at work was also something to be recorded and othered by the indigenous subject.

The added significance of that first encounter with hand milking was an introduction to a bodily skill in collaboration with an animal's body and one which seemed also to respond to, if not understand French. As a human animal, I was also relating to the named, individualized cow: 'Mère No-No'. She had been chosen for me out of the dozen others because she was more tolerant of strangers. Madame Grégoire had made me realize the specificity of cows whose treatment she made an entire way of working (Okely, 1996: 227–229).

Learning to participate through labour has also its instrumental rewards. The fieldworker is seen to be trying. His/her incompetence may enhance the hosts' sense of value. It also opens avenues. When I was meeting aged residents in retirement homes in Normandy, as part of my study, it was always a conversation opener when I revealed that I was learning to hand-milk cows. My attempts, however inept, evoked past and shared experiences among the women 'agriculteurs'. They talked of their own skills and volunteered extended narratives in mutual trust. (Okely, 1994). My bodily participation had redefined my identity by establishing rapport with manual labourers beyond the bourgeoisie.

Rolling tents

Nancy Lindisfarne (Tapper, 1991) did fieldwork among nomads in Afghanistan. She also learned that seemingly simple tasks (such as the time consuming act of rolling the felt tent) were hard without practice. As she said, 'I wasn't really very good. . . . I think that physical learning is extremely important. Because of the weight, the demandingness of it. You can't really estimate if you just looked at it. They make it look easy. Because they're good at it!'

Tree climbing

Brian Morris, in tropical forest India (1982), spoke about tree climbing for honey:

> What really surprised me – it wasn't my lack of knowledge that made me a poor hunter-gatherer. . . . I learned where the yams were . . . it was my lack of physical prowess. I could not climb these trees. I actually started practising. . . . You put your arms round the tree, as if you were going to hug it, you put your insteps on the bark, you pushed with your knees. . . . You held on with your arms as you pushed with your feet. And that created friction. And then you walked up. So the Pndaram actually walked up trees sideways . . . the children learnt, boys and girls, from an early stage. These trees were 100, 120 feet up. The honey is on the underside of the branches. They would do this just after dusk. I hadn't got a hope in the world of climbing up these trees like that . . . It wasn't common, but it was extremely dangerous if you slipped.

He subsequently realized the full extent of the risk and demands in this bodily labour when a close friend, who had acquired the skills as an indigenous member, fell to his death after years of experience.

The scholar rather than labouring body

In some instances, the anthropologist was appreciated best as scholar and manual labour would not have had the instrumental benefits. Michael Herzfeld makes this clear in speaking about his fieldwork in Greece:

> We were able to go grape picking. But they wouldn't dream of letting one do any of the heavy physical labour. Now other people have managed to do this. I think it has a lot to do with where you are and how you come in. I think that in Glendy the villagers liked the idea that they had a 'scholar', especially after I'd ceased to be a student and become in Greek terms a professor.

Similarly, Jonny Parry, when first conducting fieldwork in Northern India, was in most contexts respected as a Brahminical Scholar who did not do manual labour.

Bodily imitation

There are more subtle ways in which the fieldworker learns about the social system in which they are living through unknowing, unconscious imitation or deliberate bodily mimesis. Such imitations include ways of sitting, standing and moving to music in dance. The anthropologist may find herself closely scrutinized and instructed. S/he may risk causing offence by transgressing the boundaries of what was believed to be 'natural'. Attempts to change, however clumsy, are usefully interpreted as signs of respect. At other times, the anthropologist may, without instruction and without knowing, empathetically pick up the mood of the other person and absorb it in similar bodily posture. A photograph (Okely, 1992: 18) shows me talking with a Gypsy woman who had willingly posed for a non-Gypsy photographer whom I knew well. I had unconsciously identified with her involuntary barrier posture of arms folded. The anthropologist, if an outsider, can rarely become a native in the formal sense, but through co-residence, learning the language, in dialogue and participation in the day-to-day, can modify his/her position as complete outsider. The anthropologist's posture has to reflect and fit in with those of the hosts. It may help to merge in, to become part of the crowd, if not near invisible.

Malcolm McLeod spoke in detail about this issue when reflecting on posture in Ghana where he had done extensive fieldwork:

> It's not just a matter of politeness but communication and respect, as well as hierarchy . . . Facial expression is very important, and knowing where to look, how to look, when to show your eyes, when to look down, when to look directly at people, how to listen to them, how to sit properly. There are great subtleties there. I'm not sure how you actually learn them, except by very close and careful observation. But on the other hand, you've got to be taught how to do that. You've got to be taught that there is something worth learning there.

Also in Ghana, Louise de la Gorgendière benefited from explicit instructions on correct bodily postures from her Ghanaian research assistant before she visited people of high rank. But for Malcolm McLeod, the lessons were acquired over extended time:

> It took me *years* actually to notice, in Asante, if a court case is being tried, or people are listening to traditions being recited, or enquiring into history, there are very high levels of detailed observation to which you are subject. There is a particular form of glance at crucial moments, when you suddenly spot someone actually putting the eye on you, it's almost like an x-ray eye, and it goes right through you. And if you're not in the right position, doing the right things, when that happens, you're marked down. . . . Now, a lot of people never even become aware that is going on. I'm sure you pick it up unconsciously. You have to – . . . all the very basic things, you don't cross your legs, you're not getting lefts and rights mixed up. You don't hand people things with your left hand - the distance from which you put yourself from other people, or touching them. In many circumstances, it is closer, you should touch people, you should hold them. But it's *much* more subtle! It's the facial expressions, the posture – almost the breathing. That begins to sound very pretentious, but I don't think it is. There are

> rhythms in the speech, there are rhythms in the dance, there are rhythms in the music, there are rhythms in the way people move . . . which are very, very subtle. You do learn them unconsciously. I have seen some very eminent experts on the Asante and their culture – European experts – doing this all wrong . . . they're excused, because they're outsiders. But even if you get slightly closer to them, you begin to see things like that.

Michael Herzfeld (1985) noticed how the Greeks adjusted their bodies to linguistic subtleties and seemed to learn the same without knowing it:

> They will also stop in the middle of a sentence and savour the sound of a word, which I think is much more to do with the body, than some intellectual operation. I'm told that when I speak Greek my whole bodily appearance changes, but you'd have to ask somebody else about that.

Again, the anthropologist may pick up and absorb cultural cues through a near unconscious empathy, not only through deliberate conscious imitation.

Sitting

Malcolm McLeod spoke of Western visitors to Ghana:

> There was a Black American scholar . . . who when he was waiting to make an appointment to see the King outside the King's secretary's office, and causing this slight embarrassment. He was all slumped in a chair, chewing gum, with his legs crossed, and his feet higher than his head, in the air . . . he could've shat on the floor, that would've made it *slightly* worse, but probably not much.

The manner of sitting in a group among settled nomads in Iran studied by Sue Wright (1981, 1996) was interpreted as a reflection of a person's position in the world. The wrong posture was seen as an indication of vulnerability and loss of status and control. A person had to be 'collected'; cross-legged with hands and feet forming a circle.

> Wright: I would get this *intense* care about . . . how I behaved. So, that was shown in the body . . . an acceptable way to sit; your feet out of sight and your hands . . . your elbows on your knees, so that you've got a complete circle. . . . Little children were told by their parents, 'Collect your hands and feet together'. . . . That was the way I learnt to sit when I wanted to be in control of the situation. Because it meant that they were reading me as collected. I think the idea of balance is a crucial one. . . . You've got cross-cutting ties all around you, if you're a tribesperson. And you're trying not to offend anybody, you're trying to hold everything together, because if you can keep control, then you are not attacked . . . And again . . . particularly the way the men would sit, and would look; straight eye-contact, straight one-to-one. I didn't realize until after a while that I'd adopted this very masculine way of relating with the men. This was when I was included in men's meetings. But when walking in the alleys, I realized with a jolt that I had brought up my hand, as if holding an imaginary chador to shield myself from the gaze of a man walking towards me.

Margaret Kenna, when first doing fieldwork as a young unmarried woman on a Greek island, behaved in what she thought was a modest fashion. Only years later did she discover that sitting with crossed legs was considered to be the posture of a prostitute because apparently this twisted the womb and prevented conception (Kenna, 1992: 153). Michael Herzfeld, in contrast, learned the subtleties of the bodily position when sitting and playing cards with the men in Crete:

> I'm not a card player, or I hadn't been. I learned some of *their* games. There's a certain kind of bodily posture, because you're trying not to give things away. You're assuming a bodily posture of comfort, but also engagement. Those things I certainly was aware of and they had to do with participating.

The body culturally clothed

Nancy Lindisfarne, in Afghanistan with nomads in the 1970s, was advised by them for her own protection to wear indigenous dress. She was teased for walking like a man. She had to learn to walk with yards of billowing cloth as trousers. She learned to love the chador and the invisibility it gave. As she and her husband travelled towards Europe, she was obliged to abandon this comfort cloth. It had become part of her body and identity:

> I wore the women's clothing, which included a long black veil, a *chadari,* as they called it in Pashtu, which didn't veil my face, but which was a head covering, and that went down to the ground. I wore wide dresses, which were waisted and yoked with embroidery. And then trousers which were 10 metres of cloth . . . huge, billowing harem trousers. But I think the most striking thing which can tell how much one gets involved, are things like . . . I had this long black veil, but I was always being teased by the fact that I had a walk like a soldier . . . my style of walking was not catering for the fact that one had these very voluminous trousers, and this veil – you had to hold your head in a certain way or it would fall off. . . . When I went to the shrines I would practise trying to be invisible, so that I wasn't the foreigner. . . . Those things were exciting to learn, and completely non-verbal. I became very fond of this veil, and how one could use it to watch without being watched. . . . I still very much have this sense of what you can do with this veil. Learning to go to sleep! Because again, they have no privacy. But learning to do what women did, which was – you pulled your veil, lay down – absolutely wherever you were – pulled the veil over your head, and you could go to sleep. Because you weren't there!

Thus, contrary to Western ethnocentric presumptions, the veil is primarily learned through bodily experience to be a comfort, protection and pleasure.

The body dancing

Changing bodily movement can be an entry into ritual and cultural representations. Laura Bohannon (Smith Bowen, 1954) and Powdermaker (1967) learned in Africa and in New Guineau the deeper knowledge gained by participating and dancing in contrast to standing as unmoving spectators. Bohannon realized through the movements required how complex were the demands on the different parts of the body.

Another of the anthropologists I have interviewed; Felicia Hughes-Freeland (1997a, 1997b, 2001) has specialized in the study of dance in Indonesia. To dance became central. Her experience might be seen as a condensed metaphor for other anthropologists. She had to dance differently. The movements were slow and subtle in ways unrecognized in the cultural traditions of much Western dance.

In the 1970s, the body was still seen as something to be concealed and cerebralized in public academic interchange. At an ASA (Association of Social Anthropologists) conference on the Anthropology of the Body (Blacking, 1977), David Brookes took the subject seriously and as part of his presentation performed the Bakhtiari stick dance on the platform. A celebrated anthropology professor at a London University department, however, hurtfully declared that he brought the discipline of anthropology into 'disrepute'. It was, even in the 1970s, curiously permissible for British if not other academic anthropologists to dance in their own ballroom style at the conference evening social, but not as cross cultural performance on the speakers' platform (pc, Brookes, 1977).

Yet, as the examples of Bohannon and Powdermaker have long illustrated, dance as musical movement of the body has been integral to certain contexts in fieldwork, whether or not the anthropologist chooses to focus on dance in a subsequent ethnography. Herzfeld reflects this in his comments:

> I've always been very open to new experiences and enjoyed them and looked for them. In terms of bodily carriage, some forms of Greek dancing are quite different from anything that we do in Britain as a local tradition. I think that the performance and spontaneity is one. That's when the performance and spontaneity becomes very clear. It's no coincidence that in the film *Zorba the Greek*, dance plays such an important part, especially that final scene. I knew one or two dances. . . . I wasn't very good at picking up steps, so I tended to dance in the way that I already knew, which I partly learned when I was a student at Cambridge. There's a very fast Cretan men's dance called the *pendozalis* which I found exhilarating . . . but incredibly exhausting. I mean if you're stuck between two burly Cretan shepherds who spend all their time prancing around in the foothills.
>
> JO: Did that experience help to make sense of the dancing?
>
> MH. It certainly wasn't unhelpful. It helped in the sense of making me feel that I was part of the scene and I think making *them* feel that I was more part of the scene. But I wasn't focusing all that much on dance. That's something that Jane Cowan (1990) opened up so much more than any of us.

Helena Wulff has used her previous experience of years of dancing to make ethnographic sense of dance in the West. Here she used familiarity with aspects of her own culture but unusually exercised in years of prior balletic training through her body to interpret and produce her ethnography (Wulff, 1998). Thus dance as a non-cerebral, culturally flexible body can no longer be scandalously dismissed in anthropological academic discourse.

The senses

Anthropologists and social scientists in general, as well as those in the humanities, are reclaiming sensation for intellectual enquiry (Howes, 2003; Okely, 2001, 2006a). The anthropologist in the field, whether or not it has been fully confronted in the past, absorbs also through the skin, and learns through all the senses.

Tasting

Through hours of participating in hand-milking and shared dialogue with Madame Grégoire, I learned her views about farming and cultivation. She refused to feed her cows concentrates or use pesticides. At the end of the milking, she invited me to drink her cow's pure and uncontaminated milk. I was tasting the landscape while savouring that liquid in my mouth (Okely, 2001).

Similarly Stoller (1989) has argued for the importance of fieldwork as taste, again an anti- cerebral interconnection of all the senses with labour and vision. My exploration of taste among the small farmers in Normandy has countered the presumption by Bourdieu (1984) that only the bourgeoisie have taste or distinction (Okely, 1994).

Smell

Smells are involuntarily absorbed whether they be the evocative memory of dampened vegetation and earth in Africa, or the ever lingering odour of sheep and goats on the men with whom Michael Herzfeld associated:

> *Herzfeld*: One thing that has remained as a not very pleasant memory in my nostrils, again, given an interest in smell, was the smell of sheep. All of the men of course, their clothes smell, they reek of sheep, and goat. These people wash a great deal, they're very careful about their personal hygiene. . . . The only thing is that I recognize there's a faint tinge of nostalgia now when I think about it, because I also associate it with the marvellous times I had in the village. I think smell is a tremendously important carrier of connections between periods of one's life. It's also sometimes a way of connecting those periods of one's life with larger historical periods, which is why I try to do the smellscape as a way of introducing the embodied sense of history of the people of Rehemnos' (Herzfeld, 1991).

Louise de la Gorgendière, after her extensive fieldwork in Ghana, described what happens on her return to the continent:

> All of a sudden the smell of the *soil* of Africa just (came) comes back. And it has a *very* distinctive smell. And if I am walking in the rain, whether I am in Edinburgh, or Cambridge, or Canada, and I am in a forested area, or beside a garden, and that smell comes up, from damp soil, I am *instantly* transported to the village. *Instantly*. So, I never believed that my sense of smell was that acute. But I can just get that sense of smell, and I'm instantly transported. And if I see anything in sort of little triangle stacks, as they would have been on the tables, in Ghana, I'm instantly transported

> back. And of course the colours and the music. So I think I was far more attuned with *all* my senses than I really realized. . . . Until I closed my eyes and tried to visualize it all again. Because it wasn't just visual. It was auditory *and* sensory . . . nasal?

The body at risk

The anthropologist in the field cannot always hold back in caution but s/he may put her body, if not life, on the line. Learning through the body can be a source of pain and illness. Jonny Parry studied death rituals in Benares (1994):

> I think that what actually gave me what was diagnosed as typhoid I was certainly very ill . . . It was not Ganges water, but it was water from a particular well that was said to be sacred. It was during the beginning of the rains, so it was very hot, and that's when water tends to be most infected. And water was drawn from this well, especially for me . . . I had gone to see the well, and ask about it. What else would you do? But give a kind of honoured visitor some honorific and sacred water. It wouldn't have been impossible to refuse, but it would've been extremely difficult. People in Benares . . . were very *assertive* about these kinds of things: 'Ganges water is pure and you come here, and you claim that you have great respect, asking us all these questions about ritual and religion.' I mean, to ostentatiously refuse would not have done my rapport much good. . . . It was in Benares. It was just behind the cremation gats.

Some anthropologists have undergone rites of passage with the inevitable painful stages or subjected themselves to healing practices as embodied means of learning. Elizabeth Hsu (2005) underwent 'participant experience' in consenting to a special form of painful acupuncture in China *en route* to gaining a fuller understanding of this form of healing. Thus, pain and unforeseen risks may become participant experience extended from participant observation in the field.

Dead bodies

The cultural fate of the dead body can be a revelation into a society's priorities. Shilling and others have confronted the dominant medicalisation and privatization of death in great swathes of the West (1993). It is suggested that this is consistent with the cult of the body beautiful and secularization which gives no recompense for death in any afterlife.

But in one centre of Western classical culture, namely Greece, there are different ways of dealing with the dead. The decomposition of the body is confronted. Margaret Kenna, when I asked her about learning through the body, volunteered a stark example, namely the practice of relatives digging up the grave of their dead in an exhumation a year after the burial. The near fleshless bones are lifted out of the ground and placed in containers. This focussed Kenna on the continuity of genealogies and the significance of naming passed on from one generation to another in her Greek island fieldwork (2001). The bones were stark emblems of the end of individuals, but their collection by descendants, named after them, ensured vital continuity.

Embodied memories for the production of texts

When returning from the field and writing up, as opposed to writing down field notes, the anthropologist is faced with a mass of recorded material and months of memories (Jackson, 1990). Ottenberg has referred to 'headnotes' (1990) ie, what is not written down, remembered observations. I would prefer a less cerebral store of memory. Field notes are records for evidence, direct quotations and even quantitative data, but they may also act as mnemonic triggers of a total experience. Making sense of fieldwork is also a bodily process. The writer recognizes themes and sorts out what seemed incomprehensible puzzles because she can feel it in her bones and flesh, although s/he will be seated and relatively still, while working through the material and submerged memories (Okely, 2006b).

To conclude

Knowing others through the instrument of the field worker's own body involves deconstructing the body as a cultural, biographical construction through a lived and interactive encounter with others' cultural construction and bodily experience. This is not merely verbal, nor merely cerebral, but a kinetic and sensual process both conscious and unconscious which occurs in unpredictable, uncontrollable ways. The fieldworker may be newly marked as sexed, racialized and othered in different contexts. There are bodily risks, pains and pleasures. The anthropologist learns anew to sit, talk, stand, walk, dress, dance and labour at hitherto untried tasks. Field work contrasts with the sedentary practices of the academic. This process is often counter-intuitive when compared to the anthropologist's original cultural socialization yet, after extended participation, may become instinctive. Narratives reveal the anthropologists' transformations through embodiment and emerge as vital paths to knowledge and the writing up of cultural alternatives.

Note

1 The anthropologists with whom I have conducted extended dialogues from the late 1990s through to 2005 include those referred to in this article, namely: Michael Herzfeld, Louise de la Gorgendière, Felicia Hughes-Freeland, Margaret Kenna, Nancy Lindisfarne, Malcolm McLeod, Brian Morris, Jonny Parry, Sue Wright and Helena Wulff. This article is part of a forthcoming project *Anthropological Practice: fieldwork and the ethnographic method,* to be published by Berg.

References

Abramson, A. (1987) 'Beyond the Samoan controversy in anthropology: a history of sexuality in the eastern interior of Fiji' in P. Caplan (ed.) *The Cultural Construction of Sexuality* London: Tavistock.

Blacking, J. (ed.) (1977) *The Anthropology of the Body*, ASA Monograph, London: Academic Press.

Bourdieu, P. (1984) *Distinction: A Social Critique of the Judgement of Taste*, (transl. R. Nice) London: Routledge and Kegan Paul.

Clifford, J. and Marcus, G. (eds) (1986) *Writing Culture*, Berkeley: California University Press.

Cowan, J. (1990) *Dance and the Body Politic in Northern Greece*, Princeton: Princeton University Press.

Csordas, T. (ed.) (1994) *Embodiment and Experience: The existential ground of culture and self*, Cambridge: Cambridge University Press.

Csordas, T. (2002) *Body/Meaning/Healing*, New York: Palgrave Macmillan.

de la Gorgendière, L. (1993) Education and development in Ghana: An Asante village study, PhD thesis University of Cambridge.

Douglas, M. (1966) *Purity and Danger*, London: Routledge and Kegan Paul.

Evans-Pritchard, E. (1937) *Witchcraft, Oracles and Magic among the Azande,* Oxford: Clarendon Press.

Herzfeld, M. (1985) *The Poetics of Manhood: Contest and Identity in a Cretan Mountain Village,* Princeton: Princeton University Press.

Herzfeld, M. (1991) *A Place in History: Social and Monumental Time in a Cretan town*, Princeton: Princeton University Press.

Howell, S. (1984) *Society and Cosmos: Chewong of Peninsular* Malaysia. Oxford: Oxford University Press.

Howes, D. (2003) *Sensual Relations: Engaging the Senses in Culture and Social Theory*, Ann Arbor: University of Michigan Press.

Hsu, E. (2005) 'Acute Pain Infliction as Therapy' in *Etnofoor* 18 (1) 78–96.

Hughes-Freeland, F. (1997a) 'Consciousness in performance: a Javanese theory', *Social Anthropology* 5, 21, pp. 55–68.

Hughes-Freeland, F. (1997b) 'Art and politics: from Javanese court dance to Indonesian art', *Journal Royal Anthropological Institute,* 3, pp. 473–495.

Hughes-Freeland, F. (2001) 'Dance, dissimulation, and identity in Indonesia' in *An Anthropology of Indirect Communication* (eds) Joy Hendry and C.W. Watson, ASA Monographs 37, London, Routledge, pp. 145–162.

Jackson, J. (1990) ' "I am a fieldnote": Fieldnotes as a Symbol of Professional Identity' in R. Sanjek (ed.) *Fieldnotes: The Makings of Anthropology,* London: Cornell University Press.

Kenna, M. (1992) 'Changing places and altered perspective:research on a Greek island in the 1960s and in the 1980s' in J. Okely and H. Callaway (eds), *Anthropology and Autobiography*, London: Routledge.

Kenna, M. (2001) *Greek Island Life: fieldwork on Anafia*, Amsterdam: Harwood academic publishers.

Kulick, D. and Wilson, M. (eds.), (1995) *Taboo: Sex, identity and erotic subjectivity in anthropological fieldwork*, London: Routledge.

Martin, E. (1987) *The Woman in the Body, A Cultural Analysis of Reproduction,* Milton Keynes: Open University Press.

Mauss, M. (1936) 'Les Techniques du corps' in M. Mauss 1938 *Anthropologie et Sociologie*, Paris: Presses Universitaires de France.

Mellor, P.A. and Shilling, C. (1997) *Re-forming the Body. Religion, Community and Modernity*. London: Sage.

Moreno, E. (1995) 'Rape in the field: reflections from a survivor' in D. Kulick and M. Wilson (eds) *op cit*.

Morris, B. (1982) *Forest Traders*, LSE Monographs, London: Athlone Press.

Okely, J. (1983) *The Traveller-Gypsies*, Cambridge: Cambridge University Press.

Okely, J. (1992) 'Anthropology and Autobiography: participatory experience and embodied knowledge' in J. Okely and H. Callaway (eds), *Anthropology and Autobiography*, London: Routledge.

Okely, J. (1994) 'Vicarious and sensory knowledge of chronology and change: ageing in rural France', in K. Hastrup and P. Hervik (eds) *Social Experience and Anthropological Knowledge*, London: Routledge

Okely, J. (1996) *Own or Other Culture*, London: Routledge.

Okely, J. (2001) 'Visualism and Landscape: Looking and Seeing in Normandy' *Ethnos*, Vol. 66:1.

Okely, J. (2005) 'Gypsy Justice versus Gorgio Law: Interrelations of Difference' in *Sociological Review* vol. 53 No. 4 Nov. pp. 691–709.

Okely, J. (2006a) 'Changing senses across cultures' review of 'The Senses' (eds) R. Bendix and D. Brenneis *Etnofoor* 2005 18 (1).

Okely, J. (2006b) 'Knowing without notes' in N. Halstead, E. Hirsch and J. Okely (eds) *Knowing How to Know*, Oxford: Berghaun (in press.)

Okely, J. (2007) *Anthropological Practice: fieldwork and the ethnographic method*, Oxford: Berg. (forthcoming).

Okely, J. and Callaway, H. (eds) (1992) *Anthropology and Autobiography*, London: Routledge.

Ottenberg, S. (1990) 'Thirty years of Fieldnotes: Changing Relationships to the Text' in R. Sanjek (ed.) *Fieldnotes: The Makings of Anthropology* London: Cornell University Press.

Parry, J. (1994) *Death in Banares*. Cambridge: Cambridge University Press.

Polhemus, T. (ed.) (1978) *Social Aspects of the Human Body*, Harmondsworth: Penguin Books.

Powdermaker, H. (1967) *Stranger and Friend: The Way of an Anthropologist,* New York: W.W. Norton and Co.

Shilling, C. (1993) *The Body and Social Theory* London: Sage.

Smith Bowen, E. (L. Bohannon) (1954) *Return to Laughter,* New York: Doubleday Anchor.

Stoller, P. (1989) *The Taste of Ethnographic Things,* Philadelphia: University of Pennsylvania Press.

Tapper, N. (Lindisfarne) (1991) *Bartered Brides: Politics, Gender and Marriage in an Afghan tribal Society*, Cambridge: Cambridge University Press.

Winkler, C. (with K. Wininger) (1994) 'Rape trauma: contexts of meaning' in T. Csordas (ed.), *op cit*.

Wright, S. (1978) 'Prattle and politics: the position of women in Doshman Ziari, Iran' *Journal of the Anthropological Society of Oxford* IX (2): 98–112.

Wright, S. (1981) 'Place and Face: of Women in Doshman Ziara, Iran' in S. Ardener (ed.) *Women and Space: Ground Rules and Social Maps*, London: Croom Helm. pp. 136–57 (Revised edition, Berg, 1993)

Wright, S. (1996) 'Patterns and representations' in E. Hallam and N. Levell (eds) *Communicating Otherness: Cultural Encounters* University of Sussex, Graduate Research Centre in Culture and Communication. pp. 45–62

Wulff, H. (1988) *Twenty Girls: Growing Up, Ethnicity and Excitement in a South London Micro culture,* Almqvist & Wiksell International.

Wulff, H. (1998) *Ballet across Borders, Career and Culture in the World of Dancers,* Oxford: Berg.

Researching embodiment by way of 'body techniques'

Nick Crossley

Abstract

In this chapter I reflect upon the importance of Marcel Mauss' concept of 'body techniques' for facilitating an empirical analysis of embodiment. I begin by arguing that sociology is not guilty of mind/body dualism, in the philosophical sense, but tends rather to take the embodiment of actions and practices for granted and thus to overlook it, much as Leder suggests happens more generally in everyday, lay experience. It is the purpose, knowledge-base and normativity of actions and practices that has tended to be thematized in sociology, I observe. The importance of Mauss' concept, I continue, is that it thematizes embodiment, simultaneously drawing attention to the socio-cultural variability of particular ways of acting, without losing sight of purpose, knowledge or normativity. Indeed it draws all of these aspects of action together. Having made these points in an abstract manner, the chapter attempts to show how this innovation can and has shaped empirical work in social science. An empirical focus upon body techniques, I suggest, facilitates an empirical engagement with the embodiment of the social world.

Key words: body techniques, Mauss, dualism, absent body, diffusion

Introduction

How can we open up human embodiment to sociological research? Is it possible for the lens of sociological inquiry to reach beyond 'representations of' and 'discourses on' the body, beyond things done and attached to the body, to explore embodied agency and practice? In this chapter I suggest that it is and I propose Marcel Mauss' (1979) concept of 'body techniques' as a central tool for achieving this. I have critically discussed, used and developed this concept on a number of occasions previously (Crossley, 1995, 2004a,b, 2005). Here I limit myself to a discussion of the way in which it helps to bring embodiment before the sociological gaze, facilitating research. The chapter begins with a discussion of the absence of the body in sociology. I argue that this is not due to mind/body dualism but rather to the fact that sociologists, though dealing with human (inter)actions which are irreducibly embodied, have tended to foreground other aspects of those (inter)actions than their embodiment, for example their purposes and normative character. I suggest Mauss' (1979) concept of 'body techniques' as a remedy. A focus upon body techniques allows us to consider the purpose, normativity *and embodiment* of action as those various aspects cohere in a unified structure. The chapter then gives a brief exposition of Mauss' concept before discussing how the concept might facilitate concrete research.

Sociology does not involve mind/body dualism

The much repeated claim that sociology needs to be embodied presupposes that the body is absent within the discipline. But in what way? In the sense that sociology presupposes mind/body dualism? A great deal has been made of dualism in sociological discussions of the body, not least by me (Crossley, 2001), and I believe that the problem is an important theoretical resource that we can use to sharpen our thinking. In the final instance, however, most sociology, past and present, is not dualist. Some of the founders tackled dualism head on. Marx's (1970) engagement with idealism and materialism and Durkheim's (1974) philosophical papers are the most obvious references. More importantly, however, the conceptual architecture of dualism, centred upon mind and body, is not the conceptual architecture of sociology. Sociologists haven't talked much about 'bodies', historically, but neither have we talked about 'minds'. Ours has not traditionally been a discourse of minds and bodies. We have talked about 'behaviour', 'actions', 'interactions', 'praxis' and 'practices'; that is, about phenomena which are neutral with respect to the mind/body problematic and transcend it. Action, behaviour, interaction, practice and praxis have both embodied and mindful aspects, without any implication that these aspects derive from separate sources or 'substances'. We are talking about what people do, a physical activity, but we understand that activity to be meaningful, purposive, intelligent, relatively rational etc, and thus mindful.

In philosophy, where dualism *has* been part of the conceptual architecture, at least since Descartes, if not Plato, certain key writers have sought to resolve the problems this generates by shifting their conceptual focus away from 'mind' and 'body' and onto purposive human activity; a focus which, they believe, combines mindful and embodiment elements in a unified whole and thereby transcends dualism (eg, Ryle, 1949; Merleau-Ponty, 1965). They have called for a focus upon 'structures of behaviour' and behavioural dispositions (ibid.). Sociology, I am suggesting, inadvertently stumbled upon this 'solution' at its inception and therefore largely circumvented the problem of dualism before it arose.

Sociology therefore is not dualist. It circumvents dualism by way of its conceptual architecture. At least it did until we started talking about 'bodies'. Talk of 'bodies' is problematic because it invokes 'minds', albeit tacitly, as a necessary counter-part. Descartes' (1969) argument for dualism, we should remember, was prompted in no small part by his obsession with 'bodies' (Leder, 1988). He didn't ignore embodiment. But he separated it out conceptually, as 'the body', to a point where he mistook a conceptual distinction between the psychological and physical aspects of embodied human beings for a substantial distinction between 'mind' and 'body' (Ryle, 1949; Crossley, 2001).

Does this mean that bodies are not absent in sociology? Have we been barking up the wrong tree? I do not think so. There has been and is an absence of the body in sociological discourse but this is not because of dualism. The body has been absent in sociological discourse in the sense that phenomenological writers, particularly Leder (1990), invoke when they speak of an absence of the body in everyday embodied experience. This point needs to be unpacked briefly.

Sociology's absent body

Our embodiment is our point of view on the world for Leder (1990). It locates us in the world, putting us in a spatio-temporal relation with other beings and giving us a standpoint, literally, from which to perceive them. Our embodiment is also the basis of our consciousness, however. My body is not merely the perceptible material that you can see, smell and touch, nor even the internal organs that medical science can measure, weigh and monitor. It has another 'inside' that surgeons and neuroscientists cannot access; an inside comprising lived sensations which form the coherent and meaningful gestalt structures that are my consciousness of the world. Traditional conceptions of 'the body' focus upon its perceptible aspects and thus assume the perspective of an outside observer; an outside-in perspective. Phenomenology alerts us to the body's own, inside-out perspective, and thus to the body of the observer. Human bodies, for the phenomenologist, are both perceptible and perceiving, sensible and sentient.

Having said that, I do not *perceive* my sensations. I *have* my sensations and *only I have them* but what I *perceive* is a world beyond myself which is meaningful to me. I am having visual sensations right now but I cannot see them. I see my computer screen. Likewise I am having auditory and olfactory sensations but they are not objects of perception for me. They form my consciousness of background music and a coffee aroma. My embodied consciousness, which comprises a structure of lived sensations, *intends* a world beyond me.

This is what Leder (1990) means when he argues that the body is 'absent'. My experience is embodied but it is *not an experience of* my body. It is an embodied experience of the world around me. And for the world to be perceived by me it is necessary that my body, as a site of experience, sinks into the background and does not become the object of its own experience. This situation can be reversed in what Leder calls 'dys-appearances' of the body; that is, instances where we become aware of our bodies because they dysfunction in some way. We become aware of our visual sensations when bright lights dazzle us and cause pain, for example, when bad smells or foul tastes make us feel sick or pain and illness strike. These are reversals of the normal situation, however, whose dysfunctional nature reveals the necessity of bodily absence. As the body moves towards the foreground of our experience the world recedes into the background and we lose our grip upon it. We are blinded by the lights; feeling sick precludes our perception of the smell which makes us sick; and we find ourselves too much in pain or too ill to attend to objects and concerns in our environment. When we become aware of the sensations which ordinarily 'give us a grip' upon the world we tend to lose that grip.

I have couched this argument in terms of sensation but I might equally have focused upon perceptual organs. The eye does not see itself without mediation. It sees what lies before it. The nose does not smell itself and the ears do not hear themselves. Nor does the mouth taste itself. Each organ forms a sensuous impression of the outside world but remains its own blind spot. Touch is more complex, as one part of our body can touch another. As Merleau-Ponty (1968) notes, however, even here we see the role of the foreground-background structure. When one hand touches the other we may have a sense of touching or being touched but never both simultaneously. One experience always assumes the foreground position at the expense of the other.

The body, Leder (1990) continues, is equally absent in action. Action involves movement of the body. Typing, for example, involves movement of my fingers, arms, eyes, head etc. This is purposive, intelligent and cultured movement. To type I must know what a keyboard is and how to use it. I must know where different letters are, reaching for and tapping them in the right order. My left and right hands must work together to access upper case letters and symbols. Indeed my whole body must work together. If I lean back in my chair, for example, then my arms must reach further to hit the keys and my fingers must strike them from a different angle. I achieve all of this without being aware of how I do so, however. I know that I am typing but I don't consciously tell my hands to move or give them spatial instructions. I may only become aware of what I am thinking by way of the words I type on the screen, typing in lieu of verbalizing, but even if I say the words to myself before or as I type them I do not instruct my hands to type or guide them to the keys. I may not even know, in a reflective sense, where my fingers are going and may not have conscious knowledge of the keyboard layout. My fingers know where to go without me having to look or search but I couldn't discursively describe where individual letters are. My knowledge of the keyboard is practical, pre-reflective and embodied. And from the point of view of my consciousness, my body 'just moves' appropriately, without my interference (Crossley, 2001). At most I become aware of how I have moved after the event; for example, when I spot a typing error. Even in such cases, however, it is not my body that I become aware of but rather the error on the screen. From the point of view of consciousness, culturally appropriate bodily action and coordination 'just happens' and falls below the threshold of perception and reflective knowledge.

Again then, in action my embodiment is largely absent from experience. I do bodily things and my being consists in these bodily doings but both consciousness and action are directed at the world in which I am acting. I notice my effects upon the world but am not conscious of what I do in order to generate them. Interestingly, moreover, when we do try to concentrate upon how we do things this often decreases our competence and inhibits our action. When we become self-consciousness about how we walk, for example, we are more likely to become clumsy and awkward. Awareness of the body is linked to dysfunction. Embodied self-awareness involves dys-appearance.

Merleau-Ponty (1985) extends this notion to our experiences of others. Others exist for us, in the first instance, by way of perceptual consciousness. We see them, touch them, smell them etc. At the root of intersubjectivity and thus the social world is a 'chiasmic' intertwining of bodies: perceiving and perceptible, sensuous and sensible (Merleau-Ponty, 1968). Perception of the other, however, is not ordinarily perception of 'a body'. The other is not a physical thing for me but rather a locus of meaning. Their posture, comportment, gestures and movement communicate to me and it is the meaning of such communication which occupies the foreground of my perception. I see and hear happiness or a welcome rather than the physical movements which convey these sentiments. Moreover, this meaning is not, in the first instance, an object either. I do not reflect upon it but rather reply to it. What I perceive communicates to me. It 'affords' and generates a response from me. The smile of the other registers more within my own return smile and in the relaxation it engenders in us both than in any reflexive awareness I may have of it – unless it is inappropriate. The other only becomes an object to me, and perhaps a 'body', when this more primordial intersubjective bond is refused or disturbed in some way.

There are problems with this thesis. The body rises to the foreground of conscious experience in everyday social life for a variety of reasons and can enjoy a strong thematic presence. The objectification of female bodies in Western culture is an obvious example (Young, 2005; Bartky, 1993), as is the culture of 'body projects' encouraged by increased reflexivity in late modern societies (Giddens, 1991; Shilling, 1993; Crossley, 2006). The body, however, as a site of experience and action, is often still invisible in these situations. The lived body remains concealed in its own reflexive self-objectifications (Crossley, 2006). More to the point, the thesis of the absent body goes a long way to explaining the apparent disembodiment of sociology. The body has not been absent in sociology in the sense of literally not being there. How could it not be there when we are focusing upon behaviour, action, interaction, practice, praxis etc? But it has been pushed into the background in order to enable a foregrounding of issues which, historically at least, have assumed a greater importance: eg, purpose, meaning, goals, norms, rules etc. Like the reader who overlooks the physical inscriptions on the page before them in order to follow the meaning embodied in those inscriptions, sociologists have overlooked the embodiment of agents and actions in order better to get at the meanings, purposes, interests, rules etc. embodied by them.

The foregrounding of meaning, purpose etc. is right and proper. A sociology which pushed meaning, purpose, norms etc. into the background would be deeply flawed. We are not forced to choose, however, between meaning and embodiment. We can focus both upon the mindful and the embodied aspects of social life. A key conceptual tool which can help us to achieve this is Marcel Mauss' (1979) 'body techniques'.

Body techniques

Mauss (1979) arrived at the concept of body techniques after having observed both that certain embodied practices (eg, spitting and eating with a knife and fork) are specific to particular societies and that others vary considerably in style across societies and social groups. Women walk differently from men, for example; the bourgeoisie talk differently from the proletariat; the French military march and dig differently to British troops, etc. Building on these observations, Mauss defines body techniques as 'ways in which from society to society men [sic] know how to use their bodies' (1979: 97). This definition is potentially problematic. It can seem to suggest that 'men' and 'their bodies' are different. Mauss, however, pursues his point in a way that clearly transcends dualism. Indeed, the concept of body techniques pulls the physical, mental and social aspects of human being together as an irreducible whole (see also Levi-Strauss, 1987). Let me briefly demonstrate how these three aspects are mutually intertwined in the concept:

(1) The historical and cross-cultural variability of body techniques reveals their social aspect. If French soldiers march and dig differently from English soldiers then marching and digging must be techniques that have emerged within the collective life of these groups, by way of the inventiveness and interaction of their members. They are neither universal, which might point to 'hard-wiring', nor individual and idiosyncratic. They are properties of the collective. Moreover, they are social in two respects. Firstly, they are 'external' to the individual in the Durkheimian sense; that is to say, at any given time they exist only in and through the actions of concrete individuals but they pre-exist and will outlive those particular individuals; have been learned and passed on; embody a logic or principle which is initially alien to the agent and which must be learned; and to a degree constrain the agent (although see Crossley, 1995, 2004a). Secondly, they are the product of collective labour. They emerge out of interactions and are not the *ex nihilo* invention of specific individuals.

(2) The biological aspect of body techniques is, in part, a matter of human beings enjoying the innate intelligence, sociability and plasticity that enables us to invent, teach and learn specific techniques. Equally as important, however, the ways in we 'use' our bodies reflect the facts of our bodies. We walk as we do, in part, because we are bipedal and because our joints and muscles move in some directions but not others. Anatomical structure both constrains and potentiates particular uses of the body.

(3) The mindful aspect of body techniques consists in the fact that they are not mere movements; that they embody knowledge and understanding. To learn to swim is not merely a matter of reproducing mechanical patterns of movement, for example. Indeed good swimmers can improvise with their stroke, refuting any sense that swimming is reducible to specific, mechanical patterns of movement. To learn to swim is to grasp principles of buoyancy and propulsion which different strokes utilize in different ways and which competent swimmers can orient to in improvised play. We could specify these principles intellectually in a physics lab. The swimmer grasps them in a different way, however; that is, practically and in an embodied fashion. They do not know the theory and do not need to know it. Their understanding of the principles consists in the 'instinctive' movements that keep them afloat and propel them through the water.

Mauss uses the concept 'habitus' to conceptualize the collective knowledge involved in 'body techniques'. 'Habitus', he explains, is the Latin translation of the Greek 'exis' (the English translation is 'disposition'), a concept which Aristotle (1955) uses to capture the practical wisdom and reason of everyday life and of ethical conduct in particular. Body techniques, as habitus, are forms of practical reason. They are forms, however, which, in Mauss' words 'vary between societies, educations, proprieties and fashions, prestiges.' (Mauss, 1979: 101)

Body techniques are embedded in cultural contexts where they have a symbolic significance, are normatively regulated and perhaps also 'rationalized'. Access to certain sporting techniques (eg, boxing techniques) has been limited for females in the past, for example, because they are regarded as unladylike and have therefore been subject to prohibition. Moreover, the technique of contemporary athletes is subject to a high level of scientific scrutiny and correction. Modern competitive swimming styles, for example, are fine tuned in the laboratory. These are important aspects of body techniques and we must attend to them. It is important, however, that we do not allow a focus upon these aspects, which we are more familiar with as sociologists, to overshadow the embodied knowledge and understanding that the concept of body techniques brings to light. Swimming is a form of practical understanding in its own right, as is holding a baby, using a screwdriver, writing a letter or a list, applying lipstick etc. To study body techniques is to elucidate this level of practical understanding.

The 'mindful' aspect of body techniques is not very well developed in Mauss' work and its lack of development is one amongst a number of problems. We need to engage more seriously with the embodied subjectivity and agency he hints at; to recognize more flexibility and room for improvisation in bodily action than he allows for (see also Crossley, 1995, 2004a); and do more to grasp the link between the use of body techniques and the intercorporeal contexts in which they are used (ibid.). None of this detracts from the importance of Mauss' innovation, however. 'The body' and 'embodiment', despite their concrete connotation, are very vague, broad and abstract concepts that do not define a researchable object. 'Body techniques', by contrast, does. More importantly, it effectively translates 'embodiment' into a researchable format. By way of a focus upon body techniques we can explore the embodiment of the doing of a wide range of practices and processes that are of interest to us. In addition, as I explain in more detail below, the concept attends to issues of meaning, understanding and normativity in action, pulling them into the foreground of sociological perception without thereby pushing embodiment into the background. Indeed, Mauss accesses meaning, knowledge and normativity by way of embodiment, through the concept of body techniques. In this way Mauss resolves the root problem of the absence of the body in sociology, as diagnosed above. He analyses human knowledge in a way that does not necessitate the absence of embodiment. Finally, the concept serves as a hinge which links together the subjective life of the body with its objective, sociological situation. Body techniques are forms of understanding and knowledge. They generate meaning (see below). But they are also 'social facts', characterized by a sociological distribution, social origin and by their diffusion through social networks. By way of body techniques we can explore at least certain aspects of the social moulding of bodily life.

In what follows I want to expand upon these points, demonstrating the versatility and usefulness of 'body techniques' as a concept. In addition, I want to reflect briefly upon the methodological approaches conducive to a proper study of body techniques. In this way we will see, also, that body techniques both demand and facilitate 'mixed methods' research. 'Body techniques' defines an object of research that can be explored both quantitatively and qualitatively and which therefore facilitates the integration of these two approaches.

Exploring embodied understanding

Can we analyse embodied understanding and knowledge by way of body techniques? Don't they always remain elusive at the crucial point where we attempt to grasp them? Embodied knowledge is not discursive knowledge and cannot be put into discourse without distorting it. The knowledge of the swimmer is not that of the physicist, even if the buoyancy and propulsion of the swimmer can be explained by reference to physics, and the physicist's formulas are not, therefore, a translation of the swimmer's knowledge. Nor do we capture the principles grasped by the swimmer by describing her movements, at least not as mere movements. And there is no point in asking the swimmer how they do it because they 'just do it' without knowing what distinguishes them from the novice, who appears to do as they do but sinks all the same. Practical principles can only ever be practical; that is, grasped in practice by a being capable of doing so. These are not limits to research, however, so much as characteristics of embodied knowledge and understanding. Knowing how to swim just is being able to do it. The swimmer is not holding back on us when they tell us that they 'just do it' and there is no reason to believe, as cognitive science sometimes suggests, that they unconsciously model and calculate. To study body techniques is to study knowledge and understanding in the only form in which exist: that is, in the form of embodied and practical competence. There is nothing hidden here.

Moreover, Mauss reminds us that, as body techniques, these embodied forms of knowing and understanding are social, which means that their principles are communicated and passed on through networks. He thereby offers us a clue as to how we might open up these principles to analysis. If the principles of a technique can be communicated from a teacher to a novice then they can also be communicated to a researcher, who can subject them, and their transmission, to analysis. The researcher can observe the process of learning and/or involve themselves in it by way of what Wacquant (2004) calls 'observant participation'. S/he can observe the process whereby 'moves' are executed and copied, the imperfections of this process and the move from incompetence to competence. This can be instructive on many levels. Here I will briefly discuss three.

In the first instance the teaching and learning process tends to throw the principle embodied in a body technique into relief. Because the student doesn't always 'get it' the teacher is forced to find ways of making 'it' more explicit. They are forced to be more reflexive. And researchers therefore have a greater chance of 'getting it' too. For example, in some 'observant participation' that I did in a Muay Thai (Thai boxing) class, the principle of using one's hip to generate power in a particular kick came to light through the failure of students to grasp this principle and the repeated efforts of the teacher to explain it. The teacher made the class wiggle their hips like disco dancers, for example, in an effort to help us to find our hip action, and made reference to 'whipping' the leg out from the hip, invoking an image with a clear motile resonance; we can all simulate a whipping action with our hand and should be able to, by extension, with our leg and hip. To experienced fighters the technique is taken for granted. It feels natural and, as such, tends not to be known in such a reflexive fashion. At the point of transmission, however, it often has to be made explicit or at least more explicit.

Secondly, this helps to emphasize the point that body techniques are both technical and bodily. They are revealed as technical because it is not obvious to everyone how to do them and they must be learned, sometimes with difficulty. They are revealed as specifically body techniques and embodied forms of knowledge and understanding because what matters is the ability to do them. Some people can do the technique without having a reflexive, intellectual grasp upon how they do it or what it is that makes a technique work; they 'just do it'. Others may appear to grasp the principle intellectually or discursively but still fail to execute the technique properly. It is the technically correct performance of the technique, however, which tends to count as knowing or understanding it for those involved. The knowledge and understanding involved in body techniques consists in embodied competence.

Thirdly, this process can reveal interesting aspects about the corporeal schema and thus the embodied agency of the 'body subject' (Crossley, 2001). My above discussion of learning to use the hips to generate powerful kicks in

Muay Thai, for example, illustrates how agents can learn to find parts of their body and mobilize them in new ways. The average social agent knows, at the level of their corporeal schema, that they have hips and knows how to use them, but getting them to do new things can involve relearning how to localize and mobilize them and indeed learning new uses for them. This learning has an element of transferability to it. One does not have to relearn the use of one's hips for each martial arts technique in which this principle is deployed. The ability to use the hips to generate powerful kicks is the same as that used to generate powerful elbow strikes, for example, and the same skill can be transferred from one to the other. The effort required to find the hips and re-learn to use them in the first place points to limits of transferability within the corporeal schema however. We learn certain principle of use and these are transferable but acquisition of new principles may involve significant relearning.

To consider a different example of the way in which the transmission of body techniques illuminates aspects of the corporeal schema, the inability of novices to detect errors in their own technique and the necessity for teachers or other students to point this out reveals the limits of the corporeal schema, at the individual level, and the necessity that it be completed by feedback from others. It thereby reveals the social nature of the corporeal schema. Like Cooley's (1902) 'looking-glass self', the corporeal schema depends upon social feedback and reinforcement for its proper construction. Moreover, body techniques are revealed to have a normative aspect. In addition to their practical effectiveness (or not), they are subject to social definitions of correct form.

The more general point here is that 'body techniques' draws 'embodiment', 'knowledge' and 'understanding' together in a researchable fashion. The legitimate sociological concern to engage with agents' knowledge and understanding does not lead to an overlooking or absenting of the body but is rather re-routed through embodiment in a novel and potentially fascinating manner.

Embodied meaning

In addition to knowledge and understanding, the concept of body techniques affords us access to embodied meanings. Traditionally, sociological analysis of the process whereby meaning is conferred upon situations has focused upon language use. In a strict sense language use is itself a 'body technique'. If, following Mead (1967, 2002), we maintain that material objects acquire social meanings by way of the uses to which they are put, however, then we might equally analyse the process whereby situations are defined and meaning conferred by way of other body techniques. Body techniques, we can maintain, 'intend' situations and objects, in the phenomenological sense, and thereby confer meaning upon them. The handling of cups and candlesticks in religious ritual, for example, bestows a sacred significance upon them. This becomes obvious if we compare such ritual handling with the mundane use of cups and candlesticks in everyday life. Similarly, the dancing styles of different youth subcultures, such as the trance-like swaying of the hippy or the slam dancing of the skinhead, reveal aspects of their orientation towards others and the world (or their otherworldliness). Finally, we can observe how the techniques of the martial arts have transformed the ordinary rice flail (*nunchaku*) from a traditional farming implement to a weapon. The object becomes something different, it acquires a different purpose and meaning, in virtue of the way in which it is used and, more specifically, by ways of different techniques of usage.

This is not merely a matter of appearance, which might be adequately dealt with by way of a semiotics of the gestures involved. As I have noted elsewhere, body techniques 'put' an agent 'in situation'; that is to say, they modify perceptual, affective and cognitive structures (Crossley, 2004b). And they may be used specifically for these purposes. Meditation, for example, may be used to achieve a state of calmness and a more harmonious experience of the world. Likewise in religion, as Durkheim (1915) notes, rituals induce a religious attitude and even an ecstatic experience amongst those who perform them, for the duration of their performance. The world takes on a spiritual hue because the conscious experience of the agent is transformed by action. Finally, premeditated displays of anger in protest can generate genuine feelings of anger, constructing political elites and opponents, affectively, in new ways (Crossley, 2004b; see also Hochschild, 2003). How we act in situations affects our conscious experience of them, thus further affecting our subsequent actions. And body techniques, which structure the way in which we act, thus play a crucial role in rendering the world meaningful for us.

It is important to add a note on perception here. Body techniques are also involved in the conferral of meaning in the respect that they include specific technical modalities of perceiving. Merleau-Ponty offers us a few clues as to how we might begin to access this process. In the first instance he defines perception as an active bodily process structured through learning:

> In the gaze we have at our disposal a natural instrument analogous to a blind man's stick. *The gaze gets more or less out of things according to the way in which it ranges over or dwells on them.* To learn to see colours is to acquire a certain style of seeing, *a new use of one's body; it is to enrich and recast the body image.* (Merleau-Ponty, 1962: 153, my emphasis)

Merleau-Ponty doesn't use the term 'body technique' here but the phrase 'use of the body' clearly echoes Mauss. In addition, Merleau-Ponty emphasizes the practical nature of much perception. What I see is shaped or framed by the activity in which I am involved and serves that activity by indicating how it can be furthered. What the mid-game footballer sees, to use Merleau-Ponty's own example, is openings, opportunities and their opposites. A groundsman surveying the pitch might see something quite different, not noticed by the footballer. This is because learning to play football involves training 'the gaze' to interrogate and read its environment in particular ways. This is not just a matter of football or sport. In addition to learning to read their native language, agents have to learn to read others in their environment, traffic on the road, SPSS output, financial tables, graphs, CT scans, microscope slides etc. We learn different ways of seeing and reading the world. Perception therefore involves body techniques and perceptual meaning is shaped by such techniques.

As with embodied knowledge, then, the concept of body techniques draws meaning and embodiment together in a researchable manner. We can study meaning by way of embodiment and the two are not, therefore, mutually exclusive as foreground concerns. The study of meaning need not absent the body.

Diffusion and emergence

The meaning generated by body techniques and the knowledge and understanding they embody is best grasped by way of observation or 'observant participation', to use Wacquant's (2004) phrase. The devil is in the detail and the detail may not always be reflexively available to the lay agent in an interview situation. It must be observed in practice. *In situ* observation only reveals certain aspects of body techniques to us, however, and in particular it fails to reveal the social diffusion patterns of particular techniques, patterns which are essential to Mauss' definition of body techniques and to his sense of their social facticity. We know that we are in the presence of body techniques *qua* techniques, for Mauss, by virtue of inter-group or cross-time variability; because uses of the body manifest particular patterns of social diffusion. A comprehensive treatment of any body technique or cluster of techniques therefore involves some effort to survey their pattern and process of diffusion.

Of course ethnographic research captures aspects of the diffusion process. As noted above, one of the key ways of accessing the knowledge and understanding embodied in body techniques is by analyzing their transmission in learning situations; that is, their diffusion. This can teach us about the diffusion process in at least two respects. Firstly, it can teach us about the pedagogic mechanisms by way of which techniques are passed on. In my above discussion of learning a Muay Thai kick, for example, I noted that novices benefit from the 'mirroring' feedback of others, which compensates for the blind spots in their own bodily self-perception. Mirroring might thus be identified and studied as an aspect of the process whereby techniques are diffused. Moreover, my reference to the use of 'disco dancing' and to an instructor's mention of 'whipping' the leg both point to a role for analogy and metaphor in the learning process. Clearly there are many other mechanisms and dynamics of learning that could be explored and we must be aware of variations in the learning process. The point is clear enough, however; ethnographic research affords us purchase on the diffusion process. Secondly, whether or not techniques are acquired will depend upon the meanings and identities attached to them, and upon balances of both power and resources in the relations which comprise diffusion networks. Men are unlikely to acquire 'female' techniques of 'making up', for example, even if they enjoy considerable exposure to those techniques, because the techniques of making up have a feminine meaning and identity attached to them. Women, on the other hand, may feel forced to learn and use those techniques because specific sanctions attach to female non-compliance (Bartky, 1990; Young, 2005). Having said that, they may enjoy differential levels of access to certain techniques and the resources (eg, cosmetics) they presuppose on account of their variable levels of financial, cultural, symbolic or social resources. All of these factors are accessible at the ethnographic interface, and perhaps also in certain interview contexts. Still, however, to be sure about diffusion patterns it is necessary to quantify techniques and survey their demographic profile. The devil may be in the details but the details sometimes obscure broader patterns that are as important to an understanding of techniques as they are themselves.

The concept of body techniques is important in this respect because whilst it lends itself to a variety of qualitative research approaches it is equally amenable to quantification. The concept of body techniques allows for binary headcount comparisons of who does and doesn't practise a particular technique, for content analytic comparisons of technical style and for interval level measurement of, for example, frequency or duration of practice. Although there will always be methodological decisions to make about what counts as, for example, the presence or absence of a technique in any given situation, the concept maps on to something which is both concrete and individuated and which, as such, can be identified and counted.

Quantification is not the be-all-and-end-all, of course, nor the only indication of the social facticity of particular techniques. Observing the manner in which techniques are judged right and wrong in learning situations, and thus their normativity, may be sufficient to establish them as social facts. The group specificity of particular techniques, which can only be established through quantification, may provide important clues as to unintended effects and dynamics of techniques, however; their latent meanings and functions. Furthermore, group specificity is an important element in studying the process of diffusion, which is an important sociological issue in its own right.

In addition, and finally, the concept of body techniques poses the question of the evolution of particular uses of the body. I use the term 'evolution' rather than 'origin' because it is often very difficult to trace an exact origin of techniques. New techniques mutate out of old, by way of the improvisation of social agents; they may evolve over time; they may be simultaneously invented across numerous sites and their evolution may entail diffuse collectives. Nevertheless, in the case of some techniques it is possible to identify crucial moments in their history and, to return to my above point, in their diffusion. I have already used the example of the martial arts in this chapter and these again provide a good example. Whilst the lineage of the ancient martial arts recedes beyond recorded history, their modern forms, including such well known variants as Judo, Karate and Aikido, have well documented histories which can be explored from the point of view of an investigation of the evolution of the body techniques they involve. Moreover, the migration of these arts and techniques, from an Eastern to a Western context, is a fascinating aspect of globalization. Quantitative surveys may play an important part in such research. We want to know just who, in Western societies, practises these Eastern arts, and knowing who may help us to address the question of why. Clearly, however, archival research will play an important role too.

It is not only the martial arts of the Orient that might be explored in such ways. Elias' (1984) study of Western civilizing processes and Foucault's (1979) study of discipline both stand as important examples of how the evolution of a range of body techniques might be studied via archival sources. Neither Elias nor Foucault use the concept 'body techniques' but they are clearly looking at culturally variable uses of the body and, as such, covering the same ground. Identifying their respective foci as 'body techniques' has the added advantage, moreover, that it invites us to consider how their historical work might be rejoined and complemented by ethnographic and survey research which picks up their story in the present. The same techniques can be studied historically, quantitatively and qualitatively, affording us a multi-dimensional purchase upon them.

Conclusion

Many sociologists have called for an embodiment of the discipline. In this chapter I have attempted to diagnose the nature of our disembodiment and have identified Marcel Mauss' concept of 'body techniques' as a useful remedy. Sociology often becomes disembodied, I have suggested, because it overlooks the body in an effort to access the meanings, norms and understanding that are integral to an understanding of what human beings do in collective contexts. Mauss allows us to keep embodiment in the picture because he allows us to see the embodied nature of meaning conferral, understanding and norms. In this respect Mauss sensitizes us to the details of *in situ* interaction and practice. This is important but Mauss also encourages us to look beyond the local practice of particular techniques to grasp both the evolution of techniques and their diffusion through social networks. Moreover, his concept enables this shift of focus. Body techniques facilitate both the depth of ethnographic interrogation and the breadth of survey and archival analysis. Where such lines of enquiry will lead remains to be seen but they are clearly of importance if we are to embody sociology.

References

Aristotle (1955) *The Ethics*. Harmondsworth, Penguin.

Bartky, S.L. (1990) *Femininity and Domination. Studies in the Phenomenology of Oppression.* New York: Routledge.

Bourdieu, P. (1992) *The Logic of Practice*. Cambridge: Polity.

Cooley, C. (1902) *Human Nature and the Social Order*, New York, Charles Scribner's Sons.

Crossley, N. (1995) 'Body Techniques, Agency and Intercorporeality: On Goffman's *Relations in Public*', *Sociology* 29(1), 133–49.

Crossley, N. (2001) *The Social Body*. London, Sage.
Crossley, N. (2004a) 'The Circuit Trainer's Habitus: Reflexive Body Techniques and the Sociality of the Workout', *Body and Society* 10(1), 37–69.
Crossley, N. (2004b) Ritual, Body Technique and (Inter)subjectivity, in Schilbrack, K. (ed.), (2004) *Thinking Through Ritual: Philosophical Perspectives*, London: Routledge, 31–51.
Crossley, N. (2005) Mapping Reflexive Body Techniques, *Body and Society* 11(1), 1–35.
Crossley, N. (2006) *Reflexive Embodiment in Contemporary Societies*. Buckingham: Open University Press.
Descartes, R. (1969) *Discourse on Method and the Meditations*. Harmondsworth, Penguin.
Durkheim, E. (1915) *Elementary Forms of the Religious Life*, New York: Free Press.
Durkheim, E. (1974) *Sociology and Philosophy*, New York: Free Press.
Elias, N. (1984) *The Civilising Process*. Oxford: Blackwell.
Foucault, M. (1979) *Discipline and Punish*. Harmondsworth: Penguin.
Giddens, A. (1991) *Modernity and Self-Identity*. Cambridge: Polity.
Hochschild, A. (2003) *The Managed Heart*. Berkeley: University of California Press.
Leder, D. (1998) A Tale of Two Bodies, in D. Welton. (ed.), *Body and Flesh*. Oxford: Blackwell, 117–30.
Leder, D. (1990) *The Absent Body*. Chicago: University of Chicago Press.
Levi-Strauss, C. (1987) *Introduction to the Work of Marcel Mauss*. London: Routledge.
Marx, K. (1970) Theses on Feurbach, supplementary essay in K. Marx. and F. Engels. (1970) *The German Ideology*. London: Lawrence and Wishart, 121–3.
Mauss, M. (1979) Body Techniques, in *Sociology and Psychology*. London: RKP, 95–123.
Mead, G.H. (1967) *Mind, Self and Society*. Chicago: Chicago University Press.
Mead, G.H. (2002) 'The Physical Thing', supplementary essay in *The Philosophy of the Present*, New York: Prometheus, 135–52.
Merleau-Ponty, M. (1962) *The Phenomenology of Perception*, London: RKP.
Merleau-Ponty, M. (1965) *The Structure of Behaviour*. London: Methuen.
Merleau-Ponty, M. (1968) *The Visible and the Invisible*. Evanston: Northwestern University Press.
Merleau-Ponty, M. (1985) The Experience of Others, *Review of Existential Psychology and Psychiatry* XVIII, 33–72.
Ryle, G. (1949) *The Concept of Mind*, Harmondsworth: Penguin.
Shilling, C. (1993) *The Body and Social Theory.* London: Sage.
Wacquant, L. (2004) *Body and Soul*. Oxford: Oxford University Press.
Young, I. (2005) *On Female Bodily Experience.* Oxford: Oxford University Press.

Breathing like a soldier: culture incarnate[1]

Brian Lande

Abstract

Breathing appears to be so natural and organic that it hardly seems worth analyzing. Yet to inhabit an institution can mean having to learn to breathe in culturally distinct ways. This chapter presents the findings of an ethnographic study of 'learning to breath like a soldier' in the army. I focus on the processes by which the body is transformed and new disciplinary techniques are developed, and present the body as an alternative category of cultural analysis to a vision of military culture as the internalization of norms, values and beliefs that shape identities and provide cognitive frames for social action. Cultural patterning in the army is not an abstract intellectual process, but takes place at the level of the body as it engages in practical activity in the training environment, and becomes adapted to the military milieu.

Key Words: socialization; military; body, pedagogy

Introduction

Two platoons are lined up in front of the first sergeant, a young female cadet who has just been rotated into a leadership position. The cadets chat loudly, standing 'at ease,' while waiting to begin marksmanship training. The first sergeant stands at attention and says, 'ATTENtion.' It comes out sounding more like a question than a command. The platoons come to attention, but do not do so with the sense of urgency and assurance that is customary when a sharp, loud and correctly intoned command is given by one of the Non-Commissioned Officers (NCOs). One of the upperclassmen runs to the front of the formation and tells the first sergeant, 'don't speak from your throat. No-one will hear what you say as a command. Breathe from your stomach.'

Throughout the remainder of her time as first sergeant the young cadet is corrected on how she breathes when she speaks, but problems remain. When calling cadences while marching, the young cadet can't coordinate the movement of the company because she can't project her voice. When she is giving commands to execute movements, only some hear her voice.

> Toward the end of the week the cadet battalion commander finally pulls the cadet to one side to explain to her that she still has not learned the 'command presence.' 'You have to speak like a leader,' says the battalion commander. Another cadet, a third year, stands beside the battalion commander, who says to the first sergeant, 'So the deal is you got to learn to speak from your diaphragm, not your throat. It's like, you know, when you get punched in the stomach and you feel how the air comes out of you from your stomach, that is how you have to learn to talk.' The other cadet, who till then had been standing by listening concernedly, jumps in saying, 'ok, say "attention." But when you say it I am going to push your stomach in like you were being punched so you get the feel.' Together the three cadets repeat this exercise until the cadet is able to produce the command with the right kind of breathing and therefore the prosody to speak with authority. (September 2004, Field notes)

The body is a crucial foundation of the military world. This excerpt from my fieldwork notes on cadets in the United States Army's Reserve Officer Training Corp shows that even something as simple as giving a command requires a good fit between bodily structures and social structures. That fit arises through a collective labour upon the body of cadets. In the army, breathing 'properly' is a key embodied prerequisite for such practices as firing a rifle, running long distances, and even projecting authority on the drill ground. Without being able to breathe like a soldier, participation in military activity is severely restricted.

This chapter focuses on how soldiers move in and out of social relationships through the movements and processes of their bodies. The intertwining of bodies in social relationships is important in explaining how soldiers enter into and become committed to their social worlds. In crossing the threshold between civilian and soldier, the body not only takes on new meanings (as a 'weapon,' 'vehicle,' and 'protective armour') and value (physical performance is a principle of hierarchy), it is lived differently and thus changes its form. Changes in form to what phenomenologists call the 'corporeal schema' (Merleau-Ponty, 2002) entail the addition of new dispositions and kinetic and sensory powers that alter the very foundations of social interaction and conduct. This is not how sociologists have envisaged the socialization of soldiers.

Following Parsons and Merton, scholars of the military have conceived of socialization into military culture as the internalization of institutional values, norms, and role expectations (Caforio, 2003; Franke, 2000; Priest, 1998; Stevens *et al.*, 1994). In the more clearly Durkheimian tradition, some have looked at the rituals through which new recruits are integrated into the armed forces: military stories, songs, jokes, rites of passage and even clothing shape a shared set of beliefs and identities (Burke, 2004; Winslow, 1999). Other sociologists emphasize soldiers' cognitive scripts and schemas in accounting for how they interpret their worlds as meaningful, while ethnomethodologists focus on the everyday methods through which soldier's construct their sense of the world (Ben-Ari, 1998; Herbert, 1998). Finally, discursive theories of culture look at how people entering into a military role adopt discursive practices that shape their identities (Sasson-Levy, 2003).

While symbolic structures shape the meaning of the social world, where in these accounts is the embodied agent or the cadet who has learned to speak from the stomach or who has shaped his or her body into a long range 'weapons platform'? In order to understand these achievements, we need to appreciate that 'military culture' is largely a *military habitus* (a system of transposable and durable dispositions that generate *body techniques*, or traditional and efficacious ways of using the body) that allows for proficient participation according to the symbolic divisions and valuations of the military world (Bourdieu, 1990, 2000; Mauss, 1979). Simply, before we can discuss what people think or value about their worlds, we need to consider how the articulation of their bodies acts as the foundation for those beliefs and values. Before cadets can reflect on their world through acquired symbols they are 'always already there' in their world through their feeling and acting bodies. Embodiment is thus a crucial but missing theme from traditional sociological accounts of military life.

The military world demands that its members exert themselves constantly, master fatigue, suffer, and exhibit physical dexterity and skill. Moral categories emphasize physical readiness and technical competence. In this world the categorization of a 'good soldier' is less a matter of the imposition of representation upon the body than a reference to a kind of embodiment that army cadets struggle, with more or less success, to achieve. When cadets and cadre (the army officers and NCOs in charge) point to a soldier and say 'he's a good cadet', they are referring to a stable set of features of the *soldier's body* – an upright posture, chin up, chest forward, 'head on a swivel,' running hard – that are durable across a variety of settings. Understanding what is involved in the production of a 'good soldier' requires that we appreciate both the bodily logic of soldiering and how the corporeal schemes of the *habitus* are passed on from experts to newcomers within chains of interdependence.

Of course, what takes place in the military is an extreme form of how social life is conducted everywhere. The body is the very medium by which a person comes to enter into a collectively inhabited world (cf. Wacquant, 2004 on boxing; Sudnow, 2001 on learning an instrument; Benner, 2001 on becoming a nurse; Charlesworth, 2000 on learning working class language; Csordas, 1990, 1994 on pentecostal religions). The cadet, like a dancer or boxer, is a carnal being of flesh and blood, inhabited by the demands and necessities of the social world in the form of incorporated habits and skills that make it possible for him or her proficiently to develop the body as an instrument of social life.

In exploring the process by which social membership of the army is established in and through bodily activity, I draw on Bourdieu's (1990; 2000) analytic tools to describe how the process of teaching enjoins soldiers to act and breathe like they 'should.' My investigation focuses on the importance of breathing for two physical activities that are integral to being a military officer: running and shooting. I focus on how breathing in both of these situations serves as the foundation of social interactions. I conclude by discussing the implications of my study for the study of culture in general. In short, breathing is far from being a taken-for-granted physical activity. It is the social sinew that holds together social institutions by anchoring norms and beliefs in viscera.

Research design

Different cultural phenomena mandate different methodological postures. I wanted to know how one can *be* a soldier and this meant prying into the sentient, lived, and breathing body. This chapter draws on ethnographic and experiential data produced over 18 months of intensive fieldwork in the United States Army Reserved Officer Training Corp. I enrolled in ROTC as an army cadet, because I was interested in comprehending the cultural logic of bodily practices that often 'go without saying' in the United States army, and spent my time in the field, training and living with cadets and soldiers on a college campus, in the barracks at Fort Knox and in the woods of North Carolina with a group of soldiers training for the Special Forces. I spent an average of fifteen to twenty hours a week in the field while at my home battalion and twenty-four hours a day, seven days a week, while at Fort Knox and in North Carolina during a summer.

The approach I took was that of an apprentice to a profession. I wanted to undergo a 'moral and sensual conversion to the cosmos under investigation' (Wacquant, 2004: vii) so as to be able to grasp practically what it meant to act and be like a soldier. Passive participant observation and interviews would not suffice because what I wanted to know about was often pre-thetic and inarticulate. Most participant observation attends to what people say and do, but this does not capture the 'sensorimotor, mental, and social aptitudes' or 'total pedagogy' that 'tacitly guides social agents in their familiar universe' (Wacquant, 2005: 465). In contrast, I learned the ins and outs of becoming a soldier, on the rifle range, at my four days a week of physical training, on the parade grounds at Fort Knox with Drill Sergeants yelling, and during tactical exercises in the mountains of California. I kept detailed diaries and field notes of my training, recording my observations on the events, practices, people and rhythms of my field site at home after training and furtively under my covers or in the bathroom in the barracks after 'lights out.' I will often refer to both field notes and my personal reflections, and I often write in the present tense to preserve some sense of the immediacy and sensuousness of a situation.[2]

Wacquant argues that the value of apprenticeship, 'considered as an activity', is that it 'enables us to pry into practice in the making and to realize that the ordinary knowledge that makes us competent actors is an incarnate, sensuous, situated "knowing-how-to" that operates beneath the controls of discursive awareness and propositional reasoning' (Wacquant, 2005: 466). Such a method was adequate to the task in hand as it helped me explain the *production*, not the products, of the military *habitus* and the coordinated body techniques and patterns of social relations that form it.

I don't pretend to have emerged from this apprenticeship with a singularly representative 'native's point of view' but I was finally accepted as a competent and even highly proficient cadet. As one army lieutenant, then a cadet, frankly put it to me, 'you disgusted me. You couldn't do a push up, you were skinny, wore glasses. I was wrong. You pushed it every day at PT, hitting failure, now you're probably one of the most "squared away" cadets here.' Having 'pushed it' and 'put in the time' to acquire the skills and competencies necessary to be recognizably proficient I occupied a position within the world of army officer training that gave me one of many possible perspectives on the production of a soldier.

Breathing and soldiering

By describing two situations (running, and shooting) where a specific technique of breathing anchors the soldier's body in the military world, I explore how institutional dilemmas and imperatives become addressed by and absorbed in the body. For cadets, running and shooting constitute two aspects of basic soldiering skills: movement and combat. A sociological analysis of breathing allows us to describe the relationship between bodily transformation and social activity.

Running

Cadets are embedded in a social world that demands physical prowess and dexterity. To a surprising degree cadets are defined and evaluated in terms of their potential for movement. Everywhere cadets go they are expected to move fast and for as long as it takes to get to their destination. Soldiers often refer to the need for the rigorous and speedy movement that saturates training as 'moving with a purpose.' Strenuous movement is a basic feature of the soldiers bodily being. The very notion of leadership, to 'lead from the front' or to 'drive on', presupposes a shared kinetic culture adjusted to the demand for strenuous activity. This means cadets must transform their sensorimotor structures and expand their limits so that they can run farther, faster, and longer than would be possible for the vast majority of civilians. These demands are institutionalized in physical training and frequent Army Physical Fitness tests that evaluate and rank cadets *vis-a-vis* one another in terms of their abilities for strenuous and vigorous movement. Day by day, cadets also learn – by being insulted, berated, and demeaned – that certain kinds of breathing are desirable and demanded:

> On one of my first runs, while running with another cadet at the back of formation and nearly hyperventilating, a senior cadet, with prior military service, runs besides us. He says, 'Mr. Lande. How are you going to be a leader . . . *a lieutenant*, if you can't *lead from the front*. How do you think your soldiers are going to feel when you're *huffing it* at the rear of formation when you're on a mission?' (August 2003, Field notes)

> Running with some female cadets toward the rear, I overhear them say to a new cadet who is gasping for air, 'come on, you gonna let a woman outrun you?' (August 2003, Field notes)

And:

> I am pushing hard. I am toward the rear of the fastest ability group—not good since I am leading physical training today. Each step requires effort. I get into a rhythm breathing. In, out, in out. It is almost meditative and it helps with boredom. . . . By

the last half-mile I am working hard to keep up. I have to force my breathing to stay regular. I am doing OK until I have to get everyone in my ability group into formation to run while calling cadence. Trying to call cadence with a loud bellowing voice and run at an 8-minute a mile pace is too much. I start gasping for breath and breaking up the cadence. I direct another cadet to call cadence . . . After I have dismissed the company formation, an upperclassmen [a cadet who in the advanced course of officer instruction] comments to me about my cadence calling and says, *'this is why you got to stay fit. If you can't breathe you can't keep your composure*, that doesn't look so good as a leader if you are huffing it at the rear.' (December 2003, Personal diary)

In each of these situations, breathing is encountered as something that is moralized or criticized and therefore experienced as urgent. Breathing is not neutral but is confronted as a culturally meaningful aspect of activity. To be a moral member of the community is, following Durkheim, to have 'a bodily consensus' (as opposed to a 'logical consensus,' [Durkheim, 1995]). When cadets engage in dialogic acts such as tactical movements, rhythm and cadence are essential. Each apt action is attuned through a shared sense of movement and time. When this is lost, the group falls into confusion, people fall out of formation and the integrity and security of the group is lost. More explicitly, when the bodily consensus on breathing fails we see the coherence of social interactions and the 'mutual-tuning-in' (Schutz, 1964) of bodily rhythms fall apart.

As part of an escape and evasion course, 3rd squad, 4th platoon has just escaped from the POW camp where we have been held for the last several hours as POWs. Low on ammunition, our point man runs in front of the squad. We have to run 3k through the hot humid climate of Fort Knox before hitting safe territory. Out of breath, we stop to take a break and regroup. The squad leader gets accountability for everyone. We had been taking sporadic fire from the opposition force. But now that we have stopped the intensity of the fire has increased. I duck behind a tree as paint balls splatter around me. This is the second time so far that this has happened. Every time we stop the intensity of fire increases. The point man screams to the squad leader to get us moving. The point man lays down suppressive fire and we start running again, tree-to-tree, taking cover as we bound forward as a group. But there is a problem. One of the cadets, a newcomer to the Army, is hyperventilating. 'I . . . I can't. I can't breathe.' 'Slow down your breathing, just take deep breaths' the Squad Leader says. Angrily, the cadet replies, 'Look I'm trying, but I can't!' The lane walker [an experienced soldier who evaluates performance] says, 'OK, you [pointing at the cadet] are out of shape, you are a casualty.' Because Baxter can't recoup her breath we have to carry her the remaining 2k. We quickly grab two large branches and take off our shirts to make a stretcher. We run through the woods carrying Baxter but it comes at a cost. Because of our slow speed we are all shot by high velocity paintballs. (June 2004, Field notes)

The ability to breathe is morally valued not as an end but as something negatively reacted to in the form of classifications of the cadet who can't breathe as 'ate up', 'jacked', and a 'buddy fucker'. These categories of stigma refer to the 'the person who can't keep up' or who 'isn't fit and so gets everybody screwed.'

The technique of breathing coordinates bodies-in-time. As such it is vital for the 'sharing of the other's flux of experiences in inner time, this living through a vivid present in common' that constitutes 'the mutual tuning-in relationship, the experience of the 'We' (Schutz, 1964: 173).[3] To breathe the 'right' way is to conduct ones self virtuously. Hyperventilating, like being flustered in face-to-face interaction (Goffman, 1967: 100), threatens the very capacities that coordinated tactical activity presupposes. As Goffman (1967: 47–113) has shown, the moral qualities of interactive life hinge upon 'demeanour' and 'poise' or, as here, upon the more primordial consensus between coordinated corporeal schemes that function as the taken-for granted background of successful collective action.

The body invested with value, that can 'drive on' and 'lead from the front', is created in pedagogical encounters where cadre demand that cadets 'push it.' A master sergeant who has cadets doing a timed run says to the runners,

> you got to push it [your limit]! You only run harder when your lungs burn and the only way to stop your lungs from burning next time is to run harder. Quit complain'n and suck it up. (June 2004, Field notes)

But how do cadets learn to 'push it?' The command 'push it' has its effect against a background of monotonous situations of visual, verbal, and bodily contact where strenuous exertion is absorbed into the cadets corporeal structures. Cadets new to running are given small pointers on how to keep the pelvis over the heels, to have shoulders back, back erect, and chin up while running, which are all meant to shape the ability to breathe.

> As we came toward the third mile of the run I was spent. My lungs and shins hurt. I begin to hyperventilate, breathing in and out in quick succession. I feel nausea washing over me. One of the upperclassmen runs alongside me and asks how I am doing. I don't think I replied as much as I grunted. He says 'Whoa, Lande, you got to control your breathing. Take deep slow breaths. In through your nose, out through your mouth. With me, in . . . out . . . in . . . out.' He does this for a few more seconds until I get my breathing back under control. He also corrects my posture saying, 'Chin up, back straight, you'll get more air.' We get back to the battalion. I am sweating profusely, and still near hyper-ventilating. Another cadet tells me to walk around in circles to 'cool down.' But as soon as I stop running I am hit with a wall of nausea. I race over to the trash can and dry-heave [I had not eaten yet] and try to catch my breath. (October 2003, Personal diary)

Similarly, an army major describes trying to instruct a female cadet on the correct way to breathe,

> I was running with a cadet and she was hurting and I was telling her to breathe, to fill herself up like a bottle and hold it, breathe in through your nose for four seconds breath out through your mouth for two, and I kept telling her to do it but she just keep breathing at her own pace. I kept telling her, if you want the pain to stop you have to listen and hold your breath in. (May 2004, Field notes)

Thus, to breathe like a soldier means not breathing 'at her own pace' but breathing in through the nose and out through the mouth in time with the Major. Learning to breathe is a social activity that demands active participation and openness to the conduct of others. In the situation described by the Major we have an example of where enlistment in breathing fails.

Breathing is learned and experienced in situations in which bodies of instructors and peers perceive each other's bodily presence. Against a backdrop of constant categorization that threatens cadets with humiliation but also holds out the promise of acquiring practices that make it possible to be well regarded, cadets incorporate a bodily being that is adjusted to the evaluations and expectations of those around them.

Shooting

Just as all army cadets must be able to engage in vigorous activity requiring stamina and endurance, all army cadets are expected to have the dexterity and calm to be able to use a rifle. It is a basic feature of military training and a competency in which all soldiers are expected to have minimum proficiency. It is therefore no surprise that cadets represent this fact about their world in terms of metaphors of the body as a 'vehicle', 'platform', and 'weapon' of combat. But these beliefs about the body as a weapon do not themselves generate the competency required to fire a weapon well. As with running, the martial qualities of the cadet are the result of the embodiment of the objectified practices of instructors. Even though learning to shoot a rifle involves doctrinal texts and codified practices, the transmission of practical schemes involves a combination of imitation, direct physical contact, an array of visual and textual artifacts, and disciplinary techniques. Producing a soldier who handles a rifle well involves creating a *bodily sensitivity* that is the result of a protracted and diffuse process (a 'figuration' to use Elias's term) rather than the product of a deliberate will.

If cadets want to hit what they aim at with their rifle, they have to breathe 'rightly.' Aligning sites on a rifle and pointing it in the direction of a target is not enough to establish a 'good shot.' Irregular breathing and breathing that moves the body up and down too much will lead to misplaced shots. In order to create effective and efficient marksmen, army officer training deliberately targets cadets' breathing. For example, an army field manual (Army, 2003: section 4–5) specifies that cadets should become sensitized to the 'normal respiratory pause' that occurs at the end of the exhale (Figure 1). This way of breathing is meant to be used to 'zero' a weapon, ie, make sure that there is a harmony between the target and the cadet's movements, posture, gaze and aim. Regulated breathing is necessary to ensure that the body is not interfering with the correct aligning of the gaze and bodily posture. This style of breathing is preferred when a cadet has plenty of time to take a shot, but soldiers are often in situations where they must shoot under time constraints. Cadets in this context acquire the habit of coordinating the pause of their inhale or exhale with the other bodily movements that go into firing a rifle, as shown in Figure 2. A background aspect of bodily being is thus verbally and visually articulated in the foreground of action so that it can be integrated into an actional gestalt (the linking in practice of schemes for breathing, perception, and fine motor

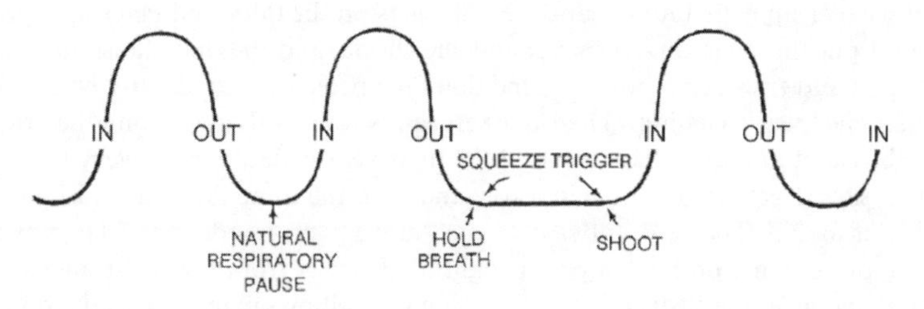

Figure 1. *Breathing to 'zero' and to take timely shots. (Army 2003: section 4–5)*

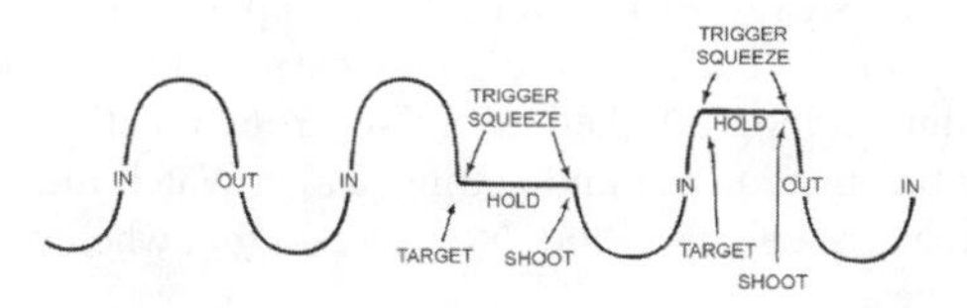

Figure 2. *Breathing in order to shoot rapidly and stability. (Army 2003: section 4–5)*

movements like trigger pulls). This is accomplished through the social organization of training into 'the four fundamentals of marksmanship': breathing, trigger pull, position, and aiming. Each stage has its practice station, instructors, texts, and bodily targets, and each is initially taught as separate in order to sensitize the cadet to parts of his or her body that are typically ignored. Once learned according to 'spec' these aspects of the body are pushed to the background.

> At the dime-and-washer station the goal is to become very sensitive to one's body movements while shooting. It is the same five cadets but this time only one instructor. The instructor says 'OK, we are going to work on trigger squeeze and breathing. When you shoot you want to reduce your movement as much as possible. Even a little movement can send a bullet off in the wrong direction. Who here knows the right way to use the trigger?' A hand goes up and a cadet says, 'You squeeze slowly and don't jerk it.' She continues, 'Also you use the meaty part of your finger [points at the center of the tip of her index finger].' The instructor says 'Right. How about breathing, when do you hold your breath?' A cadet answers 'at the top of your breath.' The instructor corrects, 'you can do it that way but the best way is to hold at the bottom of the exhale [he demonstrates by taking a big breath and exhaling]. Now all of you take a breath and just pause when you have emptied your lungs of air. Good. That is when you want to shoot.'
>
> Next he has us lay on the floor in the prone unsupported position and has us team up with a partner. 'What you are going to do now, with your partner, is take turns dry-firing your rifle. Your partner is going to put a dime on the barrel of your rifle and you need to dry-fire without knocking the dime off the tip of the barrel. You need to do this five times consecutively to get a "go".'

> I partner up with a first-year cadet. She gets on the floor and takes up a prone position. I put the dime on her barrel and she shoots and the dime falls. She charges the weapon and tries again but the same thing happens. I try to identify what is wrong to give some 'peer coaching.' The First Sergeant who is walking among the groups stops by the cadet and says, 'How is my MSI [first-year cadet] doing?' Very frustrated, the cadet says 'I get two or three in a row and then the dime falls off and I have to start all over again!' The sergeant says to me, 'move over, Lande man.' He gets down on the ground, lying on his belly at a slight angle away from the cadet and watches her shoot and gives her instruction. 'OK, bring your elbows in more. Good, good. It hurts, I know, but you won't fatigue your muscles if you use your bones. OK now move your whole body around more so it is easier to have your natural point of aim pointing straight ahead at your target. Make sure that your ankles are splayed inward, yeah that will keep you steady. Bring your right leg up and crook it OK. See, that's better, isn't it? I am going to put a dime on your barrel and I want you to shoot [dry fire] without the dime falling off the barrel. No! Your breathing is all jacked up. You're holding your breath too long and getting shaky. Watch me. Hold your breath at the end of the exhale. Show me. Good. Now just do that when you're shooting.' (October 2003, Field notes)

The whole story of this body pedagogics is not contained in army field manuals but requires situating training doctrine in the modes of coparticipation in which it is embedded (Lave and Wenger, 1991). These manuals contain rules, proscriptions, and descriptions of how to fire a rifle correctly, but they do not contain the kinds of bodily skills and shared corporeal knowledge that enable cadets to follow rules and fully grasp verbal instructions. For example, the field manual for rifle training is used against a backdrop of verbal injunctions ('no!', 'bring your elbows in!', etc.) that permeate training but are not specified in the manual; they are implicit. They take place against the background of a gestural, visual, mimetic and physical engagement (Wacquant, 2004: 100). Goffman (1981) calls this 'embedding.' As he puts it, 'Every utterance and its hearing have gestural accompaniments, these under some control of the actors' (1981: 3–4). That is, the utterance 'breathe with me' acquires its meaning as a consequence of it being made by an authorized instructor who is breathing in a manner that provides the cadet with an example of what it means to breathe 'correctly'. Cadre and advanced cadets are constantly touching and manipulating the bodies of novice cadets to accomplish a corporeal understanding. They demonstrate and act as bodily mirrors. Instructors create the proper movement and have learners follow along until they are regularly adjusting their bodies to that of the instructor. These nonverbal practices give cadets a practical understanding of what it means to 'hold your breath at the bottom of the exhale' or a feel for how unregulated breathing makes the rifle's muzzle move away from what it is aimed at.

When an instructor has his hand on the back of a cadet and is saying 'breathe with me . . . pause . . . inhale, don't hold it!' this *physical contact* is part of the meaning of the utterance. The cadet understands the command to breathe in a certain way only when he or she has incorporated the proper rhythm. Acquiring this rhythm is done through a process similar to what Wacquant (2004) has called 'the dialectic of visual and corporeal mastery' except that we ought to expand that account to include auditory and gestural contact.

An example of how trained capacities are passed on in and through practice can be found in the first weapons training lab of the second semester, when cadets are being reintroduced to the fundamentals of marksmanship.

> One of the third-year cadets is leading the instruction, 'There are two ways to control your breathing when shooting. First, when you are stationary try to shoot at the top of your breath or at the bottom of your exhale. If your chest is moving you will move and your aim will be off. Try to get a feel for it. Take up the prone position and watch how much your weapon moves while breathing normally.' We all get down on the ground. I assume a prone position. I have my left leg out at an angle and my right leg cocked to provide added stability. I bring my elbows in and center them as much as possible under my chest. I scoot my body out at a slight angle so that it is not in a straight line with my rifle. More comfortable this way, I find. I take aim at a spot on the wall and watch my movement. Up and down, up and down. I try breathing and holding. My movement is reduced. I then try breathing and holding on my exhale, it works even better. But if I hold on to the exhale too long I start to move again because I get stressed by not having enough air. I try again. I find that after about five seconds of pausing on the exhale my movement begins to increase steadily. The instructor says: 'OK, now if you are dealing with moving targets or have to acquire a target quickly you're not going to wait to breathe, so since you are spending most of your breathing time not at the top of your breath or at the bottom of your exhale just pick a comfortable spot and hold your breath.' (September 2004, Field notes)

These pedagogical situations, which occur early in marksmanship training, emphasize the tacit bodily knowledge that is necessary to grasp what is being discursively taught. When breathing is learned there is a literal 'harmony between what we aim at and what is given, between the intention and the performance' (Merleau-Ponty, 2002: 167). The crucial point, however, is that transmission of symbolic information is not enough for cadets to comprehend their activity because without a shared sense of the body, indexical statements about breathing have little meaning. This is why a labour of direct bodily manipulation and training has to occur in order to incorporate verbal utterances into the body schema. The display of texts and images (see Figures 1 and 2) have 'symbolic efficacy' only when embedded in practices of pointing, verbal utterances and reprimands, and body-to-body contact that are meant to link different modalities of perception, comprehension, and movement in order to coordinate bodily movements *as a whole*. Images and texts don't work by imparting representations. They derive their meaning from their *use* as one instrument among many.

Conclusion: from foreground to background – training to embody culture

Culture is bodily as much as it is symbolic: 'When the properties and movements of the body are socially qualified, the most fundamental social choices are naturalized' (Bourdieu, 1990: 71). The effect of bodily learning is the incorporation of new competencies and dispositions that modify the *habitus*. Cadets, like any person entering a new social microcosm, undergo a collective pedagogy that does more than remake their mental representations, deliberative ends, self-concept, role, or discursive repertoire. New cadets literally become something different. In doing so, in learning how to breathe like a soldier, cadets become anchored in their field, able to respond appropriately to events in the world through acquired skills.

To inhabit the military world, cadets must incorporate into their own flesh the habits and capacities that are the 'products of collective history'. Breathing is exemplary of how cadets inhabit their world through the ways that they are possessed by the practices of the military world. These techniques of the body arise from a preobjective intersubjectivity rooted in the bodily practices that orient people to one another. The motor function of breathing 'is both individual and systematic, because linked to a whole system of techniques involving the body and tools, and charged with a host of social meanings and values' (Bourdieu, 1977: 87).

The technique of breathing in through the nose and out through the mouth is learned by cadets who are attentive to what it takes to become an accomplished cadet. They learn this by seeing and hearing stories of how others succeeded, are praised, or criticized. Military styles of breathing become practical strategies for negotiating disparate reprimands, threats of shame, practices of evaluation and ranking that constitute and implicitly define the basic stakes and rewards of a field. Cadets' practical sense is effected collectively and often diffusely through instruction that is far from deliberate or fully thought out. All the injunctions to 'breathe through your nose and out through the mouth' or 'no no! Breathe with me' are never spelled out, justified, or debated. Nor do they fit together according to a 'deep structure.' These utterances and the gestures that accompany them are so many examples of hundreds of islands of instruction, spread out across time and people. Even in marksmanship, where there is some codification, much of the pedagogical work is tacit and suffused in body-to-body contact that is embedded in summary descriptions given about how to breathe that are not written down in any manual. The end effect is to cultivate the body as the background of social action. The body is only momentarily thrown to the foreground of action, when it becomes problematic, and then it recedes from view as it once again become the medium of interaction.

We better understand what is meant by military culture, and culture more generally, when we foreground the backgrounded kinetic and sensorial structures of the body. In this way we are able to construct a more inclusive definition of culture that is sensitive to how practical competencies are acquired in and for action. Techniques of the body, incorporated in the form of dispositions to use the body in socially approved ways and postures, are coextensive with the socially generated practices and utterances that orient the body to its world. When the pre-objective structures of the cadets fit the structures of world so that demands to run are met by a body that *can* run, we are able to understand better how social beings tacitly commit to their social worlds by an incarnate collusion.

Notes

1 I would like to thank Loïc Wacquant, Nancy Scheper-Hughes, and Arlie Hochschild for their remarks on early versions of this paper and also Heather Haverman, Chris Shilling and Nicholas Wilson for their comments. I also want to acknowledge the thoughtful comments and advice that I received for a different version of this paper from the organizer and presenters of the *Embodying Sociology* sessions at the 37th World Congress of the International Institute of Sociology, Stockholm, Sweden. July 5th–9th, 2005.

2 Also note that I alternate between 'operational' and 'presentational' data. Operational data refers to the 'running stream of spontaneous conversations and activities engaged in and observed by the ethnographer while in the field' and pertains to the 'everyday problematics' of group members (Van Maanen, 1979: 542). This data includes the actual situated practices whereby people engage one another to shape breathing as well as the verbal injunctions and admonishments meant to alter their behavior. Presentational data refers to the 'ideological, normative, and abstract, dealing far more with a manufactured image of idealized doing than with routinized practical activities actually engaged in by members of the studied organization' (ibid). In other words, some data includes what people say and do in situations where the body is foregrounded, especially descriptions of how the body is collectively worked upon, and other data emphasizes the primary meanings that group members attribute to the body and their accountings of what a certain kind of body means to them.

3 The reciprocal coordination of action is based on the sharing of inner time, the coordinated rhythms of bodies, through socialized organismic activities like breathing that create a 'vivid present together' (Schutz, 1964: 177). 'Only within this experience does the Other's conduct become meaningful to the partner tuned in on him—that is, the Other's body and its movements can be and are interpreted as a field of expression of events within his inner life . . . Facial expressions, gait, posture, ways of handling tools and instruments, without communicative intent [or significance], are examples of such a situation' (ibid).

References

Army, Department of the. (2003) 'FM 3–22.9: Rifle Marksmanship M16A1, M16A2/3, M16A4, and M4 Carbine.' Washington, D.C.: Department of the Army.

Ben-Ari, E. (1998) *Mastering Soldiers: Conflict, Emotions, and the Enemy in an Israeli Military Unit*, vol. 10. New York: Berghahn Books.

Benner, P. (2001 [1984]) *From Novice to Expert: Excellence and Power in Clinical Nursing Practice, commemorative edition*: Prentice Hall.

Bourdieu, P. (1977) *Outline of a Theory of Practice*. Cambridge: Cambridge University Press.

Bourdieu, P. (1990) *The Logic of Practice*. Stanford, CA: Stanford University Press.

Bourdieu, P. (2000) *Pascalian Meditations*. Stanford, CA: Stanford University Press.

Burke, C. (2004) *Camp All-American, Hanoi Jane, and the High-And-Tight*. Boston, Beacon Press.

Caforio, G. (2003) 'Military Officer Education.' in *Handbook of the Sociology of the Military*, edited by G. Caforio. New York: Kluwer Academic/Plenum Publishers.

Charlesworth, S.J. (2000) *A Phenomenology of Working Class Experience*. Cambridge: Cambridge University Press.

Crossley, N. (2001) *The Social Body*. Thousand Oaks, CA: SAGE Publications.
Csordas, T.J. (1990) 'Embodiment as a Paradigm for Anthropology.' *Ethos* 18: 5–47.
Csordas, T.J. (1994) *The Sacred Self: A Cultural Phenomenology of Charismatic Healing*. Berkeley, CA: University of California Press.
Durkheim, E. (1995) *The Elementary Forms of Religious Life*. Translated by K.E. Fields. New York, NY: Free Press.
Franke, V.C. (2000) 'Duty, honor country: The social identity of West Point cadets.' *Armed Forces and Society* 26: 175–202.
Goffman, E. (1967) *Interaction Ritual: Essays on Face to Face Behavior*. New York: Pantheon Books.
Goffman, E. (1981) *Forms of Talk*. Philadelphia: University of Pennsylvania Press.
Herbert, M.S. (1998) *Camouflage Isn't Only for Combat*. New York: New York University Press.
Lave, J. and Wenger, E. (1991) *Situated learning: legitimate peripheral participation*. Cambridge England; New York: Cambridge University Press.
Mauss, M. (1979) *Sociology and Psychology Essays*. London: Routledge and K. Paul.
Merleau-Ponty, M. (2002 [1962]) *Phenomenology of Perception*. London: Routledge.
Priest, R.F. (1998) 'Value changes in four cohorts at the U.S. Military Academy.' *Armed Forces and Society* 25: 81–102.
Sasson-Levy, O. (2003) 'Feminism and Military Gender Practices: Israeli Women Soldier in "Masculine" Roles.' *Sociological Inquiry* 73(3): 440–465.
Schutz, A. (1964) *Collected Papers: Studies in Social Theory, Volume II.* The Hague: Martinus Nijhoff.
Stevens, G., Rosa, F.M., and Gardner, S. (1994) 'Military academies as instruments of value change.' *Armed Forces and Society* 20: 473–482.
Sudnow, D. (2001 [1973]) *Ways of the Hand: A Rewritten Account*. Cambridge, MA: MIT Press.
Van Maanen, J. (1979) The Fact of Fiction in Organization Ethnography. *Administrative Science Quarterly* 24(4): 539–550.
Wacquant, L. (2004) *Body & soul: notebooks of an apprentice boxer*. Oxford ; New York: Oxford University Press.
Wacquant, L. (2005) 'Carnal Connections: On Embodiment, Apprenticeship, and Membership.' *Qualitative Sociology* 28: 445–474.
Winslow, D. (1999) 'Rites of Passage and Group Bonding in the Canadian Airborne.' *Armed Forces and Society* 25(3): 429–457

Listening to the dancer's body

Anna Aalten

Abstract

This article examines the occupational culture of ballet, specifically looking at body awareness and body experiences. Using a phenomenological approach, complemented by ethnographic interview data, the experiences of the ballet dancer's body, in its daily training process, are described and analysed. Focusing on the dancer's attitudes to and dealings with pain and injuries, but also looking at the issue of eating disorders, the implications of this analysis for theorizing the body as a material and only contingently elusive phenomenon are explicated. Drawing on contemporary body theory, the meaning of injuries and pain are analysed in the context of ballet culture. The concept of the phenomenologically 'absent body' is used to understand the temporary disappearance of the body from awareness, while the notion that pain and illness can be considered a form of communication offers an insight into the relationship between the individual body and the social and cultural worlds it is part of. The use of an ethnographic perspective ensures an attentiveness to the dancer's agency, informing and enriching the analysis.

Key words: ballet, occupational culture, absent body, phenomenology, agency.

Introduction

Ballet dancing is a physical profession and like all physical professions it involves specific health risks. The ballet technique, with its use of *pointe* shoes and the extreme turn-out of the legs and feet, invites dancers to

> defy the principles of human design. (. . .) Human toes were not designed to stand on. Unfortunately, dancers know this very well, but they stand on them anyway. (. . .) When dancers learn to turn out 180 degrees from the hips, to dance on pointe, to hold their torsos high off their waists, to arch and point their feet unnaturally, the muscles involved in these operations are strengthened in one way, but weakened in others (Mazo, 1974: 230–231).

But the health risks for ballet dancers, and female dancers in particular, are not only the consequence of the physical character of the profession and its associated techniques. More than twenty five years ago Lawrence Vincent, an ex-dancer and long-time physician with the New York City Ballet, already pointed to a third factor: the occupational culture of the ballet world. In a critical review, with the compelling title *Competing with the Sylph*, Vincent (1979) discussed the aesthetic ideal in the ballet world and its consequences for the health of female dancers. Vincent described the obsessive ways in which the ballet world dealt with the body weight of female dancers and related this to the frequent occurrence of eating disorders among them. Ten years later Vincent, in his introduction to the special issue on eating behaviour of *Dance Medicine & Science*, concludes that the situation has not improved since then: 'The reason', Vincent writes, 'is our failure to confront the root of the problem, because it is a *cultural and aesthetic*, not a scientific or medical one' (Vincent, 1998: 4, my emphasis).

Every occupation has its own culture. People in the same profession usually share a moral belief system and a behavioural code, telling them how to behave and what, usually unwritten, rules to obey (Hochschild, 1983; Clark, Chandler & Barry, 1994). In *Competing with the Sylph* Vincent laid bare the rules concerning the shape of the female dancer's body and directed attention to the dangers these rules presented to her health. But the development of eating disorders is not the only health risk resulting from the occupational culture of the ballet world. The dominant attitude towards pain and injuries is equally hazardous.

Research in the world of professional dance has repeatedly and convincingly shown that most dance injuries are not the consequence of trauma, but the result of chronically overburdening the body. Because pain is often ignored, a minor physical problem eventually turns into a serious one (Krasnow, Kerr & Mainwaring, 1994; Brinson and Dick, 1996; Liederbach and Compagno, 2001; Mainwaring, Krasnow & Kerr, 2001; Schärli, 2005)[1] According to the British dancer Darcey Bussell

> Dancers are always so desperate not to miss any part of their careers that we find it tempting to work through injuries if we possibly can. When we first join the company we're especially determined to prove ourselves, and I know many dancers who have been injured but who have carried on working without telling anyone (1998: 149).

Bussell continues her story by telling us that she knows it is not healthy to continue working while suffering from an injury and it will makes matters worse, but that she herself still does so every now and then. But 'every time, afterwards, I cannot believe I've taken such a stupid risk' (Bussell, 1999: 150).

For the anthropologist studying body discourses and body practices in the ballet world, the ruthless ways in which dancers and dance teachers often treat the body is bewildering. In an occupation where the body is so all-important one would expect the practitioners to treat it with the utmost respect to keep it healthy and in shape. Like eating disorders, however, overburdening and exhaustion are considered by many dancers unavoidable risks of the profession. Why do dancers not take better care of their bodies? What are the moral beliefs that bring forth such an attitude? Which behavioural codes do dancers adhere to when it comes to pain? And what does 'listening to the body' mean within the context of ballet?

This chapter examines the occupational culture of ballet, looking specifically at body awareness and body experiences. Using a phenomenological approach, complemented by ethnographic interview data, the experiences of the ballet dancer's body, in its daily training process, are described and analysed. Focusing on the dancer's attitudes and dealings with pain and injuries, but also dealing with the issue of eating disorders, the implications of this analysis for theorizing the body as a material, only contingently elusive, phenomenon are explicated.

Theorizing the Body

In the last two decades the body has become an important and well-respected subject of anthropological and sociological scholarship (Turner, 1984; Csordas, 1990; Turner, 1992; Synnott, 1993; Lupton, 1995; Nettleton, 1995; Williams & Bendelow, 1998; Shilling, 2003).[2] While initially the body tended to be treated as an 'object' controlled by government or 'discourse', researchers interested in bodily experience and a 'more meat-and-bones approach' to the subject (Foster, 1997: 235) often turned to phenomenology, and more particularly to the work of Merleau-Ponty, in advocating embodiment as a paradigm for anthropology and sociology (Nettleton and Watson, 1998; Csordas, 1990). The phenomenological approach holds much promise for the study of ballet dancers, given the extent to which their work is bound up with their bodies. Professional dancers present an interesting case in that they generally treat their bodies as objects controlled by their minds, and are highly selective about which features of their physical experiences they focus on. In this respect Drew Leder's (1990) account, of how it is that people's bodies can become 'absent' from their awareness but also force themselves to the front of it, is highly relevant to the study of ballet dancers.

In everyday life most people, while depending on their bodies to engage with the world, are usually not aware of their bodies. When I try to catch a ball, my attention will be focussed on the ball and not on the many complicated physical processes that allow me to catch it successfully. When I eat a sandwich I will be aware of the taste and structure of the food, but probably not of my mouth's movements to make the food enter my body or my stomach's efforts to digest it. The elusiveness of the body or, as Csordas (1994: 8) has formulated it, this '*disappearance* from awareness' is the reason why Leder (1990: 69) speaks of the 'absent body', stating that 'it is *the body's own tendency toward self-concealment* that allows for the possibility of its neglect'.

The tendency toward self-concealment, however, is disrupted when there is illness, pain or a sudden confrontation with physical failure. When I tear a muscle trying to catch the ball, when I burn my tongue because the food is too hot or when my stomach rejects the shrimp salad that has gone bad, causing me to vomit for hours, I am suddenly very aware of my body. Then the body leaves its mode of absence, making its presence known.

> A region of the body that may have previously given forth little in the way of sensory stimuli suddenly speaks up. . . . Even body regions that are ordinarily perceptible still present a heightened call when in pain (Leder, 1990: 71).

Taking Leder's statement that when the body is in pain it 'speaks up' one step further, pain is one of the ways the body escapes its elusiveness, making itself heard and thereby becoming undeniably material.

In their influential article 'The Mindful Body' the anthropologists Nancy Scheper-Hughes and Margaret Lock (1987) add a cultural dimension to Leder's concern with the reappearance of the body by proposing to see pain and illness as a form of communication. They suggest that illness and pain come into being and are expressed as a result of interaction between embodied individuals' feelings and thoughts, on the one hand, and the social relationships and cultural belief systems of which they are part, on the other. Through illness, which Scheper-Hughes and Lock call 'the language of the organs', nature, society and culture make themselves heard all at the same time (1987: 31). Here Scheper-Hughes and Lock explicitly draw attention to the relationship between the body, its 'owner' and the social and cultural worlds it is part of. To grasp the meaning of pain and illness it is not enough to look at the body's presence or absence in the individual's consciousness. Understanding the 'language of the organs' is only possible if the body is positioned firmly within the cultural symbolism and the context of the social groups it is part of.

This becomes clear if we delve further into the occupational culture of ballet, a culture that offers its participants not only a moral belief system and behavioural codes, but also a specific language that enables individual dancers to understand and communicate with each other. As such, this culture impacts upon how dancers are socialized into the beliefs dominant in the ballet world, and helps us to understand the meanings they attribute to pain, injuries, and bodily shape and weight.

Ethnographic perspectives

The present analysis is based on an ethnographic study of body discourses and body practices in ballet conducted between 1993 and 2000 in The Netherlands (Aalten, 2002).[3] Formal in-depth interviews with male and female ballet dancers, informal conversations backstage and during touring trips, and interviews with professionals like nutritionists, physiotherapists and doctors specializing in dancer's injuries, were held over the years. Observation was another important method in the research: I attended daily classes and rehearsals at Het Nationale Ballet, the major ballet company of The Netherlands, and numerous ballet classes at other companies and professional ballet schools. In addition to the formal and informal interviews and observations, extended biographical interviews were conducted with twenty-five female professional ballet dancers and nine dance students at professional schools. The life stories that were written on the basis of this interview material were complemented by a collection of dancers' autobiographies.[4] In both the biographical interviews and the autobiographies, the attitude towards pain and injuries was a focus of the analysis, but much was also revealed about weight and body shape. These ethnographic and biographical methods complemented each other well. While the former allowed for an exploration of the subculture of ballet, exposing the context where injuries occur and body norms are established, the latter offered more insight into the individual identities of dancers.

Creating the dancer's body

In their years of training, professional dancers are confronted with 'two bodies: one, perceived and tangible; the other, aesthetically ideal' (Foster, 1997: 237).[5] The perceived and tangible body is the body they experience daily, with the toes that hurt because they are being forced into *pointe* shoes, the stomach aching for a meal, and the muscles that are tired after a long working day. This experienced body is also one that struggles to fulfil the demands placed on it in terms of being able to do the difficult pirouette after endless hours of trying, keeping balanced at the right moment, and physically forcing itself into harmony with the long lyrical lines the choreographer is asking for. The second body is the ideal body that is presented to a dancer by her teachers, ballet masters and choreographers. This ideal body has a specific form and the ability to perform specific movements endlessly and with ease. In ballet this bodily form is well described and its movement patterns are known (Lawson, 1979; Jowitt, 1988; Warren, 1989). Within the power relations of the ballet world, teachers, ballet masters, choreographers and artistic directors are the ones who operate as gatekeepers to the profession and dictate which bodies approximate most closely to the ideal.

These two bodies, the perceived and tangible, and the ideal, constantly interact.[6] During the first ten years of education and training, the years in which the dancer's body is created, the nature of this interaction is highly unequal.[7] Throughout these years, training is aimed at *creating* a dancer's body, using the ideal body as yardstick. The dancer who works with her body is constantly aware of the ideal. She is also aware of the fact that working, and working hard, can bring the ideal closer. Dancer Tessa Cooke had legs that did not fit the necessary 'ballerina look'.

> I really needed to mould my body into the required shape. I have literally formed my legs through training and dancing. In my case the malleability is proven. When your body is your instrument you can do that. When you really put your mind to it, you

can change your body. Not only by getting thinner, but also in other aspects. It's simply a matter of focussing strongly enough.

With the right kind of training and exercises and enough will power, bodies can be moulded. Dancers know this because this is what they are told by their teachers and because they come to experience the relationship between constant hard work and physical change and improvement.

During their training years, in short, dancers learn that the body is indeed malleable. The steps that seemed impossible at the outset can now be mastered, constant exercises have effect and the ideal body can be created. A young dancer told me how she put her lessons into practice: 'Every night I sat down in front of my bed and pushed my legs wider until they really hurt. The next day I could go a bit further.' This dancer literally felt how the body could be moulded. But in the process of creating the dancer's body she also learnt another lesson. Discovering that pushing her legs 'until they really hurt' would bring her closer to the desired ideal, she learnt to regard pain as a sign of improvement. In the pain of her hurting legs nature, society and culture came together, telling her the story of her own physical boundaries, the social constraints of her profession, and the symbolic meaning of the necessity of discipline and suffering all at the same time.

If dancers encounter lessons in pain, so too are they subject to lessons in weight. In ballet the keyword is lightness (Jowitt, 1988). By using their will power and technique, dancers challenge the law of gravity, creating the illusion of doing so without any effort. When female dancers get 'on *pointe*', make endless turns or jump into the air, they seem to be weightless. The beauty of ballet is not in the presentation of the human body as it is, struggling, sweating and subjected to gravity, but in the stylization of it. As the American dance scholar Roger Copeland states:

> In the tradition from Plato to Freud, art is conceived as a mode of sublimation, an alchemical conversion of lower or bodily energy into a higher, mental or spiritual state. To create a work of art is to transcend the lowliness of the body. Hence the odd paradox that dance – the only art form whose raw material is the human body – began to idealize the image of the disembodied woman (Copeland, 1990: 27).

The ideal of the disembodied woman has concrete consequences for the ways in which female dancers treat their bodies. The most obvious consequence is the constant striving to be slim. In the daily life of female dancers, the ambition to weigh as little as possible and the specific attitude towards food that is related to this ambition are omnipresent and eating disorders are frequent.

Female dancers working in companies that present nineteenth-century ballets cannot escape the ideal of the disembodied sylph. In 1995 Esther Protzman, a soloist with Het Nationale Ballet in Amsterdam, confessed to her suffering from serious eating disorders since early puberty in one of the nation's major newspapers. She had just started training again, after a total collapse several months before. Esther Protzman said:

> I could not do anything any more. I had no energy left. My obsession with non-eating had completely taken over my dancing. I thought I would be a better dancer if only I could be extremely thin and it has taken me a lot of effort to realize that I had gone too far in that.

A year after the publication of this admission I interviewed Esther Protzman. She told me that her problems had already started at school. After finishing her training she was accepted into Het Nationale Ballet, the most prestigious ballet company of the Netherlands, and it was at this stage that she became obsessive about her weight. The staff of the Het Nationale Ballet did not offer any help and she did not ask for it. On the face of it nothing was wrong, because for years Esther Protzman danced beautifully and was promoted steadily until she became a first soloist. It was only after a complete collapse that she herself and the staff of the ballet company realized that something was very wrong.

This dancer is certainly not alone in her struggle. International research shows that female dancers in particular engage in unhealthy eating patterns, especially when the physical strain of their daily activities is taken into account (Benson *et al.*, 1988; Warren, 1989; Brinson & Dick, 1996; Haight, 1998; Wolman, 1999; Koutedakis & Yamurtas, 2004).[8] Yet, for years the dance world would not acknowledge this problem. The aesthetic ideal and the body practices that followed from it were so much part of the occupational culture of ballet that people closed their eyes to its negative consequences (Gordon, 1983; Vincent, 1979, 1998). In recent years eating disorders and their consequences are on the agenda. Nevertheless, the fact that the aesthetic ideal can be the cause of serious eating disorders for female dancers, disorders that constitute a general health risk for the profession as a whole, is only slowly being acknowledged (Benn & Walters, 2001).

Coping with pain and hunger

In 1995, at an international conference of dance scholars, Susan Foster told an anecdote about a female dancer visiting her physician. The doctor asked the dancer where she felt the pain and for how long she had been feeling it. The dancer looked at him with a look of complete incomprehension. When the doctor asked her what it was that was so incomprehensible, she answered: 'But I feel pain all the time!' This little story may be exaggerated, but it touches on a fundamental element in the life of all dancers. Physical pain is part of the daily life of dancers, and is considered an inevitable aspect of the profession. Writing about the occupational culture in four ballet companies the anthropologist Helena Wulff even speaks of a 'culture of injury and pain' (1998: 105). Most dancers find this so obvious that my questions about pain were met with a shrug of the shoulders. When I persisted I was usually given stories of funny accidents or really serious injuries, before we finally arrived at the day-to-day experiences with pain.

Psychological research shows that dancers, despite their continuous complaining, actually have a high level of pain endurance (Tajet-Foxell & Rose, 1995; Ramel & Moritz, 1998). This strange junction of experiencing and complaining about pain, on the one hand, and being able to endure a high level of pain, on the other, can only be understood within the framework of the ballet culture and the dancer's relationship with her body. Listen to what Yoko van der Tweel told me about her relationship with pain in our first interview, when she had been with Het Nationale Ballet for four years.

> I remember having a corn once and I still needed to go on *pointe* for the ballet we were doing at the time. Then I discovered that it is possible to focus yourself mentally up to the point where you do not feel the pain anymore the moment you get on stage. In a way you surpass the pain.

Seven years later I talked to her again and asked her how she looked at pain now. She told me the following anecdote.

> I think you feel pain when you are doing nothing. That's when you feel it. But when you are dancing you do not feel any pain. Once, during a rehearsal one of my *pointe* shoe ribbons broke. I put it together with a safety pin and while I was dancing the pin started to bend and the point of it went through my foot. This had been going on for some time and the bleeding was heavy. But I did not feel a thing! Because I had been dancing and concentrating on the dancing. Therefore you do not feel pain in that situation.

All dancers I interviewed had comparable stories about being able to ignore pain and physical problems. They accepted pain as an inevitable part of their profession, while at the same time experiencing a certain level of control over it.

In the dance world there are 'easy' bodies and 'difficult' bodies. An easy body is a body that can be moulded into the required dancer's body without too much effort and pain. Slim, supple, a good turn-out, long legs that can go upwards in a straight line, beautiful feet and a straight back. With a difficult body the distance between the body of the dance and the ideal body is greater. Many dancers, even the ones with the so-called easy bodies, used the term 'fighting' when they talked about their relationship with their bodies. As journalist Joseph Mazo so aptly put it: ballet dancers have to teach their bodies to do things that 'defy the principles of human design' (1974: 230). The word 'defy' can be taken literally here. For dancers physical boundaries must be crossed and bodily limitations are seen as challenges.

A dancer's attitude toward pain has to be understood within this context. Every dancer knows: if you want to be good, you have to suffer. For a dancer the experience of pain is not only negative, precisely because of this heroic aspect. Pain can be a sign that you are working hard or that you are improving yourself physically. Therefore pain is often even welcomed (Wulff, 1998: 106–107). Most dancers gave descriptions of this attitude towards pain that went far back into their training years.

> At school you were never allowed to show if something hurt. There was this little note in the dressings room saying: 'Blood is good, no pain no gain'. That really said it all.

> Crying if you were in pain was absolutely forbidden. When you did, the reaction was always: 'Keep smiling! You are the one who wants to be here, if you don't like it you can leave. If you want to stay, stop whining!' So you simply did not dare to stop, you just went on. There was a time when I had terrible cramps, but I never stopped. Never! (Nienke Bonnema).

Dancer Mariët Andringa had a 'difficult body'. In school, however, she learned how to diminish the distance between the two bodies, her own and the ideal.

> I had a good feeling when I left school. I felt like a winner. I was a fighting machine. I was so strong that I pulled my tendons until they snapped. Looking back now I know that I treated my own body with hatred. I danced when I was in pain or injured. After a holiday I would do thirty-two *changements* straight from a grand *plié*. And the next day, with legs like this, I would do them again. Or *frappés* for at least half an hour. While the teacher sat at my feet to make sure I would not give up. The tears would be streaming down my face, but I would keep going. That was the only thing that mattered: not giving up. You will definitely develop a specific kind of mental strength. But physically? What you learn is to close off all feeling. This can be good in some situations. But it takes you away from your ability to feel pain.

In both stories these dancers describe how during their training years they were socialized to accept the body's suffering as an inevitable part of their profession.

The denial of food, the necessary fuel for the body, is also part of this. Every one of the dancers I interviewed had some personal experience with eating disorders. Most managed to overcome them, but for some food and eating were always fraught with emotions. The problems usually started during puberty in school. Numerous dancers told me the story of how a teacher would point at the thinnest girl in the class, telling the others to follow her example. They talked about the 'contagiousness' of disordered eating behaviour; even when no remarks were made about one's own body, criticisms of the bodies of friends was enough to start dieting. Yoko van der Tweel told me:

> I have never had any trouble to stay thin. But at school I was surrounded by girls who were obsessed by their weight and had problems. So I sort of went along and started to have doubts about myself. As a consequence I gained weight and had to go on a diet as well. So for a time I went up and down. Fortunately that has changed after I became a professional dancer. Ever since I joined the company I have been okay.

Another story I was often told was that when a dancer had lost weight as the result of an illness, she would receive praise and be encouraged to continue dieting.

Dieting can be seen as part of the constant work on the body that is part and parcel of the ballet world. All dancers had the capacity to loose some weight whenever it was really necessary, for example if a ballet with very revealing costumes was staged. For some, not eating became a way of life.

> When I had just joined the company I experimented with diets and even with pills. But after a while I stopped that and since the birth of my daughter I have never been on a diet again. But even now, after leaving the company, I still don't like to eat. I

> never feel hungry. I don't eat three meals a day, I hate feeling full (Nicolette Langestraat).

The ability to control one's appetite and to go without food in order to reach the ideal of the disembodied woman was all part of the socialization of a dancer.

The necessity of crossing physical boundaries and the definition of pain and suffering as heroic bring forth a mode of bodily absence that is specific for ballet dancers. In ballet it is not 'the body's own tendency towards self-concealment' that is responsible for its absence in the dancer's consciousness. Dancers work with and on their bodies in a highly conscious manner and therefore do not experience the taken-for-granted, passive absence of the body that is common for non-dancers. As became apparent in the life stories, the absence of the dancer's body is an *active* absence, an absence that is *forced* upon the body. The body's ability to make itself known, by crying out in pain or hunger, is taken away by the dancer in her struggle to achieve the required technique and bodily perfection. When the body 'speaks up' it is habitually silenced into a mode of bodily absence to allow the dancer to continue working, thereby denying the body its materiality. In an occupational culture that on the one hand believes in the malleability of the body, striving for disembodiedness, and on the other hand gives a heroic status to pain, the neglect of the body of the dancer is the result of a conscious act. But this act does not go unpunished. Despite the dancer's discipline and capacity to silence her body, it still retains some of its abilities to call attention to itself, one of which is through injury.

Listening to the body

Dancers who systematically silence their bodies run the risk of meeting the boundaries of its malleability. When Esther Protzman told the national press in 1995 about her problems with eating, she had just returned to training again after a serious collapse several months before. For years she had subjected her body to an unhealthy eating pattern and suddenly it had refused to continue. She literally could not do anything anymore and was forced to stop dancing. When I interviewed Protzman a year later, she said:

> Now I know that a dancer has to take very good care of herself. That you have to give your body what it needs. But this is difficult, because the demands are high. A dancer wants to dance. So when you are not chosen for a role, there is a problem. I always thought that my main problem was my weight and that I would be chosen more if only I would be thinner. But this is not how it works. You have to be yourself. Dancers have to work with their own bodies, not with some idealized image of it. You have to know what you are worth and accept that maybe you will not be chosen for every ballet.

The reason why it took a talented and intelligent dancer like Esther Protzman so many years to discover that she needed to take better care of her body is related to the more general belief in the malleability of the body within the ballet world. Body weight is regarded as relatively easy to control. All the dancers I interviewed told me that losing weight had never presented any difficulties. They were disciplined enough to loose the pounds that had to go, even within a very short time. But for every one of them there comes a moment when they realize that body weight cannot be manipulated endlessly. Some of them, like Esther Protzman, had to suffer a serious collapse before reaching this insight.

During my research I repeatedly interviewed Daniëlle Valk, a *corps de ballet* dancer with Het Nationale Ballet. In our first interview I asked her how she dealt with physical problems:

> Sometimes the company only has a few people available who can dance a particular role and in that case you feel responsible. I remember having a problem with the knuckle of the big toe in one of my feet. This was one of those typical problems of over-burdening. It was really painful with certain movements, but not serious enough to stop me from dancing. Before I went on stage I had to make the movements that hurt the most repeatedly to make it through the performance. That wasn't very pleasant. I would have skipped the performance, but when they tell you they do not have anybody to take your place, what can you do? And then, when you see other colleagues continuing, you do not want to disappoint them.

So she continued dancing despite the problem, which she considered a minor discomfort anyhow. But Het Nationale Ballet's repertoire contains much pointe work and the feet of Daniëlle Valk were apparently not up to this. The small problem of over-burdening that she was telling me about in our first interview went gradually from bad to worse. Inflammation of the knuckle of her big toe became chronic and caused her much trouble. Because of the company's tight schedule and a repertoire with multiple dancing styles, Valk's feet did not have enough time to heal properly. The medicines she took helped her to fight the inflammation but were a cause of serious stomach trouble. Within three years after our first interview Valk was forced to stop dancing.[9] Her body had spoken in ways that could no longer be ignored.

Within the world of ballet, Protzman's long history of distorted eating and Valk's choice to continue dancing despite an injury is not at all exceptional. Wainwright and Turner (2004: 317) state that on an everyday level 'dancing and performing with niggling injuries is the norm'. The fear of losing roles and the sense that performance is obligatory are only partly responsible for the dullness of hearing that dancers seem to suffer towards the language of their bodies. For many dancers their identity is so closely tied up with their profession that not being able to dance presents a major threat to their sense of self (Mainwaring, Krasnow & Kerr, 2001; Wainwright, Williams & Turner, 2005). This is why a serious injury, that is an injury that prevents a dancer from doing what she loves doing most, dancing, always has such a devastating effect (Macchi and Crossman, 1996).

But in an occupational culture that teaches its participants to ignore the language of the body and actively to silence it, an injury can also be a good thing. In her memoirs, the American dancer Merrill Ashley, who had a 30-year career with the New York City Ballet, expresses a view on injuries that seems to go against the grain of dominant thinking within the world of ballet. According to Ashley an injury can be positive, because it heightens the awareness of the dancer towards her body. Ashley states:

> After an injury, a dancer learns, at least for a short time, to heed his body if only because pain speaks a language almost anyone can understand. This heightened awareness should not disappear once the dancers returns to form; rather it should help him continue to learn about the ways in which the body moves and reacts (1984: 217–218)

It is possible that Ashley's views have more to do with wishful thinking than with an accurate description of ballet reality. When interviewing twenty-six dancers of the professional division of the Royal Winnipeg Ballet School in Canada, the researchers discovered that the majority of them did not change their way of working after an injury. A considerable minority, however, (eleven) did actually modify their exercises, were more careful and aware of their bodies and used better technique (Macchi & Crossman, 1996).

In the course of my research I met several dancers whose stories resonated with Ashley's view on injuries. Mariët Andringa, who described herself as a 'fighting machine', told me:

> I used to be that dancer who could almost die of pain and still go on smiling. So typical. That enormous distance between how you feel and what your body tells you. I have had to learn how to discover my own boundaries. I really needed my injury to teach me that. Now I know what I can do and this is so much better, because now I can prevent myself from getting injured. But I needed the injury for that.

Another dancer described a similar experience. Cora Bos-Kroese was a dancer with the Nederlands Dans Theater when I first interviewed her. She told me how happy she had been when she was accepted in the company immediately after she had finished her education. To prove her worth she worked extremely hard and managed to dance a lot. But then she was struck by a serious back injury in her second year with the company, making it impossible for her to walk for a week. The shock of the injury and its consequences changed her attitude towards her work. Bos-Kroese:

> Before the injury I worked from positions. I had this *arabesque* that I wanted to get right and I simply worked as long and as hard as possible to get there. Every day I stretched and pulled. Then suddenly I could not do anything anymore. All the vertebrae were irritated, all the muscles were hard. It was as if my body had created its own defense against my working it. Imagine, I could not walk for a whole week! That really made me think. I realized I could try to work differently. I decided to start listening to my body. To work with what it can do instead of with the ideal. Now I stretch and I consciously feel how far I can go. It's a matter of consciousness. But I needed the injury before I could do that.

Stories such as these show how the silencing of the body is so much part and parcel of the occupational culture of the ballet world that 'listening to the body' has to be learned actively. Paradoxically, an injury can serve as an impetus to start this learning process.

An injury that prevents a dancer from dancing is the worst that can happen to her. But my research shows that within an occupational culture that systematically silences the body, an injury can also be a good thing. I have interviewed dancers who were confronted with the boundaries their bodies set to them early in their careers and others for whom this experience came later. But to all of them it offered the same lesson: first they had forced their bodies to fit to the ideal image but then this injury happened and made them realize that there was an end to the malleability of their bodies. Or, as dancer Esther Protzman formulated it: 'You have to be yourself. Dancers have to work with their own bodies, not with some idealized image of it'. Once this message hit home, the dancer started to work differently. The nature of the interaction between her own body and the ideal changed. Instead of the unequal subordination of the perceived and tangible body by the ideal came an interchange between the two bodies. The perceived and tangible body was given a voice and was allowed to be present in the discussion on the goals that the dancer was striving for.

Conclusion

At the outset of this article I was looking for answers to the question of why so many dance injuries are the result of a chronically overburdening of the body. Why do dancers not take better care of their bodies? As an anthropologist studying the unwritten rules and regulations of the ballet world I was bewildered by the often harsh ways in which many ballet dancers treat the instrument they depend on most. Eating disorders, overburdening, exhaustion and dancing with pain and minor injuries are considered by many dancers unavoidable risks of the profession. What are the moral beliefs that bring forth this attitude? Which behavioural codes do dancers adhere to when it comes to pain? And what does 'listening to the body' mean in the context of ballet?

Drawing on contemporary body theory I aimed to analyse the meaning of injuries and pain in the context of ballet culture, while my use of an ethnographic perspective allowed me to be attentive to the dancer's agency. The concept of 'the absent body' helped me to understand the disappearance of the body from awareness, while the notion that pain and illness can be considered a form of communication offered an insight into the relationship between the individual body and the social and cultural worlds it is part of.

Professional dancers are in an extremely demanding occupation when it comes to physical capabilities and strength. The daily reality of classes, rehearsals and performances forces them to work themselves literally into a sweat and to defy 'the principles of human design'. The physical demands of the profession, however, are not the only reason why dancers suffer from serious health risks. Another reason can be found in the occupational culture of the ballet. The belief in the malleability of the body creates a world where a dancer's body is always under construction. Dancers are well aware of the notion that continuous practice and perseverance will lead to a change and improvement of their own perceived and tangible bodies towards the required ideal. The pain and suffering that are involved in the process is considered to be necessary and even somewhat heroic.

Because of their profession, dancers relate to their bodies differently from non-dancers. Dancers do not have the same kind of disappearance from awareness of the body that is common for most people. During their training their bodies are present as the focus of the dancer's attempts to incorporate the specific ballet technique and master the necessary skills. Their bodies are quite literally the building material for their art. On the other hand, the dancer's training also creates a particular absence of the body. The constant repetition of well-known movement patterns in the daily class brings dancers to a state where they can do them unconsciously. After having mastered the skill of performing a *battement frappés* the dancer does not have to think about her body anymore when she is asked to execute this particular movement, as it has become part of her basic 'techniques of the body' (Mauss, 1973).

The 'absence of the body' in the ballet world is not passive and taken-for-granted, but an absence that is actively achieved. In their attempts to create the ideal ballet body, professional dancers knowingly silence their own material bodies. Many female dancers develop eating disorders while striving to become the disembodied sylph that is the ideal in ballet. They purposely misunderstand the 'language of the organs', ignoring their hunger and lack of energy. Pain and injuries are not viewed as signs of the materiality of the body and the necessity to listen to its needs, but as boundaries that have to be crossed.

The process of silencing does not always go unpunished, however. Sometimes the body speaks up in a way that cannot be ignored, by confronting the dancer with an injury that is so serious that she has to stop dancing. Paradoxically, a serious injury can incite a dancer to start 'listening to her body', working in a different and probably healthier way.

Notes

1 According to dancer's self-assessment in a recent quantitative study in The Netherlands 60% of their injuries were chronic, due either to fatigue, overwork, ignoring early warning signs, an incorrect technique or a combination of these (Schärli, 2005: 18–20).

2 According to Chris Shilling 'the body has moved to the very centre of academic analysis', serving as 'an enormously productive focus for theoretical and, increasingly, empirical work' (2003: viii, 211).

3 The results of the study were published in a book that was written in Dutch (Aalten, 2002). See for publications in English on the methodology Aalten, 2005, on body images in ballet Aalten, 1997 and on body practices in relation to dominant beliefs in the ballet world Aalten, 2004.

4 Most important were De Mille, 1951; Fonteyn, 1976; Bentley, 1982; Brady, 1982; Seymour, 1984; Ashley, 1984; Kirkland, 1986; Porter, 1989; Farrell, 1990; Kent, 1997; Bull, 1999 and Bussell, 1999.

5 The reader is reminded of 'the two bodies', the physical and the social body, as described by the anthropologist Mary Douglas in her well known work on natural symbols. According to Douglas

(1970) it is the social body that constrains the way the physical body is perceived and experienced. However, this is not a one-way process: the social and physical body continually exchange meanings, each reinforcing the categories of the other.

6 The anthropologist Lewis, who took Leder's concept of the absent body as his starting point and analysed the bodily modes of Brazilian *capoeira* players, says that learning a physical skill requires the individual to mediate between an embodied and a disembodied state, claiming that 'body practitioners such as dancers, athletes, and actors in our world are in this intermediate mode more of the time than are others, and thus their worlds of embodiment are different from the norm' (1995: 229).

7 In an interview I had with the French dancer Sabine Chaland she said that 'it takes ten years to make a dancer's body'. Other dancers made similar statements.

8 It is impossible to give exact figures on the occurrence of eating disorders among female dancers as the information available and the definitions used in the different studies vary widely. In the latest quantitative study among professional dancers in The Netherlands nearly half of the female dancers report having suffered from an eating disorder at least once (Schärli, 2005: 34). The sample of this study, however, was based on a majority of modern dancers working freelance, while there is some evidence that eating disorders occur more frequently among ballet dancers than among modern dancers.

9 Thanks to the growing body of literature on dancer's injuries there is much more information available now than there was twenty years ago. One of the interesting findings in relation to the subject of this chapter is the strong correlation between injury occurrence, fatigue and (the lack of) social support (Patterson, Smith, Everett & Ptacek, 1998; Liederbach & Compagno, 2001; Adam, Brassington, Steiner & Martheson, 2004).

References

Aalten, A. (1997) 'Performing the Body, Creating Culture.' *The European Journal of Women's Studies* (4) 2: 197–217.

Aalten, A. (2002) *De bovenbenen van Olga de Haas. Achter de schermen van de Nederlandse balletwereld.* Amsterdam: Van Gennep.

Aalten, A. (2004) 'The beliefs we work with – health and occupational culture in Dutch ballet.' in: Mirjam van der Linden (ed.), *Not Just Any Body & Soul. Health, well-being and excellence in dance*, pp. 58–66. Amsterdam: Uitgever International Theatre and Film Books.

Aalten, A. (2005) 'We Dance, We Don't Live'. Biographical Research in Dance Studies.' *Discourses in Dance* (3) 1: 5–20.

Adam, M.U., Brassington, G.S., Steiner, H. and Martheson, G.O. (2004) 'Psychological Factors Associated with Performance-Limiting Injuries in Professional Ballet Dancers.' *Journal of Dance Medicine* (8) 2: 43–46.

Ashley, M. (1984) *Dancing for Balanchine*. New York: E.P.Dutton Inc.

Benn, T. and Walters, D. (2001) 'Between Scylla and Charybdis. Nutritional education versus body culture and the ballet aesthetics: the effects of the lives of female dancers', *Research in Dance Education*, (2) 2: 139–155.

Benson, J. *et al.* (1988) 'Nutritional considerations for ballet dancers', in Clarkson, P. and Skrinar, M. (eds), *Science of Dance Training*, pp. 223–237. Champaign: Human Kinetics Publishers.

Bentley, T. (1982) *Winter Season. A Dancer's Journal*. New York: Random House.

Brady, J. (1982) *The Unmaking of a Dancer. An Unconventional Life*. Washington: Washington Square Press.

Brinson, P. and Dick, F. (1996) *Fit to Dance? The report of the national inquiry into dancers' health and injury.* London: Calouste Gulbenkian Foundation.

Bull, D. (1999) *Dancing Away. A Covent Garden Diary*. London: Methuen.

Bussell, D. (with Judith Mackrell) (1999) *Life in Dance.* London: Arrow Books.

Clark, H., Chandler, J. and Barry, J. (1994) (eds), *Organizations and Identities*. London: Chapman and Hall.
Copeland, R. (1990) 'Duncan, Graham, Rainer, and Sexual Politics', *Dance Theatre Journal* (8) 3: 6–30.
Csordas, T. (1990) 'Embodiment as a Paradigm for Anthropology', *Ethos* 18: 5–47.
Csordas, T. (1994) (ed.), *Embodiment and Experience: The Existential Ground of Culture and Self*. Cambridge: Cambridge University Press.
de Mille, A. (1951) *Dance to the Piper: Memoirs of the Ballet*. London: Hamish Hamilton.
Douglas, M. (1970) *Natural Symbols: Explorations in Cosmology*. London: Barrie and Rocklif, the Cresset Press.
Farrell, S. (with Bentley, T.) (1990) *Holding on Air. An autobiography*. New York: Summit Books.
Fonteyn, M. (1976) *Autobiography*. New York: Warner.
Foster, S. (1997) 'Dancing Bodies', in J. Desmond (ed), *Meaning in Motion. New Cultural Studies of Dance*, pp. 235–259. Durham and London: Duke University Press.
Gordon, S. (1983) *Off Balance. The Real World of Ballet*. New York: Pantheon Books.
Haight, H.J. (1998) 'Morphologic, Physiologic, and Functional Interactionsin Elite Female Ballet Dancers', *Medical Problems of Performing Artists* (13) 1: 4–13.
Hochschild, A.R. (1983) *The Managed Heart*. Berkeley, CA: University of California Press.
Holstein, J.A. and Gubrium, J.F. (2000) *The Self We Live By: Narrative Identity in a Postmodern World*. New York: Oxford University Press.
Jowitt, D. (1988) *Time and the Dancing Image*. New York: William Morrow.
Kent, A. (1997) *Once a dancer. An Autobiography*. New York: St. Martin's Press.
Kirkland, G. and Lawrence, G. (1986) *Dancing on my Grave*. New York: Doubleday.
Koutedakis, Y. and Yamurtas, A. (2004) 'The Dancer as Performing Athlete: Physiological Considerations', *Sports Medicine* (34) 10: 651–661.
Krasnow, Kerr and Mainwaring (1994) 'Psychology of Dealing with the Injured Dancer', *Medical Problems of Performing Artists* (9) 1: 7–19.
Lawson, J. (1979) *The Principles of Classical Dance*. London: Adam & Clarks Black.
Leder, D. (1990) *The Absent Body*. Chicago: Chicago University Press.
Lewis, J. (1995) 'Genre and Embodiment: From Brazilian Capoeira to the Ethnology of Human Movement', *Cultural Anthropology* (10) 2: 221–243.
Liederbach, M. and Compagno, J.M. (2001) 'Psychological Aspects of Fatigue Related Injuries in Dancers', *Journal of Dance Medicine and Science* (5) 4: 116–120.
Lupton, D. (1995) *The Imperative of Health*. London: Sage.
Macchi, R. and Crossman, J. (1996) 'After the Fall: Reflections of Injured Classical Ballet Dancers', *Journal of Sport Behaviour* (19) 3: 221–234.
Mainwaring, L.M., Krasnow, D. and Kerr, G. (2001) 'And The Dance Goes On: Psychological Impact of Injury', *Journal of Dance, Medicine and Science* (5) 4: 105–115.
Mauss, M. (1973 [1934]) 'Techniques of the body', *Economy and Society* 2: 70–88.
Mazo, J. (1974) *Dance Is A Contact Sport*. New York: Da Capo Press.
Nettleton, S. (1995) *The Sociology of Health and Illness*. Cambridge: Polity Press.
Nettleton, S. and Watson, J. (1998) (eds), *The Body in Everyday life*. London and New York: Routledge.
Patterson, E.L., Smith, R.E., Everett, J.J. and Ptacek, J.T. (1998) 'Psychological Factors as Predictors of Ballet Injuries: Interactive Effects of Life Stress and Social Support', *Journal of Sport Behaviour* (21) 1: 101–112.
Porter, M. (with Dunhill, A.) (1989) *Ballerina. A Dancer's Life*. London: Michael O'Mara Books.
Ramel, E.M. and Moritz, U. (1998) 'Psychosocial Factors at Work and Their Association with Professional Ballet Dancer's Muscoskeletal Disorders', *Medical Problems of Performing Artists* (13) 2: 66–74.
Schärli, A. (2005) *Fit to dance? – The Netherlands. A national inquiry into professional dancers' health and injury*. Amsterdam: MA thesis Vrije Universiteit.

Embodied knowledge in glassblowing: the experience of meaning and the struggle towards proficiency

Erin O'Connor

Abstract

Becoming a proficient glassblower involves an indispensable shift away from cognitive readings of practice towards corporeal readings, marking the development of proficient practical knowledge. In learning glassblowing myself in the course of an ethnography of handicrafts in New York City, the subtleties of apprenticeship, the modes of reading and understanding the practice, both cognitive and corporeal, have emerged, complexifying our understanding of the transmission, development, and modalities of practical knowledge. Such ethnographic dissection brings phenomenological considerations to bear on the question of achieving proficient practical knowledge, and enables us to sharpen our understanding of the role of meaning in practice.

Key words: glassblowing, apprenticeship, intentionality, body, practical knowledge, Bourdieu

Introduction: Coming to glassblowing

Embodiment characterizes our experience of the world. It is through embodied relations with the world, tacitly understood, that we accrue practical knowledge. Thus, when concretizing a research design for a project on craft skills, I situated myself in the field of craft, hoping to unearth and access in practice itself the tacit understandings of practical knowledge rather than pursuing purely aesthetic debates. While my research began as a comparative ethnography of ceramics, fibre arts and glassblowing, the impossibility of gaining proficiency within all three fields simultaneously soon became apparent. This is the context in which I focused on glassblowing, conducting field research at New York Glass, a not-for-profit glassblowing studio in New York City since September 2003.

New York Glass is the largest and most comprehensive public educational glass facility on the east coast.[1] Though the use of the facility is rumoured to have declined over the last seven years due to political struggles for power within the board of directors, which resulted in loss of endowments and consequent

Scheper-Hughes, N. and Locke, M.M. (1987) 'The Mindful Body. A Prolegomenon to Future Work in Medical Anthropology', *Medical Anthropology Quarterly* (1) 1: 6–41.
Seymour, L. (with Gardner, P.) (1984) *Lynn. The autobiography of Lynn Seymour*. London: Granada.
Shilling, C. (2003) *The Body and Social Theory. 2nd Edition.* London: Sage.
Synnott, A. (1993) *The Body Social: Symbolism, Self and Society*. London: Routledge.
Tajet-Foxell, B. and Rose, F.D. (1995) 'Pain and Pain Tolerance in Professional Ballet Dancers.' *British Journal of Sports Medicine* (29) 1: 31–34.
Turner, B.S. (1992) *Regulating bodies: essays in medical sociology.* London: Routledge.
Turner, B.S. (1984). *The Body and Society: Explorations in Social Theory*. Oxford: Blackwell.
Vincent, L.M. (1979) *Competing with the Sylph: Dancers and the Pursuit of the Ideal Body Form.* New York: Andrews and McMeel.
Vincent, L.M. (1998) 'Disordered Eating: Confronting the Dance Aesthetic.' *Dance Medicine & Science* (2) 1: 4–6.
Wainwright, S.P. and Turner, B.S. (2004) 'Epiphanies of embodiment: injury, identity and the balletic body', *Qualitative Research* (4) 3: 311–337.
Wainwright, S.P., Williams, C. and Turner, B.S. (2005) 'Fractured Identities; injury and the balletic body', *Health: An Interdisciplinary Journal for the Social Study of Health, Illness and Medicine* (9) 1: 49–66.
Warren, G.W. (1989) *Classical Ballet Technique*. Tampa: University of South Florida Press.
Williams, S.J. and Bendelow, G. (1998) *The Lived Body: Sociological Themes, Embodied Issues.* London and New York: Routledge.
Wolman, R. (1999) 'Body Weight and Bone Density' in Y. Koutedakis and G. Sharp (eds), *The Fit and Healthy Dancer*, pp. 249–265. New York: John Wiley and Sons.
Wulff, H. (1998) *Ballet Across Borders. Career and Culture in the World of Dancers.* Oxford and New York: Berg.

difficulty in maintaining the facilities, New York Glass is still a-bustle, used by both artists and students alike.[2] The studio offers courses throughout the year, including basic to advanced glassblowing, hot casting, kiln casting, lampworking, fusing, neon, stained glass, coldworking and bead-making. There are weekend intensive courses, one-day courses, demonstrations by visiting artists, glassblowers in residence and, of course, the daily workings of self-employed production glassblowers and glass artists.

A glassblowing studio consists of a furnace (which 'cooks' and holds molten glass at approximately 1800 degrees Fahrenheit, the glory hole (a small cylindrical furnace located in front of the workbench of the glassblower in which the glass is continuously reheated while being worked upon), and an annealer (an insulated box usually at least eight cubic feet with heating elements in which finished glass pieces are placed and then slowly brought down to room temperature). For public access use, New York Glass has two large furnaces, as well as numerous glory-holes and annealers. When arriving at New York Glass, one typically finds glassblowers at their benches, blowing vessels or sculpting objects, their assistants hustling about, top-loading finished pieces into the annealer and opening the furnace door for the glassblower to gather out glass. In a moment, one glimpses the ever-emergent inferno-like orange of molten glass from the furnace, is mesmerized by the blaze of the glory-hole at which the undulating glass is reheated to be shaped, and overwhelmed by the heady smoky scent of burning newspaper and pure unadulterated heat.

I had been blowing glass for six months when I attempted to blow a rudimentary goblet. I had accrued through practice a basic set of glassblowing skills which utilized numerous hand tools. These included gathering glass from the furnace, blowing a bubble, and forming shapes such as cylinders, bowls and plates. Though blowing a goblet called upon these skills, the process required both new skills as well as new configurations of those previously acquired. The challenge of blowing the goblet therefore was to combine learned with unlearned skills, a situation which afforded me the opportunity to evaluate how glassblowing is read by the glassblower, in varying stages of proficiency, and to reflect upon the ebb and flow of sensations, techniques, and modes of consciousness.

Reading the practice

A goblet begins with that invariable gather of glass from the furnace. I withdrew the blowpipe, a broomstick-length hollow steel tube, from the warming rack where its tip rested in a row of low blue-orange gas flames, and walked, the pipe's hot tip down, towards the furnace to gather. At the furnace my partner for the evening, Heather, slid open the coal-chute-sized iron door at hip height. I quickly dipped the heated tip of the pipe into the water bucket to remove any carbon, sending small streams of steam to my knees from the sizzling water. Between the door and the vat of molten glass was a small ledge, about six inches wide. I lifted the pipe with both hands to a horizontal position level with the ledge and gently rested the pipe, nearly at its tip, upon it. Withdrawing my left hand, I pushed the warm tip into the furnace until the edge of the ledge reached the pipe's mid-point where my left hand had been, effectively becoming a mid-point of balance. It was here, at the ledge's edge, that I felt the pipe. Just as the child tries to become more buoyant on the see-saw so that her friend may come to the ground through her effect on the mid-point of balance, I let my right hand, which still gripped the steel at the pipe's other end, become light until the pipe's warm tip within the furnace lowered toward and into the slightly undulating molten glass. Seized by the viscosity of the glass, the pipe, without a counterforce from the right hand outside, would have sunk. Instantly, my right hand set to work, the left too taking up a place just below the right, quickly rotating the pipe clockwise so as to both keep the pipe from sinking beyond three inches deep and to 'gather' the glass through twirling – much as one would gather honey by twirling a teaspoon in the honey-jar at the breakfast table. I gathered with a sense of confidence, though the over-zealousness of the grip of the glass on the blowpipe told me that the blowpipe had gone too deep. Pushing directly down on the end of pipe closest to me with my right hand, I brought the other tip out of the glass and swiftly withdrew the pipe with a mango-sized gather of glass at its tip from the furnace – the gather would be adequate for the task at hand. Heather slid the furnace door closed.[3]

I had seen gathering demonstrated, had been instructed in how to gather, and had gathered many times prior to the above-mentioned gather to blow the goblet. By the fifth week of a beginner's intensive class in the winter of 2004, we had stopped following Rob, the instructor, to the furnace to watch his initial gather. The technique of gathering had been broken down into successive moments as I had noted in my field notes during my first glassblowing days:

> We were asked to step forward individually to the furnace with our blowpipes and 'gather'. 'Just rest your pipe on the little ledge here,' Rob advised, 'just like you would on a windowsill and then just lower the tip into the glass with your right hand on the end of the pipe. Watch the reflection of the pipe in the glass rise to meet the pipe, then lower it in just a few inches and give it a few swift twirls – one, two, three – that's all you should need. Keep it on the ledge, and bring the tip of the pipe up. Place your left hand on the pipe just beneath the right, pull it up and out. Don't worry, you'll do it quick enough, because this isn't the sort of place you want to hang around too long' (Field notes, October 19, 2003).

Bringing the blowpipe into the proper holding posture, twirling the blowpipe strongly and with a steady cadence, placing it at the proper leverage point on the ledge, lowering it at the proper speed and placing its tip into the glass at the proper depth – these were all vital components to gathering successfully. We would practise these component skills independent of each other, abstracted from the actual process, as when Paul, my glassblowing instructor in the fall of 2003, recommended that we twirl broomsticks while watching TV at home to improve our finger dexterity. Although, however, the steps of the gather are

Gathering from the furnace.

explained and sometimes demonstrated distinctly, like successive points on a line, to gather proficiently is not just a matter of linking together these successive actions.

The difference in moving from one step (lifting) to the next (lowering) to the next (twirling) and yet the next (lifting again) and so forth, and being able to 'gather' begins to differentiate the gather of a novice and the gather of a proficient glassblower: the novice tends to proceed in distinctive, successive steps. Here we already see two possible sets of objects of attention for the glassblower to read amidst her practice: 1) the part that is an end in itself and 2) the part as it serves a project, a whole. When gathering for the goblet, I looked to the gather's mass and its position on the tip of the pipe in anticipation of working on it towards a goblet. Towards this end, I registered the efficacy of the gather, not the successive components or techniques of the gather, upon which my attention had been riveted in my first days of glassblowing. I did not consciously decide to continue to twirl when removing the blowpipe from the furnace, only sensed that, though a bit deep, the gather had been proficient for the purpose of blowing a goblet. This is a marked progress for the novice, who accustomed to serving the instrument then finds the 'instrument through techniques' actually becoming a part of her. In *Personal Knowledge*, Michael Polanyi discusses this process through which instruments recede from consciousness and become extensions of the body: '[T]ools . . . can never lie in the field of . . . operations; they remain necessarily on our side of it, forming part of ourselves, the operating persons. We pour ourselves out into them and assimilate them as parts of our own existence. We accept them existentially by dwelling in them' (Polanyi, 1962: 59). I had developed what Polanyi terms, a *subsidiary awareness* of the blowpipe.[4]

The objects of our subsidiary awareness 'are not watched in themselves; we watch something else while keeping intensely aware of them' (Polanyi, 1962: 55). Though my technical capability enabled my gather, I did not pay heed to each step, the distinctness of which had been insisted upon in my early days of glass-blowing, but rather attended the gather itself, the correctness of which informed, if necessary, immediate adjustments to my techniques. I knew my gathering had been apt by virtue of the gather. The objects of subsidiary awareness were not objects of attention, but rather instruments of attention. As I began the process of gathering the glass, my awareness of the blowpipe's weight in my palm receded and in its stead advanced the sensation of the ledge's edge at the blowpipe's mid-point followed by the weight of the gathering glass on the blowpipe's tip, and finally the gather towards a goblet. David Sudnow discusses the shift away from an awareness of the particularities towards the whole in regard to his jazz piano playing as an 'express aiming' or 'melodic intentionality': 'The emergence of a melodic intentionality, an express aiming for sounds, was dependent in my experience upon the acquisition of facilities that made it possible, and it wasn't as though in my prior work I had been trying and failing to make coherent note-to-note melodies' (Sudnow, 1978: 44).

As our awareness of a practice shifts into focal awareness, so too does that practice take on a *lived* character, a graceful extended movement, an arc of embodied techniques. Rob and Paul's instruction, intentional or not, had consistently encouraged a shift towards this *lived* type of awareness. While Rob may instruct, 'Bring the pipe up level with the ledge' or Paul may instruct, 'Twirl the pipe at an even pace' – bringing our attention to what had been subsidiary – they often countered this with a quick counter-instruction to refocus on the project at hand, in this case, blowing the goblet. So while Paul, observing me warming my gather in the glory-hole as prior preparation for blowing out into a bubble, would call my attention to the pace of my twirling – 'Slow it down there cowgirl. Keep it steady.' – he would also quickly thereafter refocus my attention to the task of getting the glass to the desired end, calling out over my shoulder, 'But keep your eyes on the glass!! Don't take your eyes off the glass! It's starting to hang.' By bringing the technique into focal awareness, we could hone that technique. But we were quickly urged to allow what had become a momentary object of focal awareness, the technique and tool, to slip back into subsidiary awareness, a movement of attention which, having consciously attempted to mimic the correct technique, forged a slow process of restructuring.

This is the defining exercise of apprenticeship: the apprentice fashions her practice by making an implicit technique explicit, improving and re-aligning that technique with its intended purpose, and allowing the revised technique to again recede into unconsciousness, with the effect of shaping the still nascent glassblowing element of her *habitus*, 'the system of structured, structuring dispositions' (Bourdieu, 1990: 50). Paul and Rob's direction of our attention towards technique is an abstraction of a moment from the process in which it is embedded; a moment of reflection, evaluation and decision, a moment to which we may properly refer to as reading, that process through which we retrospectively discern the meaning of, in this case, our actions or technique. That an evaluation of the gather, a reading of the glass, would necessarily be retrospective leads me to suggest that reading a skill, like glassblowing, may be the mark of the novice and, while it can improve technique through bringing it into a state of exception, it can never be an operative mechanism of proficiency. When gathering for the goblet, I did not need to evaluate each of its constitutive moments to understand the deftness of the gather. Sense-making happened otherwise than through this retrospective meaning-making.

Meaning in practice

To understand the gather was not an intellectual synthesis of successive acts by a discerning consciousness. Rather, it was bodily intentionality: 'practical, non-thetic intentionality, which has nothing in common with a *cogitatio* (or a noesis) consciously orientated towards a *cogitatum* (a noema), is rooted in a posture, a way of bearing the body (a *hexis*), a durable way of being of the durably modified body which is engendered and perpetuated, while constantly changing (within limits), in a twofold relationship, structured and structuring, to the environment' (Bourdieu, 2000: 143–144). Moreover, this bodily intentionality 'is a kind of necessary coincidence – which gives it the appearance of a pre-established harmony' (Bourdieu, 2000: 143). When I understood I effectively aligned the particular techniques with the whole intended end through bodily intentionality: 'to understand is to experience the harmony between what we aim at and what is given, between the intention and the performance – and the body is our anchorage in a world' (Merleau-Ponty, 1962: 144). The body is itself able to assimilate new significances – the 'body is that meaningful core' (Merleau-Ponty, 1962: 147). Thus, in virtue of bodily intentionality, the particular techniques become '*sense-full*'.[5] That is, the meaning of the particular lies in its incorporated lived service to, or functioning towards, the whole, not within the abstracted retrospective interpretation and consequent understanding of its function. When the interpretive effort of 'reading' the practice, understanding how the parts fit into the whole, remains salient to that practice (as essentially a semantic understanding of meaning) it forms an immense barrier to the *lived* experience of the craft as meaningful.[6]

It is not so easy as either/or, however. In fact, both types of meaning are often co-existent for novice and master. We have discussed how semantic readings of meaning are more or less necessary, depending upon the extent of incorporation of the practice. For the novice, her lived experience is likely to be informed, not from a lived practice of the meaning of the particular technique as it serves the whole, but rather from other areas of her life which help her to handle the newly encountered situation. Her adaptation is not wholly conscious; it happens at the level of the body. Her body 'catches' already-known components of glass-blowing, like heat and retrieval and with some adjustments handles and gets through the new situation with greater or lesser degrees of success. These adaptations are specifically in response to what she finds herself confronted with and, in this sense, lack an anticipatory quality. They do, however, in re-positioning the body, set up the opportunity for the restructuring of the novice's *habitus*, that system of dispositions that can anticipate, in accord with the *field*, those rules of glassblowing. Thus, through the adaptations, the glassblowing *habitus* begins to take shape and she develops a 'feel for the game' (Bourdieu, 1990: 66). As the novice progresses, her adaptations to newly presented situations in glass-blowing are grounded less and less in previous non-glassblowing experiences and more and more in her solidifying glassblowing skills, accomplished through a process of bodily restructuration.

In my attempt to blow the goblet I found that while I was able to complete the first steps (the gather and blowing the initial bubble proficiently), attaching the stem and foot were extremely difficult. Sensing the inevitability of the upcoming technical difficulty, anxiety flowed into my hands as I carried the gather on the blowpipe back to the workbench from the furnace. I blew out the bubble, paddled its bottom flat and asked my partner, Heather, to bring me a *bit*. A bit is made by gathering a small amount of glass onto the tip of the punty and shaping that gather into a slightly tapered cylinder by rolling it, called *marvering*, on a steel table, called a *marver*. I would then attach this finger-like piece of glass to the bottom of the bubble to serve as the goblet stem.

> When Heather returned with the bit I was waiting with my blowpipe positioned vertically before me, mouthpiece resting on the top of my right shoe, bubble positioned right in front of my face, left hand holding the diamond sheers that are used to pull, attach, and cut through the still hot glass bit. Heather positioned herself to my left, aligning her right shoulder with my left and centered the punty vertically in front of her body, the hot bit of gathered glass hovering just above her feet. 'Check your hands,' I called to her, attempting to linger on that sense of assuring composure and exaggerated confidence that accompanies the initial posture of a practice. She did, consciously shuffling her feet forward, closer to me, lining up our shoulders, testing that the width between us equalled the length of the punty. She placed her left hand above the right on the punty and set it into a pendulum-like swing (Field notes, April 8, 2004).

It needed to happen in a blink of an eye, as Rob and Jane, his teaching assistant, had demonstrated. It hadn't and we had to re-heat our already-too-cold pieces.

Re-positioned, Heather again swung the hot bit. Intense anticipation filled my body: 'Rob and Jane were both calling out to me, "Take it with the shears! Pull it onto the bubble!"' (Field notes, April 8, 2004). Their words called for action: I knew I needed to do as they had demonstrated – I needed to take hold of the punty with the diamond shears (imagine large scissors with curved blades that leave a diamond-shaped hole in the middle when closed), pull it towards

Popping the bubble.

Letting the bubble blow out.

Paddling the bottom of the bubble.

Marvering the bit for the stem.

the bubble before me and set the glass bit onto the bubble. I had no established rhythm, such as I had when gathering, to carry my actions. I was seized by a type of stage-fright: my body could not anticipate the right moment. Consequently, I *looked* for it: 'My eyes jumped between my stagnant bubble, Heather's swinging punty swinging with the bit and the space passing in between. I felt impotent standing there, waiting for, rather than bringing about, the correct alignment of the swinging punty and bit with the standing blowpipe and bubble' (Field notes, April 8, 2004). I visually scanned the arrangement of the object's positions, for the proximity necessary to take the punty with the diamond shears, guide it towards center of the bubble, and finally with a straight downward pull, bring the bit into contact with the bubble. I could feel the rapid movement of my eyes – it made me even more nervous – they couldn't keep the tempo, were not the proper organ, could not anticipate, but waited to receive.

I did not and in fact could not catch the spatial synthesis for which I waited. I wrote in my field notes that day:

> Heather delayed the punty in its downswing, it was stagnant. I grabbed onto it with the diamond shears, with the unease of catching baited game, and pulled it towards the bubble, and attempting to center the bit on the bottom of the bubble, began to

> pull it down. The irrevocable touch down of the bit upon the bubble happened before I could notice and Rob and Jane were already calling, 'Pull off! Pull off! You've got to pull the bit up and off the bubble!' My body was both numb and abuzz in the agitation of the unknown, hands shaking, heart racing. I drew the punty away from the bubble with the diamond shears so that the bit elongated into a semblance of a stem. They continued, 'It's going cold! Cut it! Don't wait to cut it!' Not seeing the cold of which they spoke, but knowing that I had to act immediately, I hurriedly took the shears with my right hand, clumsily positioned them on my fingertips for leverage and clamped down onto the glass: quartz-like veins of opacity broke through its clarity, as I exerted as much brute pressure as I could muster; the glass moaning under the bandying shears like paper-thin ice of a frosted sidewalk puddle under foot on a February morning (Field notes, April 8, 2004).

In my attempt to take the bit for the stem of my goblet, I had lost the ability to synthesize the movements of my hand with a greater whole body movement toward the goblet and found myself unable to attend to the technique as a whole, let alone to the goblet (something which had been possible in the initial gather and blowing of the bubble). There was no recession of a trained body into unconsciousness, operating of its own accord, as I had experienced in the gather for the goblet. In its stead, arose the bare punty, blowpipe and glass – each distinct – seemingly unrelated, but needing to be brought together as had been demonstrated. My efforts, however, to read spatially for the right moment of bodily intervention, to see when the time was right, were doomed to fail: 'Motion perceived visually remains purely kinematic. Because sight follows movement so effortlessly, it cannot help us to make that movement an integral part of our inner lives' (Bachelard, 1971: 8). Such efforts forsake what is essential to practice: temporality. Practice, whether novice or proficient, must be temporally not spatially motivated, the hallmark of non-reflective corporeal readings. Rob and Jane, in their efforts to instruct with their calls to action, set me into motion, made me temporal – my temporality needed to be primary to my corporeal configuration. Though I answered their calls with motion, I could not find quite the right way to handle the situation and therefore crassly mimicked what I had seen in the demonstration – the reaching out for the swinging punty and adherence of the bit to the bubble – gauging this spatially with my vision not temporally with my body. In my interjection into the process I seemed out-of-time, an interloper.

The inability to experience the particulars within a lived relation to the whole – when the glass, pipe, and shears become separated from blowing the goblet – when we are frozen in a moment of *ek-stasis* from the practice – lacks corporeal comprehension. Until the moment of taking the bit for the stem, we have seen that the embodied knowledge accrued was informed through a certain guided instruction that led my body to a better practice – a 'practical mimesis (or mimeticism) which implies an overall relation of identification and has nothing in common with an *imitation* that would presuppose a conscious effort to reproduce a gesture, an utterance or an object explicitly constituted as a model' (Bourdieu, 1990: 73). Similarly, Loïc Wacquant deemed mimesis the vehicle of transmission of pugilistic knowledge: 'Pugilistic knowledge is thus transmitted by mimeticism or countermimeticism, by watching how others do things, scrutinizing their moves, spying on their responses to DeeDee's [the coach's] instructions, copying their routine, by imitating them more or less consciously – in other words, outside the explicit intervention of the coach' (Wacquant, 2004: 117). Imitation, for Wacquant, like Bourdieu, is not the reproduction of an object in an image, but rather is the transformative process, both dynamic and corporeal, by which the novice translates visual observations into corporeal action and incorporation: 'It's exhilarating to be shadowboxing next to the Illinois state champion! I watch Curtis like a hawk out of the corner of my eye and try to reproduce all of his gestures: hooks and short jabs; nervous, fast, sharp movements with a "give" of the shoulder; nimble and precise footwork. I imitate him as best I can, and in the enthusiasm of the moment I frankly feel like a real boxer' (Wacquant, 2004: 118). It is this corporeal comprehension through practical mimesis that lacked in my practice, such that following my attempt to take the bit, I daydreamed while heating at the glory hole – an additional form of *ekstasis*, non-integrated and irrelevant to the task at hand.

Placing the bit onto the bubble had been gruelling and I was exhausted. I turned, pipe with glass in hand, towards the comforting glory-hole, that blazing barrel-like furnace, where the glassblower warms the glass on the end of her pipe with soothing rhythmic rotations.

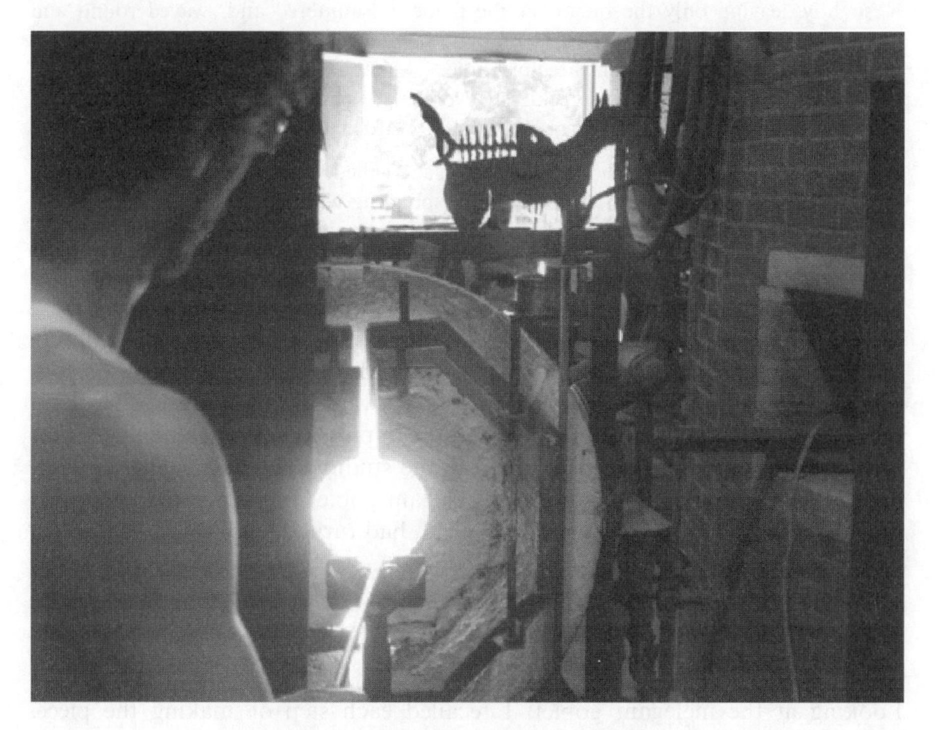

Heating the piece at the glory hole.

I was immensely relieved and my body fell into that familiar mode, my fingers automatically twirling the pipe to that long-established rhythm, my eyes looking nowhere into the glory-hole. Slowly becoming caught up in the flickering texture of heat – its white, orange and grey hues running around the furnace's walls, framing the rotating glass – I became mesmerized and I day-dreamed:

> During the process of reheating the bit three times in order for me to 'shorten' it, I had amazing visions at the glory hole. Not amazing visions, but I can't escape the glass constantly conforming to phallic or sexual images. The glass started to move, the heat of the glory hole awakening its fluidity, its rounded end making gentle revolutions. I could not act on it; it was too charming, too intimate: I wanted to follow it, to see where it was going, where it could take me. I just stared at these still timid revolutions, pleased that it answered within a moment my own gestures. I kept the bubble, the goblet's bowl, and the bit, the goblet's stem, rotating. My body faded away – into the rotating blowpipe, my eyes becoming increasingly captivated by the movements of the softening glass. My bubble became testicles, flaming orange, and the bit, the stem, on the end became a searching penis, swirling around as it softened with the heat. Though attached to my pipe it seemed to swim outwards, bounded within the course white-peach-tangerine walls of the glory hole – the breathing red embers below, the roar of the bathing gas flame – was it nice in there? Why did I seem to be cutting through the lake? Moving ever-outwards within the brilliant fiery red of the glory hole, the bit shortened and the penis reformed to a sperm, swimming towards me, the short tail struggling to propel the head up my blowpipe. I withdrew the blowpipe slightly, leaving only the bit under the flame: it sauntered and swayed round and round, directing the piece towards me. The sauntering amused me – I didn't mind. I wanted to keep the glass in the glory hole: I was relieved to become a spectator, to become captivated. The stem recklessly overheated, sauntered and swayed round and round – an enraged white sperm swimming towards me. (Field notes, April 8, 2004).
>
> 'Ok, flash! You're going to lose the piece' Jane called, waiting for me at the bench. 'Oh yeah,' I thought, both jumping and responding with lethargic reluctance to the call to make myself vulnerable once again to the unknown of blowing the goblet. (Field notes, April 8, 2004).

Jane called my attention back to the piece, directing me to heat the stem – reasonably – and then to shorten it by holding the pipe, glass up, when coming out of the glory hole so that the hot glass sagged. I began to once again recognize the piece as a 'goblet' and eagerly worked toward that end, sincerely evoking my skills to the best of my ability – I had the impression of finishing an elegant piece. To my surprise, when I returned to the studio a few days later to pick it up, my goblet in no way resembled the elegant goblet I remembered placing in the annealer to cool. My goblet, Rob joked, had turned 'globlet'.

Proficiency in pactice

Looking at the inelegant goblet, I recalled each step of making the piece, blowing out the bowl of the goblet, attaching and pulling out the stem,

The 'globlet'.

humming a smooth rhythm for the turns of the pipe to fall into, pressing the small glass disc for the foot of the goblet – in the end everything had seemed to fall together, but these memories and impressions were at odds with what I held in my hand. How did I go wrong?

We have already discussed how a reading of the practice cannot be an operative principle of proficiency, as it calls for an interruption of practice, in virtue of the abstraction and reflection it requires. We have also seen that confronted with the new, a type of interruption, an individual will draw from previous experience in order to manage the new situation, a type of corporeal adaptation anchored in the person's already established *habitus*. Proficient glassblowers have often said that glassblowing is not about blowing the perfect piece of glass, but coming up with effective solutions to all the problems that consistently present themselves in the process of glassblowing (Field notes, March 19, 2004). They nudge towards the idea that *non-reflective anticipation* is the force of proficiency, neither non-reflective, nor reflective adaptation. It is '[that] almost miraculous encounter between the *habitus* and a field, between incorporated history and an objectified history, which makes possible the near-perfect anticipation of the future inscribed in all the concrete configurations' (Bourdieu, 1990: 66).

This anticipation that marks proficient practical knowledge is not a reflective forward-looking gesture. It is a non-reflective corporeal forward-going movement beyond adaptation achieved through training: 'Training teaches the movements – that is the most obvious part – but it also inculcates in a practical manner the schemata that allow one to better differentiate, distinguish, evaluate, and eventually reproduce these movements. It sets into motion a dialectic of corporeal mastery and visual mastery: to understand what you have to do, you watch the others box, but you do not truly see what they are doing unless you have already understood a little with your eyes, that is to say, with your body' (Wacquant, 2004: 118). My body, while making the goblet, did not have this corporeal sight. Does an account, however, of corporeal anticipation achieved through training or rather the lack of it, help us fully to understand the failure of the goblet? It seems that an account of the development of proficiency must attend not only to the development of bodily techniques, those dispositions through which one can anticipate, but also to the material of practice itself and the forged sensibilities of the material's properties in practice. That is, to an account of the body of the practitioner, we must also bring an account of the body, or bodies, with which he or she works – whether glass, or other boxers.

Consider Jane's direction of my attention towards the heats of the glass to form the stem. She bid me to pay attention to the material in hand, to attend to the glass. The greater part of my focus, however, was towards vision of a goblet of elegance and grace. Perhaps, this vision itself was immature and Jane's encouragement to tend the glass not only directed my attention towards technique, but towards understanding the properties of the material itself, such as the relationship between degrees of heat and the ability to lengthen or shorten a piece. While the blindness of my body surely limited my ability to achieve the goblet, so also, it seems in retrospection, did my inability to 'see' despite how eagerly I 'looked' and 'saw'.

The image towards which I consciously executed techniques was itself, despite its exquisiteness before me, a caricature: a big ballooned goblet from a Crate & Barrel window, or a festive wedding scene from Boccaccio's *Decamerone*. I wanted to see, but perhaps could not yet see that which had animated my nascent envisioned piece, the glass itself. As Bachelard writes of the poet in his contemplation of nature, of which fire, heat and glass surely belong, '[C]ontemplated nature aids contemplation, [in] that it already contains some means of contemplation' (Bachelard, 1971: 77). In making the goblet, my imagination, though reaching towards, was not yet animated by the glass. It was not yet material – material imagination is 'this amazing need for penetration which, going beyond the attractions of the imagination of forms, thinks matter, dreams it, lives in it, or, in other words, materializes the imaginary' (Bachelard, 1971: 37). It is not the positing of material, or substance, or content, but the opening of a material dimension within training, within mimeticism and countermimeticism, that simultaneously opens the possibility for proficiency in glassblowing.

When we write that the proficiency of corporeal knowledge is defined by the interrelatedness of habitus and field and the body's consequent ability to anticipate and that this anticipation is possible only when the practitioner understands the world's imminence in which she operates and is therefore able to act immediately, we must flesh out the flesh of that world, its materiality.

Conclusion

I now remember the hesitance that flitted across the face of my instructor, Rob, when I suggested that he demonstrate how to blow a goblet:

> 'Anything but that,' he said slightly bowing and waving his hands as if before a daunting task, 'For a goblet, I have to be warmed up. Maybe at the end of class.' Since no one else had another suggestion, however, Rob begrudgingly began the demonstration, 'I guess that I could show you how to blow out the bottom for a goblet at least.' But, he did it all and the demonstration was more daunting than any of us could have foreseen; the complexity of blowing the piece was unparalleled to anything we had done before. I felt amazed and moved by something completely new. When Rob asked what I was going to blow, I answered with a semi-shrug – 'A goblet, I guess.' (Field notes, April 8, 2004).

The shrug came not from my indifference, but rather from the humility brought on by the complexity of the demonstration. I was unsure of my ability to navigate myself through the making journey.

I had not yet realized that 'navigation', though perhaps seeing me through to the end, and consequently landing me with a stout 'globlet', involved an extremely complex set of readings, informed by sensation, reverie, imagination, memory, reflection, adaptation. Nor had I realized that it was not and never would be any of these readings, though necessary as they may be to the dialectic of apprenticeship, through which the *habitus* is restructured. Only through the arduous process of developing that corporeal sight, a indubitably materially embedded endeavor in glassblowing, does the glassblower become proficient and house the capacity to anticipate the necessary.

Acknowledgements

I am very grateful to everyone at New York Glass for allowing me to carry out my research in their facilities and for the time they have taken for casual discussions and interviews. Special thanks to my beginning glassblowing instructors, Rob Panepinto and Jane Royal. Their patient instruction was the backbone of this article. I am incredibly indebted to the ongoing support and valuable insights of Craig Calhoun, Richard Sennett and Terry Williams. I would also like to thank Edward S. Casey, Michael Jackson, Chris Shilling and Loïc Wacquant for their encouragement and constructive comments. A version of this chapter was first published in Ethnography.

Notes

1 Glassblowing requires a serious commitment as well as a significant financial investment. The facilities needed to blow glass are too expensive for but a few to afford for themselves, so studios tend to be shared by both novices and experts, hobbyists and professionals. Few students continue the practice beyond a beginning level and even fewer intend to become professionals. The professionals work freelance, generally selling their pieces for resale in department stores or boutiques in the city or to private individuals. They also subsidize their freelance earnings through teaching enrolled courses or as a private instructor. Many are also artists in other mediums, such as music, painting and drawing. The students vary from dissatisfied bankers to retired physics teachers to searching hipsters. For most students a general yearning to create, to make, to express themselves, coupled with some previous exposure to and consequent fascination with glassblowing, a TV programme or a demonstration seen in a tourist artisan village, brought them to glass. Most glassblowing in the United States is 'studio' glassblowing, as distinct from Venetian style.

2 New York Glass claims use of its facilities by over 350 artists and 900 students a year. The number of 'regulars' is not nearly so high.

3 This particular gather was in April 2004. By the fall of 2005, my understanding of how to gather had dramatically changed. Rather than gathering by lowering and raising the pipe like a see-saw, one should push the pipe into and pull out of the glass. By pulling the pipe out of the glass with a rather quick motion the glass 'falls' off the end of the pipe, meaning that while some of the glass is wrapped around the pipe itself, most of it is 'off' the end of the pipe, like a push-up popsicle is frozen not around, but 'off' the stick.

4 Merleau-Ponty's famous discussion of the incorporation of the blind man's stick from an object in hand to an extension of his phenomenal body: 'The blind man's stick has ceased to be an object for him, and is no longer perceived for itself; its point has become an area of sensitivity, extending the scope and active radius of touch, and providing a parallel to sight. In the exploration of things, the length of the stick does not enter expressly as a middle term: the blind man is rather aware of it through the position of objects than of the position of objects through it. . . . To get used to a hat, a car or a stick is to be transplanted into them, or conversely, to incorporate them into the bulk of our own body. Habit expresses our power of dilating our being-in-the-world, or changing our existence by appropriating fresh instruments' (Merleau-Ponty, 1962: 143).

5 'To understand practical understanding, one has to move beyond the alternatives of thing and consciousness, mechanistic materialism and constructive idealism. More precisely, one has to discard the mentalism and intellectualism which lead to a view of the practical relation to the world as a "perception" and of that perception as a "mental synthesis" – without ignoring the practical work of construction, which as Jacques Bourveresse observes, "implements non-conceptual forms of organization" that owe nothing to the intervention of language' (Bourdieu, 2000: 136).

6 In this sense I disagree with William Sewell who, taking culture to be 'the semiotic aspect of human social practice,' argues that 'to engage in cultural practice is to make use of a semiotic code to do something in the world' (Sewell, 1999: 48–51). Tacit understandings are accrued through practice and make experience meaningful. Meaningful practice is not couched in an understanding of the relations of signs, but rather in corporeality and materiality.

References

Bachelard, G. (1971) *On Poetic Imagination and Reverie*. (edited and translated by C. Gaudin). Dallas, Texas: Spring Publications, Inc.

Bourdieu, P. (1990) *The Logic of Practice*. trans. Richard Nice. Cambridge, England: Polity Press.

Bourdieu, P. (2000) *Pascalian Meditations*, trans. Richard Nice. Stanford, California: Stanford University Press.

Merleau-Ponty, M. (1962) *The Phenomenology of Perception*. London: Routledge.
Polanyi, M. (1962) *Personal Knowledge: Towards a Post-Critical Philosophy*. Chicago: University of Chicago Press.
Sewell, W.H., Jr. (1999) 'The Concepts of Culture', in V. Bonnell & L. Hunt (eds), *Beyond the Cultural Turn*. Los Angeles: University of California Press.
Sudnow, D. (1978) *Ways of the Hand*. Cambridge: Harvard University Press.
Wacquant, L. (2004) *Body & Soul: Ethnographic Notebooks of an Apprentice Boxer*. Berkeley: University of California Press.

Vulnerable/dangerous bodies? The trials and tribulations of sleep

Simon J. Williams

Abstract

Sleep provides us with a unique vantage point on the sociology of *living in/as a body*. We are sleeping as well as waking beings. Sleeping, moreover, is *embodied* and *embedded* in the social world. Whilst many of us derive great comfort or pleasure from our sleep, this chapter explores the other face of sleep, namely the vulnerabilities and dangers it embodies and engenders, potentially at least, to self and others. This in turn provides the basis, towards the end of the chapter, for a broader series of sociological reflections on the growing problematization or politics of sleep in a 24/7 risk society where sleep is now becoming a matter of 'public concern'. Sleep, it is concluded, is a crucial yet sociologically overlooked aspect of our embodiment; a shared embodied vulnerability that, at one and the same time, unites and divides us.

Key words: Sleep, embodiment, vulnerability, danger, emotion, trust, risk, blame

Introduction

The starting point of this chapter is that we are sleeping as well as waking beings. It is only relatively recently, however, that sociologists have begun to wake up to this embodied fact and accord sleep the proper attention it deserves. Corporeal themes of *living in/as a body* do not begin and end with waking life. Sleep, moreover, is *embodied* and *embedded* in the social world. As such it merits far greater attention from corporeal sociologists than it has received to date.

In this chapter I wish to take a closer look at the particular if not peculiar *vulnerabilities* and *dangers* that sleep *embodies* and *engenders*.[1] The first part of the chapter provides what may be construed as a preliminary phenomenological sketch of sleep in terms of living in/as a body in general, and the disappearing body/self in particular. This in turn paves the way, in the second part of the chapter, for a more detailed examination of the embodied vulnerabilities and dangers of sleep in relation to self and others. Sleep, however, as I argue in the third section of the chapter, is far from simply a passive state that just 'happens' to us. Rather, it is brought under our own *partial* control through a series of sleep-related habits, routines and rituals, including (reflexive) body techniques which help facilitate safe passage into and out of the sleep role. The remainder of the chapter, building on these embodied insights, involves a broader series of sociological reflections on sleep in a 24/7 risk society as a matter of 'public concern' where themes of vulnerability, vigilance and virtue loom large across the public-private divide.

The dormant/dreaming body and the disappearing self: I sleep therefore I am (not)?

An encounter or engagement with sleep raises a host of complex philosophical as well as sociological issues. Sleep, indeed, has been the source of much philosophical speculation and debate through the ages, from the ancient Greeks to the present day. Descartes' deliberations on sleep and dreams are particularly instructive in this respect. Sleep, for obvious reasons, posed a potential problem in terms of Descartes classic formulation *cogito ergo sum* (I think therefore I am). Either we cease to exist when we sleep (I sleep therefore I am not) given the loss of consciousness it entails, or else some other explanation or qualifying clause is necessary in the case of sleep and other states of unconsciousness. Descartes' own particular resolution of this conundrum, unsurprisingly perhaps, favoured the latter line of reasoning, namely that we are never entirely unconscious, even in the deepest, soundest sleep. We also, of course, dream. Yet dreaming, for Descartes, posed another problem as to whether or not there are any 'sure signs' or 'definite marks' that enable us to *know for certain* we are awake rather than dreaming, or dreaming rather than awake. Descartes, to be sure, was not the first nor the last philosopher to pose this problem; both Plato before him and Bertrand Russell after him raised similar doubts about the dream-awake distinction. Descartes, however, as part and parcel of his principle of 'methodic doubt', is particularly troubled by this problem in *The Meditations*. Thus in the first meditation he doubts whether there are any such grounds for distinguishing one state from the other. By the sixth meditation, however, Descartes appears to have regained confidence in his ability reliably to distinguish dreams from wakefulness, thereby dismissing his previous doubts as 'laughable', in part because God would not allow him to be so deceived and in part because dreams are 'never joined with all the other actions of life by the memory as is the case with actions that occur when one is awake' (Descartes, 1996/1641, Sixth Meditation: 89).

Another awkward philosophical question arises at this point as to whether or not sleep itself may be regarded as the necessary or indispensable condition of (self) consciousness. Johnstone Jnr (1973), for example, is a strong advocate of this claim, arguing that it is only by virtue of the 'interruption' or 'gap' in consciousness which states such as sleep afford us, that we become *aware* of being conscious at all. Without sleep, in other words, the very notion of consciousness and unconsciousness would have little or no meaning. This, to be sure, is a bold statement which accords sleep pride of place in any debate on consciousness; a kind of 'absent presence', and a profound one at that. It is equally possible if not more plausible, however, to argue precisely the opposite case, namely that it is consciousness itself which makes sleep an intelligible phenomenon, not the other way around. 'The phenomenon of sleep and related interruptions of consciousness', in other words, 'are intelligible, if and only if, one is aware of his (sic) own consciousness *prior* to such an interruption' (Galloway, 1977: 110, my emphasis).

But what precisely is sleep anyway? What are its defining hallmarks and how are we to distinguish it from waking life? Answers to these questions are not quite as simple as they seem. Certainly sleep cannot be equated with going to bed, lying down, closing our eyes or the partaking of rest. I may, for example, lie in bed, eyes tightly closed, without getting a wink of sleep all night long. It is possible moreover to sleep standing up with our eyes wide open. We are also quite busy when we sleep, including fervent brain wave activity when we dream, the maintenance of basic bodily functions such as heartbeat and respiration, and other replenishing, repair and restorative work. Two key features nonetheless, in keeping with the foregoing discussion, stand out as defining criteria: first, the *perceptual barrier* that sleep erects between us and the waking world, and; second, the relatively rapid *reversibility* of sleep compared to other bodily states such as coma or death (Dement with Vaughan, 2000). We *live through* sleep, in other words, unlike death.

Phenomenologically speaking, sleep may be regarded as a 'withrawal from the intersubjective world' through a 'radical alteration in the tension of consciousness' (Schutz, 1974: 46). Upon waking, 'my activities of consciousness begin where they left off before I went to sleep' (Ibid). Between my withdrawal from the everyday life-world and my return to it, however, 'time has not stood still' (Ibid). I live through world time, that is to say, as 'transcending "my time"' (yesterday was Sunday, today is Monday) (Ibid). Cast in bodily terms, what this amounts to is a phenomenological transition from an *ecstatic* modality in which the body projects outwards in experience to a *recessive* modality in which the body falls back into unexperiencable depth (Leder, 1990). Dreams, to be sure, as noted earlier, restore an experiential process; but a preliminary severance from waking involvement, Leder (1990: 57) rightly argues, is necessary in order to dream. It is this 'severance', this loss of consciousness to the world that is shared by all phases of sleep. We can only ever access the sleeping body *indirectly*, moreover: 'Where "it" is "I", as conscious perceiving subject, necessarily am not' (Leder, 1990: 58). Upon awakening, for example, I may fallibly piece together the nature, quality and quantity of my sleep. How do I feel, am I (still) tired, did I get enough sleep? Others too of course provide another indirect route to the nature and quality of my sleep life, whether our nearest and dearest or the technician in the sleep laboratory.

Sleep, therefore, these indirect modes of recovery or apprehension notwithstanding, involves a certain 'absence' from self and others. Sleep, moreover, is not something I can directly will, command or control, try as I might. Rather, sleep comes over us, or creeps up on us. We *fall* asleep. I may look to sleep, mimic sleep, ritually play at sleep, or indirectly try to influence its occurrence in a variety of ingenious ways but, try as I might, sleep comes of its own accord (cf. Merleau-Ponty, 1962). The harder I try to sleep, indeed, the more likely it is to elude or evade me and the worse I am likely to feel. I may even become anxious about my sleep, knowing I need it but being unable to get it. My (incessant) wakefulness, in this case, itself becomes a 'problem', thereby transforming my normal mode of corporeal *dis*-appearance into a state of corporeal *dys*-appearance (cf. Leder, 1990). Alternatively, I may actually experience my own bodily need, drive or desire for sleep as a 'problem', something to be fought against or resisted, given my own waking projects or plans, thereby transforming my body again into a state of corporeal *dys-appearance* (Crossley, 2004).

Between deep sleep and alert wakefulness, nonetheless, lie a range of 'intermediate positions' or 'transitional states' through which I 'cyclically move' (Leder, 1990). This includes light sleep, half sleep, dream states and various other twilight or hypnagogic experiences (cf. Mavromatis, 1987) that hover somewhere between the ecstastic (the I can) and the recessive (the I cannot) (Leder, 1990). Lucid dreaming is particularly interesting on this count, given the fact that people are consciously aware they are dreaming, when they are dreaming (ie, *'I am dreaming this'*), hence the term *lucid* dreaming (see, for example, La Berge, 1985). They may even, in rare or fleeting instances begin to take control of their dream world. This in turn suggests that: (i) the statement 'I am asleep', contra Malcolm (1959), is perhaps possible (ie, that people 'can and do have dream experiences in which they are aware of being asleep and dreaming' (Mavromatis, 1987: 104–5)); (ii) dreams are no mere fabrications we conjure upon waking, and; (iii) we can perhaps, to the extent that lucid dreams are influenced by us in this fashion, be 'sinful' or 'immoral' in our dreams (see, for example, Flanagan, 2000).

A further important qualification to the foregoing discussion arises at this point, namely that we are never entirely 'cut off' from or 'dead to' the intersubjective world, even when asleep. Not only is sleep a rapidly reversible state, it involves a *partial* or *selective* rather than total screening of external stimuli. Some things may not wake us but others surely will: the gentle calling of our name, perhaps, or the slightest stirrings of a mother's newborn baby. A strong enough stimuli, if all else fails, will usually arouse us and bring us back into the waking world, happily or otherwise. This therefore, harking back to previous Cartesian formulations, implies a *partial* rather than a total loss of self/world in sleep: we remain, to varying degrees, socially 'attuned' or 'attentive' whilst we sleep. Our intentional threads to the intersubjective world, in short, as Merleau-Ponty (1962) reminds us, are 'never entirely severed'. We are never entirely sleepers, not even in the deepest darkest moments of sleep.

Safe and sound in our beds? The embodied vulnerabilities and dangers of sleep(iness)

Embedded in the foregoing discussion are further important questions regarding the embodied *vulnerabilities* and *dangers* of sleep(iness), both to self and others. We are all, of course, by virtue of our fleshy, mortal, embodiment, vulnerable creatures in sickness and in health: beings unto death. Sleep, it is clear, whilst undoubtedly a source of great comfort and pleasure, sanctuary and salvation for many of us, renders us vulnerable or dangerous, *potentially* at least, in all sorts of ways.

A number of points may be raised in support of this contention. For a start, the loss of waking consciousness and control that sleep involves renders me vulnerable both to other waking agents who may do me 'harm' and to my (absent) self. It is true of course that we all have to sleep at some time or other. Sleep, in this respect, may well be construed as a great leveller: 'thy indifferent judge between high and low', to quote Sir Philip Syndey's famous phrase. Waking agents, nonetheless, have a distinct advantage by virtue of their wakefulness over those who sleep. The power balance, as such, is firmly tilted in favour of waking agents whilst we sleep. Whilst I am asleep, for example, burglars may tip-toe into my house, steal my goods, and leave me with few worldly possession when I awake the next morning. I may even be attacked in the night or killed in my sleep, being caught 'unaware' or 'off my guard'. Raids too, for good reason, are often conducted in the middle of the night or early hours of the morning when people are asleep in their beds and hence at their most vulnerable. *Feigning* sleep, in contrast, goes someway towards reversing this power imbalance, lulling waking agents into a false sense of security through the guise or mantle of sleep (Schwartz, 1970).

Matters do not end here, however. We are also *vulnerable to ourselves*, given the loss of bodily control sleep effects. Sleep disorders, for example, come in many shapes and sizes, from sleep apnoea (colloquially known as the 'midnight strangler') through the horrors of the nightmare to restless leg syndrome (Kryger *et al.*, 2005). Take sleep paralysis (SP) and sleep walking (somnambulism), for instance. The former, (SP), is a sleep-wake cycle disturbance occurring in the transition *into* or *out of* sleep which involves feelings of paralysis for several seconds or minutes, often accompanied by hypnagogic experiences. This may include auditory and visual hallucinations, a sense of an evil presence or pressure on the chest (the so-called 'incubus' or 'old hag') and associated feelings of choking, suffocating, floating or out-of-body sensations (see, for example, Cheyne *et al.*, 1999). Unlike the nightmare, however, SP is a waking experience that may result in feelings of abject terror. Beliefs about demonic attacks, paranormal experiences, even alien abductions, are common, moreover, despite prevailing physiological explanations. Weisgerber's (2004) study of SP sufferers use of the Internet, for example, clearly suggests that far from dispelling these myths surrounding the disorder, the interactions of on-line bulletin board members of the SP community actually reinforced them by offering a forum for the articulation and discussion of alternative (ie, non-medical) explanatory frameworks.

Somnambulists, in contrast, may quite literally find themselves walking into all sorts of trouble. Perhaps the most recent illustration of this, reported in the British national press, concerned a 15-year-old girl who was rescued after she went sleep -walking and ended up on the arm of a 130- foot crane! On spotting the girl, a passer-by dialled 999, prompting a dramatic rescue operation by emergency services to reach the girl who was *unaware of the danger she was in*. Asked to comment on this seemingly bizarre event, a sleep expert stated that he was not at all surprised by the incident: 'I treat people who have driven cars, ridden horses and even attempted to fly a helicopter', he said (Ebrahim, quoted in Marsh, 2005).

It is not simply a case of the sleepers' vulnerability to self/others, however. Others may also be vulnerable to us when we sleep. We may, in other words, be a *danger to others by virtue of our sleeping bodies.* I may lash out at my partner in my sleep, for example, dealing her a violent, albeit unintentional, blow. Cases have also been reported of murders committed whilst asleep, acquittal hanging or falling on this dormant criterion. Jules Lowe, for example, in a recent court case in Manchester, was acquitted of murdering his father Eddie after he, with the help of a sleep expert, convinced the jury that he was sleep-walking at the time.

Bodies then, as this suggests, may behave quite 'badly' when we sleep, placing both self and others at risk. We are, in this respect, socially as well as physically vulnerable given the potentially *embarrassing* or *stigmatizing*, if not criminal, consequences of these dormant acts.

There is however a further important dimension to this picture of the embodied vulnerabilities of sleep, one hinted at earlier, which has less to do with the actual state of *being* asleep, or even the act of *feigning* sleep, than with the embodied vulnerabilities that *lack* of sleep, particularly prolonged or sustain lack of sleep, engenders. The effects of sleep deprivation, as this suggests, are likely to vary depending on the nature and type of sleep deprivation in question. *Total* sleep deprivation, for example, is a very different case from *limited* or *partial* sleep deprivation. Effects, moreover, are likely to vary from individual to individual. The longer I go without sleep, however, the more I am likely to suffer in one way or another. I am liable, for example, to feel increasingly tired and sleepy – itself variable throughout any twenty-four period due to circadian rhythms within the body – to find cognitive and motor tasks more difficult to perform, to become more sensitive to pain, to become moody, irritable or downright bad tempered, even to hallucinate or become paranoid. Body temperature, immune functioning and health status may also be affected in due course. Whether or not total sleep deprivation is lethal is difficult to assess, for obvious ethical reasons. Results from animal studies, nonetheless, clearly suggest that eventual death results (see, for example, Rechtschaffen *et al.*, 1989).

Sleep deprivation, it is claimed, is a common complaint in a 24/7 society, the costs and consequences of which are still being counted. There is, however, a darker more disturbing side to the sleep deprivation story in which our own embodied need for sleep is used against us for various dubious ends and purposes. A common theme in our pilot work on women's experiences of (not) sleeping in contexts of domestic violence (for example, Williams, *et al.*, 2004; Lowe *et al.*, 2007)[2] was being woken or stopped from sleeping as part of the abuse ('don't you dare go to sleep'). Related themes included being afraid to sleep too deeply ('sleeping on your guard'); fear of being attacked or even killed whilst asleep; sleeping with weapons of self-defence by the bed; taking/timing sleep when perpetrators of domestic violence were out or about to sleep themselves; fighting constant fatigue and other physical and emotional signs of abuse and sleep deprivation; use of alcohol, street and prescription drugs to manage sleep, and; continuing 'bad' or 'poor' sleep (including bad dreams) after the domestic violence had ended, particularly when court cases or child contact was imminent. The impact of domestic violence on children's sleep was also a prominent theme in these women's accounts, including disturbed sleep, night waking, bed-wetting and episodes of shouting and crying in their sleep.

What we see here in effect is the way in which power relations are re/constituted in and through the 'control' of sleep, thereby rendering these women and children vulnerable. Sleep deprivation in such circumstances is part and parcel of a regime to establish a docile and powerless victim whose own response is dulled or blunted through these very means (Lowe *et al.*, 2007). There are direct links here, moreover, to the use of sleep deprivation in other contexts as an instrument of interrogation, punishment or torture, a very effective one at that, given it leaves no obvious physical marks or traces on its victims. These techniques or tactics, indeed, have a long history in both the East and West. Perhaps the most recent well publicized case of these principles in practice concerns the euphemistically described 'sleep management', 'dietary manipulation' and 'stress position' techniques used by US military personnel in Abu Ghraib and Guatanamo Bay. Debates on the legality of these techniques continues. Their 'efficacy' in breaking down even the most recalcitrant of victims, nonetheless, is surely beyond doubt, the very reason indeed for their continuing deployment, legal or otherwise.

To these observations on the darker side of sleep deprivation, we may of course add the plight of those who, for whatever reason, spend their lives sleeping 'rough' on the street. Sleep, for example, as Rensen's (2003) insightful ethnography of sleeping rough on the streets of Amsterdam shows, is a 'rare privilege' for the majority of outside sleepers. Even resting is 'scarcely possible', given the nature of street life and the embodied vulnerabilities it entails. The homeless, as such, may exist in a liminal state somewhere between fatigue and half-sleep. Sleeping outside, in this respect, is almost always a 'compromise' which itself embodies 'numerous facets of homelessness'. Placing these issues in global perspective, moreover, provides a further important reminder of the precarious sleep and unenviable sleeping arrangements of those living in other adverse conditions (be it poverty, overcrowding, famine, flood or bloodshed) around the world today.

Whilst sleep then, to summarize, may well be a corporeal release or pleasure to be anticipated and savoured, it also embodies and engenders its own potential vulnerabilities and dangers, not simply when we *do* sleep but also when we *do not* sleep, both for self and others (with or without bed and abode) across the public-private divide.

Going to bed/doing sleeping: emotion, habit, trust and routine

The danger in the foregoing analysis is that it paints an overly passive picture of sleep, or perhaps more correctly the sleeper, and that it fosters a largely negative impression that sleep is all about dangers, hazards, risks and vulnerabilities. Yet sleep as I have already stressed, is a corporeal pleasure for many if not all of us, something we look forward to if not welcome as a vital social 'release'. It is also something we *actively* try to manage or 'do' (cf. Taylor, 1993) in our daily/nightly lives, thereby placing it under our own *partial* control. But what precisely does this partial control involve or entail?

A number of points may be made here with respect to 'going to bed' and 'doing' sleeping. For a start, from a physical and spatial viewpoint, we tend to sleep, 'rough' sleepers notwithstanding, in specially designated places and spaces, usually though not always in the privacy and comfort of our own homes, or our bedrooms to be more precise. Sleep and residency, as Schwartz (1970) astutely notes, are intimately related, thereby tying bed to abode and dormancy to domicile. In going to bed, moreover, I may go through a series of more or less elaborate checking routines and rituals designed to put my mind at rest and ensure, as best I can, my own (and other family members) safety and security whilst I/we sleep. I may, for example, bolt the door, close the windows, set the alarm, and check various other pieces of equipment that need to be turned off for the night are turned off. I should also, of course, if I am diligent or safety-conscious, check the smoke alarms at least once a week to make sure they perform their duty of night watchmen, alerting us to any danger, whilst we sleep in our beds.

These routines and rituals are part and parcel of other more explicit body-centred routines and rituals involved in going to bed and going to sleep, practices which help *prepare* us for sleep or *facilitate* our passage into this dormant state. In going to bed, for example, I may go to the bathroom, clean my teeth, change out of my day clothes, put on my pyjamas, climb into bed and set the alarm clock. I may also take a warm bath, have a milky drink, read in bed for a little while, listen to the radio, or perhaps if I am having particular difficulty with my sleep, take a sleeping tablet or some herbal remedy to lull me into the land of Nod. These seemingly humble bed-time rituals and routines, moreover, may be particularly elaborate in the case of young children, including bathing, bed-time stories, lullabies, tucking in or swaddling, kissing goodnight and so forth (Ben-Ari, 2005). Similarly, upon awakening the next morning, I may go through a series of more or less elaborate 'reverse' routines and rituals that help ease or facilitate my passage back into the waking world, including a return to the bathroom, the brushing of my teeth, washing, shaving and dressing, having breakfast and so forth.

What we have here, in effect, is a *status* or *role passage* which itself is mediated or facilitated by a 'transition phase' or 'interactional membrane' (cf. Goffman, 1961; Schwartz, 1970) of the utmost importance for any successful or accomplished movement to and from the waking world, or into and out of the 'sleep role' if you prefer (Schwartz, 1970). Sleep, from this perspective, is *mediated* by way of a series of body techniques, rituals and practices (cf. Mauss, 1973/1934; Bourdieu, 1984) which bring it under our own partial control: an important reminder of the learnt as well as the unlearnt, reflexive as well as the pre-reflexive, purposive as well was the non-purposive, personal as well as the pre-personal, elements of this embodied transition into and out of waking life (Crossley, 2004). It is not simply a case of the individual preparing for bed because they are tired or sleepy, however, but of *growing tired* or *sleepy* in and through these preparatory phases, processes or practices; a 'reciprocity of motive and action in the sleep role', as Schwartz (1970: 488–91) appositely puts it. These techniques and rituals, moreover, provide a crucial means of establishing *ontological security* and *basic trust* (cf. Giddens, 1984). Trust and security, reciprocally, are the important *prerequisites* or indispensable ingredients for the *effectiveness* of these very techniques and rituals themselves (Crossley, 2004). 'To sleep', in other words, 'we must be at rest, which means free of anxiety, which in turn means ontologically secure. Habits and routines are the key to such security' (Crossley, 2004: 11).

Emotions, it is clear, are intimately bound up with these issues. I will not for example, sleep soundly if I am feeling anxious, insecure or unsafe, or if I am feeling sad, angry, fearful or stressed about something. The nature and quality of my sleep, in reciprocal fashion, is likely to affect my mood and feelings in significant, though perhaps unacknowledged, ways. If I have not slept well, for whatever reason, I may be moody, irritable, bad tempered, prone to emotional outbursts or just plain unbearable to live with, particularly if my sleep problems continue unabated. Good or bad dreams too may engender a variety of emotions both during the dream itself and upon waking as we ponder and piece them back together as best we can, with or without the aid of an analyst.

There is in fact a lot of (hidden) emotion work or emotion management (cf. Hochschild, 1983) involved in 'doing' sleeping in relation both to self and other. Individuals, for instance, may attempt to resolve, or at least rehearse, some of the emotional issues of the day when they take to their beds (Pahl, 2005). Longer-term emotional issues may also be mulled over in these quieter moments, both prior to sleep and during other points of the night should we awaken. Putting children to bed and tending to them in the night provides another important dimension to the picture here – a further hidden form of emotion work which tends to fall most heavily on women's shoulders (Hislop & Arber, 2003).

We also, of course, frequently sleep *together* rather than alone. Modern day coupledom it seems is predicated on the need to sleep together as a symbol or embodied expression of the relationship; a great source of comfort if not security for many of us. To sleep with one's partner or lover, indeed, denotes a level of intimacy and trust over and above the purely physical, carnal or sexual act (Schwartz, 1970).[3] Couples who decide to sleep apart, therefore, for whatever reason, must contend with the symbolic as well as the practical significance of doing so in terms of what this says, rightly or wrongly, about their relationship. Sleeping in an empty bed, moreover, when you have been used to sleeping next to your nearest and dearest, may itself give rise to awkward, strange or uneasy feelings and hence to varying degrees of sleep disturbance. The doing of sleeping then, as this suggests, is closely bound up with the doing of emotion and the doing of intimacy: an embodied expression of mutual trust and vulnerability through which we are commonly, carnally bound.

Vulnerability, vigilance and virtue: the problematization of sleep in a 24/7 risk society as a matter of 'public concern'

The bulk of this chapter so far has been taken up with the embodied vulnerabilities and dangers of sleep(iness) and the doing of sleeping in everyday/night life. A full sociological account of these issues, however, must also contend with the manner in which sleep is becoming increasingly 'problematized' in contemporary society as a matter of 'public concern': an issue that involves both a heightened social awareness and cultural sensitivity to the 'risks' associated with lack of sleep and calls for *ever greater vigilance* in relation to sleep and alertness management. The moral equation of sleep with sloth, in this respect, is now being challenged or reconfigured through a revaluation of the virtues of sleep, albeit a revaluation which remains broadly congruent with late capitalist imperatives and agendas. We live in an era in which people, so we are told, are not getting 'enough' sleep given the pressures of life and living in 24/7 society (www.sleepfoundation.org; Dement with Vaughan, 2000; Leadbeater, 2004). The stresses and strains of work, the demands of family life, expanding leisure and entertainment opportunities and the endless possibilities of the technology revolution, these and many other factors are said to be keeping us from our beds and depriving us of our sleep. Sleepiness, as such, is becoming increasingly problematized as an *'at risk' state*; a transition, as Kroll-Smith and Gunter (2005) astutely comment, from a relatively benign, private, corporeal moment and promise of tranquil repose, into a public, clinical, measurable condition and a potentially hazardous reprobate state, both to self and others. Alongside, or opposite, the idea of sleepiness as a naturally occurring bodily state, in other words, we now find growing concerns in professional and popular culture about the consequences of sleepiness for health and public safety.

Sleepiness, it is claimed, is a prime culprit or contributory factor in many accidents, both on and off the job, from the Exxon Valdez oil spill to the Challenger Space Shuttle disaster (Moore-Ede, 1993). Drowsiness behind the wheel, moreover, is now construed as every bit as dangerous as drunk driving. It is also viewed as the enemy of creativity, productivity and performance in all walks of life. This in turn translates more or less readily into the politics of blame if not the criminalization of sleepiness in a 24/7 society – the basic message being that you too are responsible for getting 'enough' sleep. The UK Selby rail disaster, for example, resulted in a man being put behind bars on the grounds that he was wrecklessly sleepy behind the wheel. States in the US such as New Jersey are also now criminalizing drowsiness behind the wheel (Kroll-Smith & Gunter, 2005). Meanwhile, various organizations, particularly in the US, are starting to introduce 'sleep-friendly' or 'sleep-smart' policies and practices, including the seemingly humble workplace nap, thereby bringing *corporeal needs* and *corporate demands* into closer alignment through a further 'deprivatization' of sleep (see, for example, Baxter & Kroll-Smith, 2005; Brown, 2004).

What we have here then, are a series of scientific, medical, managerial and moral discourses and agendas, themselves borrowing liberally from one another and popularized through the media (Kroll-Smith, 2003), in which sleep(iness) is increasingly problematized as a matter of public concern; a problem which calls for *ever renewed vigilance*. We are, it seems, increasingly advised, encouraged or cajoled, through multiple forms of authority and expertise, to govern, regulate or supervise our sleep as well as our waking lives in the name of health and happiness, wisdom and virtue, productivity and performance in all walks of life (Kroll-Smith, 2003; Kroll-Smith & Gunter, 2005). Sleep, in these and other ways, is increasingly being put to work, both literally and metaphorically, in the interests of medicalized and managerial agendas in the 24/7 era (Williams, 2005; Brown, 2004).

One may also speculate in this vein about the future uptake of new wakefulness promoting drugs such as Provigil (Modafinil). Initially marketed for the treatment of conditions such as narcolepsy, this drug is already being used in the US for newly emergent conditions such as 'shift-work sleep disorder' and 'excessive daytime sleepiness' (EDS). It is also being trailed in the military. Is this, we might justifiably ask, the thin end of the wedge? When imagined in corporate contexts, for example, 'might it be possible that workers will be encouraged to use it and work even longer without rest', thereby helping 'overcome bodily limitations in the name of success' (Brown, 2004: 186)? Will sleep(iness), in other words, be increasingly micro-managed in this fashion in the future, both on and off the job, given the pressures of life and living in the 24/7 era? And if so, at what human cost? Something to sleep on perhaps. . . .

Conclusions

It is tempting, given the relatively embryonic state of sociological work on sleep to date, to avoid any hard-and-fast conclusions or to end on an inconclusive note. A number of points nonetheless are worth spelling out in closing.

The first, most obvious, point to note, echoing the theme of this particular section of the monograph, is that a full and proper sociological account of *living in/as a body* must of necessity include or incorporate sleep. Sleep, as we have seen, raises important further questions about the *being* and *having* aspects of embodiment. It also poses intriguing questions about consciousness, agency and selfhood. But whilst sleep, I have argued, may justifiably be construed as a corporeal pleasure and a valued 'social release', it also renders us *vulnerable* or *dangerous*, potentially at least, to self and others through this loss of waking consciousness and loss of corporeal control. In order to sleep, therefore, we need to *feel* safe, secure and at ease. Sleep, indeed, as I have shown, is intimately bound up with emotion, trust and ontological (in)security. The 'doing' or reflexive management of sleeping, in this respect, modifies these embodied vulnerabilities and dangers in important ways. The basic embodied fact remains nonetheless that we are all more or less vulnerable or dangerous when we sleep, both to self and others.

This in turn raises a broader series of sociological questions about sleep, vulnerability and human rights. If Turner (1992) is correct that human rights need to be grounded in our own embodied vulnerability then again this must surely include sleep. The fragile, fitful, fateful sleep of those in poor, war-torn, famine-stricken, disease-ridden parts of the world today, moreover, provides another powerful reminder of this basic embodied fact. Sleep, from this perspective, may very well be a great leveller and a basic human right but it is also something that unites and divides us: a sensitive existential marker or expression of (in)equality, (in)security and (in)justice, both past and present, public and private.

The other point to spell out in closing concerns the increasing problematization of sleep in a 24/7 risk society as a matter of public concern. Sleep, as we have seen, is increasingly construed and constructed as a new site of risk and a new source of governance tied to the politics of blame. Within this new configuration of meaning, *vigilance is valorized*, with or without the aid of the latest pharmacological 'fix'. As for the future of sleep, clearly, to the extent that sleep remains a valued 'social release', it will not be 'done away with' lightly, either as a designer lifestyle option or a permanent post-human possibility. That sleep is now being 'put to work' in corporate culture, however, is surely a telling sign: the final frontier perhaps of late capitalism?

In these and other ways, then, sociology has much to contribute to the study of sleep and society. The argument here, however, is not so much for a ghettoized sociology of sleep, seen as the province of the mad, marginal or maverick few, but of the relevance of sleep to the sociological enterprise as a whole, not least the sociology of *embodiment*. It is time therefore, to conclude, for sociologists to wake up to the trials and tribulations, if not the problems and politics of sleep.

Notes

1 For a fuller account of the sociological nature and dimensions of sleep, see Williams (2005).
2 Our study used focus groups to explore the sleep problems experienced by 17 women survivors of domestic violence, all but one of whom were no longer living with violent partners at the time

of the study. For a more detailed discussion of the methodology and study findings see Lowe *et al.* (2007).

3 Parent-child co-sleeping practices provide another interesting variant on these themes, themselves of course socially and culturally variable matters.

References

Baxter, V. and Kroll-Smith, S. (2005) Napping at work: Shifting boundaries between public and private time. *Current Sociology*, 53, 1: 33–55.

Ben-Ari, E. (2005) Bedtime around the world: Children, families and sleep. Paper presented at the ESRC Sleep and Society seminar, 27th June 2005, University of Warwick (www.warwick.ac.uk/go/sleepandsociety).

Bourdieu, P. (1984) *Distinction*. London: Routledge.

Brown, M. (2004) Taking care of business: self-help and sleep medicine in American corporate culture. *Journal of Medical Humanities*, 25, 3 (Fall): 173–87.

Cheyne, J.A., Reuffer, S.D. and Newby-Clark, I.R. (1999) Hypnagogic and hypnopompic hallucinations during sleep paralysis: neurological and cultural construction of the night-mare. *Consciousness and Cognition*, 8, 3: 319–37.

Crossley, N. (2004) Sleep, reflexive embodiment and social networks. Paper presented at the first ESRC 'Sleep and Society' seminar, 3rd December, University of Warwick (www.warwick.ac.uk/go/sleepandsociety).

Dement, W.C. (with Vaughan, C.) (2000) *The Promise of Sleep: The Scientific Connection between Health, Happiness and a Good Night's Sleep*. NY and London: Delacourt Press/Macmillan.

Descartes, R. (1996/1641) *Meditations on First Philosophy with Selections from Objections and Replies* (ed.) J. Cottingham. Revised edition. Cambridge: Cambridge University Press.

Flanagan, O. (2000) *Dreaming Souls: Sleep, Dreams and the Evolution of the Conscious Mind*. Oxford: Oxford University Press.

Galloway, J.W. (1977) On Johnstone's 'Phenomenology of death' and 'Philosophy of sleep'. *Philosophy and Phenomenology*, 38, 1: 107–13.

Giddens, A. (1984) *The Constitution of Society*. Cambridge: Polity Press.

Goffman, E. (1961) *Encounters: Two Studies in the Sociology of Interaction*. Indianapolis: Bobbs-Merrill.

Hislop, J. and Arber, S. (2003) Sleepers wake! The gendered nature of sleep disruption among mid-life women. *Sociology*, 37, 4: 695–711.

Hochschild, A.R. (1983) *The Managed Heart: The Commercialization of Human Feeling*. Berkeley CA: University of California Press.

Johnstone, Jnr., H.W. (1973) Toward a philosophy of sleep. *Philosophy and Phenomenological Research*, 34, 1: 73–81.

Kroll-Smith, S. (2003) Popular media and 'excessive daytime sleepiness': a study of rhetorical authority in medical sociology. *Sociology of Health and Illness*, 25, 6: 625–43.

Kroll-Smith, S. and Gunter, V. (2005) Governing sleepiness: Somnolent bodies, discourse, and liquid modernity. *Sociological Inquiry*, 75, 3: 346–71.

Kryger, M.H., Roth, T. and Dement, W.C. (eds) (2005) *Principles and Pratice of Sleep Medicine* (Fourth Edition). Philadelphia/London: W.B. Saunders Company.

La Berge, S. (1985) *Lucid Dreaming*. LA: JP. Tarcher.

Leadbeater, C. (2004) *Dream On: Sleep in the 24/7 Society*. London: Demos.

Leder, D. (1990) *The Absent Body*. Chicago: University of Chicago Press.

Lowe, P., Humphreys, C. and Williams, S.J. (2007) Night terrors: Women's experiences of (not) sleeping where there is domestic violence. *Violence Against Women*. In Press.

Malcolm, N. (1959) *Dreaming*. London: Routledge and Kegan Paul.

Marsh, G. (2005) Girl, 15, Rescued after sleepwalk up a 30 ft. crane. *Daily Express*. July 6th: 8.

Mauss, M. (1973/1934) Techniques of the body. *Economy and Society*, 2: 70–88.

Mavromatis, A. (1987) *Hypnagogia: The Unique State of Consciousness Between Wakefulness and Sleep*. London: Routledge.
Merleau-Ponty, M. (1962) *The Phenomenology of Perception*. London: Routledge.
Moore-Ede, M. (1993) *The 24 Society: The Risks, Costs and Consequences of a World That Never Stops.* London: Piatkus.
Pahl, J. (2005) Power, inequalities and resources within families. Paper presented at the 2nd ESRC Sleep and Society Seminar, 26th April, University of Surrey.
Rechtschaffen, A., Bergman, B.M., Everson, C.A, Kushida, C.A. and Gilliland, M.A. (1989) Sleep deprivation in the rat: X. Integration and discussion of the findings. *Sleep*, 12: 68–87.
Rensen, P. (2003) Sleeping without a home: the embedment of sleep in the lives of the rough-sleeping homeless in Amsterdam, in B. Steger and L. Brunt (eds.), (2003) *Night-time and Sleep in Asia and the West: Exploring the Dark Side of Life*. London: Routledge Curzon, Pp. 87–107.
Schutz, A. (with T. Luckmann) (1974) *The Structures of the Lifeworld* (Transl. by R. Zaner and H. Tristram Englehardt Jnr.). London: Heinemann.
Schwartz, B. (1970) Notes on the sociology of sleep. *Sociological Quarterly*, 11 (4): 485–99.
Steger, B. and Brunt, L. (eds.) (2003) *Night-time and Sleep in Asia and the West: Exploring the Dark Side of Life*. London: Routledge Curzon.
Taylor, B. (1993) Unconsciousness and society: the sociology of sleep. *International Journal of Politics and Culture*, 6 (3): 463–71.
Turner, B.S. (1992) Outline of a theory of human rights. *Sociology*, 27, 3: 489–512.
Weisgerber, C. (2004) Turning to the internet for help on sensitive medical problems: A qualitative study of the construction of a sleep disorder through online interaction. *Information, Communication & Society*, 7, 4: 554–74.
Williams, S.J. (2005) *Sleep and Society: Sociological Ventures into the (Un)Known*. London: Routledge.
Williams, S.J., Griffiths, F.E. and Lowe, P. (2004) *Sleep: A Feasibility Study*. University of Warwick.

Notes on contributors

Anna Aalten is Associate Professor at the Department of Sociology and Anthropology of the University of Amsterdam, The Netherlands, where she teaches general anthropology courses, gender studies, body theory and qualitative methodology. Her latest research was on body images and body practices in ballet. She is currently engaged in a research project on excellence and health at Codarts, University of Professional Arts Education in Rotterdam. Aalten has published in national and international journals in the fields of anthropology, feminist studies and body theory. Some of these publications can be found via her website: http://users.fmg.uva.nl/aaalten/ Her email address is: a.j.j.aalten@uva.nl

Nick Crossley is a Professor of Sociology in the School of Social Sciences at the University of Manchester. He has published many papers, theoretical and empirical, on embodiment, and also two books on the topic: *The Social Body* (Sage, 2001) and *Reflexive Embodiment in Contemporary Society* (McGraw-Hill, 2006). His other research interests include social networks, social movements and sociological theory.

Kathy Davis is Senior Researcher at the Research Institute for History and Culture at Utrecht University in The Netherlands. She has published extensively on contemporary feminist approaches to the body, interaction between physicians and women patients, cultural constructions of beauty and beauty practices, and the political and ethical dimensions of surgical technologies. Her books include *Dubious Equalities and Embodied Differences* (Rowman & Littlefield, 2003), *Reshaping the Female Body* (Routledge, 1995), *Power Under the Microscope* (Foris, 1988), and *Embodied Practices. Feminist Perspectives on the Body* (Sage, 1997). Her latest book is *The Making of Our Bodies, Ourselves. How Feminist Knowledge Travels Across Borders* (Duke University Press, 2007).

Brian Lande is a doctoral candidate at the University of California-Berkeley where he is also affiliated with the Center for Urban Ethnography. His research involves the comparative ethnography of institutions of violence with a strong emphasis on the embodied character of 'violence work' within institutions such as the military and police. His dissertation, "Bodies of Force" is a 'carnal ethnography' of three police training programs. This work focuses on how, from three different points of view within the field of police education, new police recruits come to know, master, embody and take for granted the state's monopoly on 'legitimate' force.

Donald N. Levine is the Peter B. Ritzma Professor of Sociology and former dean of the College at the University of Chicago. He served for fifteen years as editor of the *Heritage of Sociology* series and as chair of the ASA Theory Section in 1996–97. His publications include *Georg Simmel On Individuality and Social Forms*, *The Flight from Ambiguity*, *Visions of the Sociological Tradition*, *Greater Ethiopia: The Evolution of a Multiethnic Society*, and *Powers of the Mind: The Reinvention of Liberal Learning in America*. He holds the rank of *sandan* (3rd-degree black belt) in the art of aikido, and is founder and president of Aiki Extensions, Inc. (www.aiki-extensions.org).

Erin O'Connor is a doctoral candidate in the Department of Sociology at the New School for Social Research in New York City. Her chief interests are ethnographic field methods, social theory, cultural sociology, and the sociology of knowledge. Her Ph.D. dissertation is an ethnography of the development of practical knowledge in glassblowing. *Address*: New School for Social Research, Sociology Department, Constellations Journal, 65 Fifth Avenue, New York, NY 10003, USA. email: eeo@mac.com

Judith Okely is Emeritus Professor of Social Anthropology, Hull University, and Deputy Director of the International Gender Studies Centre, Queen Elizabeth House, Oxford University. Previously Professor at Edinburgh University, she has been visiting Professor at the Universities of Copenhagen and Vienna, the Central European University, Budapest and Egerton University, Kenya. She has conducted fieldwork in the UK and France. Topics include: Gypsies/Roma worldwide, Fieldwork Practice, Gender, Visualism and Rural Representations. Her work has been translated into Japanese, Hungarian, Chinese, French, Italian and Polish. Her forthcoming study (Berg) is based on extended dialogues with anthropologists concerning their fieldwork practice in localities around the globe.

Chris Shilling is Professor of Sociology at the University of Portsmouth, UK. He has written extensively on the body in sociology and social theory, on historical transformations of the body, and on corporeal realism, and his publications include *The Body and Social Theory* (1993, 2nd edition 2003, Sage), *Re-forming the Body: Religion, Community and Modernity* (1997, co-authored with P.A. Mellor, Sage), *The Sociological Ambition* (2001, co-authored with P.A. Mellor, Sage), and *The Body in Culture, Technology & Society* (2005, Sage). His latest book, *Changing Bodies: Habit, Crisis and Creativity*, will be published by Sage Press in 2008. Chris also coordinates the International Body Pedagogics Project.

Bryan S. Turner was Professor of Sociology at the University of Cambridge (1998–2005) and is currently Professor of Sociology in the Asia Research Institute, National University of Singapore. He is the research leader of the cluster on globalization and religion. He edited the *Cambridge Dictionary of Sociology* (2006) and published *Vulnerability and Human Rights* (2006) with Penn State University Press. Professor Turner is a research associate of GEMAS (Centre National de la Recherche Scientifique, Paris), an honorary professor of Deakin University, and an adjunct professor at Murdoch University Australia.

Simon Williams is Professor of Sociology in the Department of Sociology, University of Warwick, UK. He has longstanding interests in the sociology of embodiment/embodied sociology and has recently extended this work to the much neglected domain of sleep. His latest book is entitled *Sleep and Society: Sociological Ventures into the (Un)Known* (2005, Routledge). He currently is taking these sociological research agendas forward on a number of fronts, including a British Academy funded project on the social construction of sleep in the media and related research on the governance and biopolitics of sleep in a 24/7 society.

Name Index

Aalten, A. 11, 14, 112, 122, 123
Abramson, A. 66, 78
Adam, M.U. 123
Agamben, G. 28, 30, 35
Alcoff L.M. 56, 58, 63
Alexander, F.M. 44
Alexander, J. 64
Alexander, J.C. 17
Anderson, N. 12, 16
Arber, S. 150, 154
Archer, M. 2, 9
Ardener, S. 79
Arendt, H. 29
Aristotle, 20, 28, 29, 86, 93
Aron, R. 3, 16
Ashley, M. 119, 120, 122, 123

Babitsch, B. 53, 54, 63
Bachelard, G. 134, 138, 140
Bare, M. 39, 48
Barry, J. 110, 124
Bartky, S.L. 57, 63, 84, 92, 93
Baxter, V. 152, 154
Beck, U. 34, 35
Bell, D. 25
Ben-Ari, E. 96, 107, 149, 154
Bendelow, G. 111, 125
Bendix, R. 79
Benn, T. 115, 123
Benner, P. 97, 107
Benson, J. 115, 123
Bentley, T. 122–124
Berger, P.L. 23, 28, 35, 36
Bergman, B.M. 155
Bettelheim, B. 40, 45, 48
Birke, L. 53, 55, 56, 63
Blacking, J. 66, 74, 78
Boas, F. 21
Bohannon, L. 73, 74, 79
Bonnell, V. 141
Bordo, S. 53, 54, 59, 63
Bottomore, T. 17
Boulding, K.E. 38, 40, 43, 44, 48
Bourdieu, P. 7, 16, 29, 75, 78, 93, 97, 106, 107, 126, 131, 132, 134, 135, 137, 140, 150, 154
Bourveresse, J. 140
Bowlby, J. 43
Brady, J. 122, 123
Brassington, G.S. 123
Breckenridge, C.A. 55, 63
Brenneis, D. 79
Brinson, P. 110, 115, 123
Brookes, D. 74
Brown, M. 152, 154
Brunt, L. 155
Bull, D. 122, 123
Burke, C. 96, 107
Bussell, D. 110, 122, 123
Butler, J. 2, 10, 16, 54, 63, 64
Bynum, C. 2, 16

Caforio, G. 96, 107
Callaway, H. 66, 78, 79
Caplan, P. 78
Chandler, J. 110, 124
Charlesworth, S.J. 97, 107
Cheyne, J.A. 146, 154
Clark, H. 110, 124
Clarke, A.E. 63
Clarkson, P. 123
Clifford, J. 66, 78

Coleman, J.S. 38, 40, 41, 48
Collins, P.H. 53, 63
Collins, R. 38, 48
Compagno, J.M. 110, 123, 124
Comte, A. 3, 16, 17
Cooley, C. 89, 93
Copeland, R. 114, 124
Cornaro, L. 32, 34
Coser, L. 16, 38, 48
Cottingham, J. 154
Cowan, J. 74, 78
Creaven, S. 5, 16
Crossley, N. 11, 13, 16, 80–86, 88, 90, 93, 94, 108, 145, 150, 154
Crossman, J. 119, 120, 124
Csordas, T.J. 66, 78, 79, 97, 108, 111, 124

Darwin, C. 20, 22, 23
Davis, K. 12, 53, 62, 63
Davis-Floyd, R.E. 62, 63
de la Gorgendière, L. 67, 71, 75, 78
de Mille, A. 122, 124
Deleuze, G. 8, 16
Dement, W.C. 144, 151, 154
Descartes, R. 81, 94, 143, 154
Desmond, J. 124
Dewey, J. 44
Dick, F. 110, 115, 123
Douglas, M. 66, 78, 122, 124
Dreyfus, H.L. 27, 35
Dubos, R. 34, 35
Dunhill, A. 124
Durkheim, E. 3, 4, 5, 6, 10, 16, 17, 23, 41, 81, 85, 90, 94, 96, 100, 108

Eichberg, H. 7, 16
Einstein, A. 48
Eisenstein, Z. 7, 16
Elias, N. 27, 35, 93, 94, 102
Elliott, A. 36
Embree, L. 63
Engels, F. 6, 94
Evans-Pritchard, E. 67, 78
Everett, J.J. 123, 124
Everson, C.A. 155

Farrell, S. 122, 124
Fausto-Sterling, A. 63
Featherstone, M. 2, 7, 16, 17
Feder, M. 2, 16
Feldenkrais, M. 16, 39, 48
Fischer, J.L. 36
Fisher, L. 63
Fisher, R. 40, 44, 48
Flanagan, O. 145, 154
Fonteyn, M. 122, 124
Foster, S. 111, 113, 115, 124
Foucault, M. 8, 9, 16, 23, 28, 29, 30, 53, 59, 64, 93, 94
Franke, V.C. 96, 108
Freud, S. 41, 42, 48, 114
Frisby, D. 17
Fromm, E. 49
Fukuyama, F. 21, 35

Galloway, J.W. 144, 154
Gardner, H. 48, 49
Gardner, P. 125
Gardner, S. 108
Garfinkel, H. 8
Gatens, M. 52, 63
Gaudin, C. 140
Gehlen, A. 28
Geras, N. 16
Gerth, H. 18
Giddens, A. 84, 94, 150, 154
Gilligan, J. 49
Gilliland, M.A. 155
Giordano, C. 45, 49
Goffman, E. 6, 15, 93, 101, 104, 108, 150, 154
Goodchild, P. 8, 16
Gordon, S. 115, 124
Griffiths, F.E. 155
Grosz, E. 7, 8, 16
Guattari, F. 8, 16
Gubrium, J.F. 124
Guignon, C.B. 35
Gunter, V. 151, 152, 154

Haight, H.J. 115, 124
Hallam, E. 79
Halstead, N. 79
Haraway, D.J. 12, 24, 35, 50–53, 58, 60, 61, 63
Harding, S. 53, 63
Hastrup, K. 79
Heidegger, M. 26, 27, 28, 30, 35, 36

Heilbron, J. 3, 16
Hendry, J. 78
Hepworth, M. 17
Herbert, M.S. 96, 108
Hervik, P. 79
Herzfeld, M. 70, 72–75, 77, 78
Hirsch, E. 79
Hirst, P. 2, 16
Hislop, J. 150, 154
Hobbes, T. 3, 42, 43
Hochschild, A.R. 90, 94, 107, 110, 124, 150, 154
Holstein, J.A. 124
Howell, S. 66, 78
Howes, D. 75, 78
Howson, A. 9, 16
Hsu, E. 76, 78
Hughes-Freeland, F. 74, 77, 78
Humphreys, C. 154
Hunt, L. 141
Huxley, A. 28

Inglis, D. 9, 16
Irigary, L. 7, 16
Iyengar, B.K. 46, 49

Jackson, J. 77, 78
James, W. 41, 49
Janowitz, M. 40, 45, 48
Joas, H. 2, 9, 16
Johnstone, Jnr., H.W. 143, 154
Jones, F.P. 44, 49
Jowitt, D. 113, 114, 124

Kant, I. 29
Kapsalis, T. 62, 63
Keller, E.F. 53, 63
Kenna, M. 72, 73, 76, 77, 78
Kent, A. 122, 124
Kerr, G. 110, 119, 124
Kirkland, G. 122, 124
Klages, L. 27
Kluckhohn, C. 21, 22, 36
Kohut, H. 43
Koutedakis, Y. 115, 124, 125
Krasnow, D. 110, 119, 124
Kriesberg, L. 38, 49
Kristeva, J. 7, 16
Kroeber, A.L. 21, 22, 36
Kroker, A. 8, 16
Kroker, M. 8, 16
Kroll-Smith, S. 151, 152, 154
Kruks, S. 53, 56, 57, 59, 60, 63
Kryger, M.H. 146, 154
Kuhlmann, K. 53, 54, 63
Kulick, D. 66, 78
Kushida, C.A. 155

La Berge, S. 145, 154
Lakoff, G. 2, 16
Lande, B. 11, 14
Lave, J. 104, 108
Lawrence, G. 124
Lawson, J. 113, 124
Leadbeater, C. 151, 154
Leder, D. 80, 82, 83, 94, 111, 112, 123, 124, 144, 145, 154
Levell, N. 79
Levi-Strauss, C. 85, 94
Levine, D.N. 3, 6, 7, 11, 12, 14, 16, 17, 45, 48, 49
Lewis, J. 123, 124
Lewis, W. 25
Lidz, C.W. 37, 39, 49
Lidz, M.L. 37, 39, 49
Liederbach, M. 110, 123, 124
Linden, P. 46, 49
Lindisfarne, N. (see Tapper, N.) 70, 73, 77, 79
Lock, M.M. 112, 125
Lorenz, K. 41, 42, 49
Lowe, P. 148, 154, 155
Luckmann, T. 28, 35, 155
Lugones, M. 59, 60, 64
Lupton, D. 111, 124

Macchi, R. 119, 120, 124
Mackinnon, C. 7, 16
Mackrell, J. 123
McLellan, G. 16
McLeod, M. 71, 72, 77
McLuhan, M. 25, 26, 29
McNay, L. 53, 64
Mainwaring, L.M. 110, 119, 124
Malcolm, N. 145, 154
Malthus, T. 31, 32, 34, 36
Marcus, G. 66, 78
Marcuse, H. 6, 7, 17

Marsh, G. 147, 154
Marshall, H. 57, 64
Martheson, G.O. 123
Martin, E. 57, 58, 64, 66, 78
Marx, K. 5, 6, 15, 16, 17, 23, 24, 25, 36, 81, 94
Mauss, M. 13, 23, 66, 78, 80, 81, 85–88, 90, 91, 93, 94, 97, 108, 122, 124, 150, 154
Mavromatis, A. 145, 155
Mazo, J. 109, 116, 124
Mead, G.H. 89, 94
Mead, M. 49
Mellor, P. A. 1, 14, 17, 66, 78
Merleau-Ponty, M. 81, 83, 84, 90, 94, 96, 105, 108, 111, 131, 140, 141, 145, 155
Merton, R. 96
Mills, C.W. 6, 18
Mohanty, C. 59, 60, 64
Moi, T. 16
Moore-Ede, M. 151, 155
Moreno, E. 66, 78
Morgen, S. 62, 64
Morgenthau, H. 41, 49
Moritz, U. 116, 124
Morris, B. 69, 70, 77
Moya, P.M.L. 58, 64
Murphy, M. 62, 64

Naddaff, R. 2, 16
Nettleton, S. 13, 17, 111, 124
Newby-Clark, I.R. 154
Nietzsche, F. 27, 28, 30, 34, 36, 43

O'Connor, E. 11, 14, 15
Okely, J. 11, 12, 13, 66–71, 75, 77–79
Olesen, V.L. 63
O'Neill, J. 9, 17
Ottenberg, S. 12, 17, 77, 79

Pahl, J. 150, 155
Parry, J. 70, 76, 77, 79
Parsons, T. 6, 9, 12, 17, 22, 30, 36, 37, 38, 41, 47, 48, 49, 96
Patterson, E.L. 123, 124
Perry, R.B. 49
Peterson, D. 42, 49
Piaget, J. 39, 49
Pickering, M. 3, 17
Plato, 81, 114, 143
Polanyi, M. 15, 17, 129, 130, 141
Polhemus, T. 79
Porter, M. 122, 124
Powdermaker, H. 73, 74, 79
Price, J. 63
Priest, R.F. 96, 108
Ptacek, J.T. 123, 124

Ramel, E.M. 116, 124
Raposa, M.L. 28, 36
Rechtschaffen, A. 147, 155
Rensen, P. 148, 155
Retzinger, S.M. 44, 49
Reuffer, S.D. 154
Rickman, J. 48
Rosa, F.M. 108
Rose, F.D. 116, 125
Roth, T. 154
Russell, B. 143
Ryle, G. 81, 82, 94

Safranski, R. 26, 36
Sanjek, R. 17, 78, 79
Saotome, M. 46, 49
Sasson-Levy, O. 96, 108
Sault, N. 63
Schärli, A. 110, 122–124
Scheff, T.J. 44, 49
Scheler, M. 48, 49
Schelling, T.C. 38, 49
Scheper-Hughes, N. 107, 112, 125
Schilbrack, K. 94
Schutz, A. 100, 101, 107, 108, 144, 155
Schwartz, B. 146, 149–151, 155
Scott, J.W. 53, 57, 58, 64
Seigel, J. 29, 36
Sewell, Jnr.,W.H. 140, 141
Seymour, L. 122, 125
Sharp, G. 125
Shildrick, M. 63
Shilling, C. 1, 2, 4, 6, 7, 14, 17, 48, 49, 66, 76, 78, 79, 84, 94, 107, 111, 122, 125, 139
Shils, E. 49
Shusterman, R. 7, 17
Sica, A.Q. 36
Simmel, G. 3, 4, 5, 10, 17, 40, 44
Skrinar, M. 123

Smith, D.E. 53, 59, 60, 64
Smith, P. 17
Smith, R.E. 123, 124
Smith, S.L. 63, 64
Smith, T.S. 44, 49
Smith Bowen, E. 73, 79
Sorel, G. 43
Spelman, E. 53, 64
Springer, K. 63, 64
Steger, B. 155
Steiner, H. 123
Stevens, G. 96, 108
Stoller, P. 75, 79
Stone-Mediatore, S. 56, 59, 60, 64
Stryker, S. 8, 17
Sudnow, D. 97, 108, 130, 141
Suleiman, S. 2, 17
Synnott, A. 111, 125

Tajet-Foxell, B. 116, 125
Tapper, N. (see Lindisfarne, N.) 70, 79
Taylor, B. 149, 155
Taylor, W.W. 36
Tazi, N. 2, 16
Tinbergen, N. 41, 42, 48, 49
Turner, B.S. 2, 10, 11, 17, 28, 30, 36, 111, 119, 125, 153, 155
Turner, S. 36

Ueshiba, M. 46
Urry, W. 40, 44, 48

van der Linden, M. 123
Van Maanen, J. 107, 108
Varikas, E. 56, 64
Vaughan, C. 144, 151, 154
Vincent, L.M. 110, 115, 125
Virilio, P. 24, 36
Vogler, C. 55, 63
Vogt, E.Z. 36

Wacquant, L. 14, 17, 88, 91, 94, 97, 98, 104, 107, 108, 134, 135, 138, 139, 141
Wainwright, S.P. 119, 125
Walters, D. 115, 123
Warren, G.W. 113, 115, 125
Watson, C.W. 78
Watson, J. 13, 17, 111, 124
Weber, M. 3, 4, 5, 6, 11, 17, 18, 27, 30, 36, 38, 41
Weisgerber, C. 146, 155
Welton, D. 94
Wendell, S. 55, 56, 64
Wenger, E. 104, 108
White, E.C. 63, 64
Whittle, S. 8, 17
Whyte, W.H. 30, 36
Wiedmann, A.K. 27, 36
Williams, C. 119, 125
Williams, S.J. 15, 111, 125, 148, 152–155
Wilson, M. 66, 78
Wininger, K. 79
Winkler, C. 66, 79
Winnicott, D. 43
Winslow, D. 96, 108
Wolman, R. 115, 125
Woolley, P. 2, 16
Wrangham, R. 42, 49
Wright, S. 72, 77, 79
Wulff, H. 68, 74, 77, 79, 115, 116, 125

Yamurtas, A. 115, 124
Young, I.M. 2, 18, 57, 64, 84, 92, 94

Subject Index

actional organism 37, 41, 43, 47, 48
actor network theory 8
Afghanistan 65, 70, 73
Africa 33, 65, 73, 75
agency 12, 54, 59, 60, 62, 80, 86, 88, 109, 121, 153
age 38, 61, 66, 69
ageing 32, 33, 35, 55
aggression 37–48
– aggressive impulses 4, 40–43, 45, 46, 48
aikido 46, 92
alienation 5, 11, 23, 28
animal/human dualism/distinction 11, 19, 20, 22–24, 28, 35
animal instinct/character 3, 4, 5, 11, 22, 28, 42
ancestors 23, 30, 41, 67
ancient Rome 45
ancient/archaic Greece 24, 26, 45, 143
anomie 11
anthropology 1, 3, 11–13, 15, 19–23, 28, 65–77, 110–112, 115, 121–123
arbitration 47
army 14, 95–107
– Cadets, 14, 95–106
– NCOs 95, 97
– US Army Reserved Officer Training Corp 14, 96, 98
asana 46
attack/counter-attack 4, 40, 42, 43, 72, 146, 148
autobiography 66, 113

ballet 14, 74, 109–123
– aesthetic ideal 110, 115
– artistic directors 113
– choreographers 113
– culture 14, 109–123
bathing 66, 67, 149
behavioural
– capacity 39, 43, 117, 118
– codes 110–112, 121
– organism 38
– system 37, 39
biological determinism 9, 20, 30, 53, 55, 56, 61
biology 3, 13, 20, 22, 30, 31, 34, 38, 42, 53–56
bio-technology 23, 31, 34
blame 142, 152, 153
bodily imitation 65, 71, 72, 102, 134, 135
bodily rhythms 72, 99, 100, 104, 107, 133, 136, 147
body
– as an absent-presence 2, 80–85, 87, 89, 91, 92, 109, 111, 121, 123, 144, 146
– biological 52, 53, 55, 56, 63
– biologically sexed 7, 53, 66
– blank screen 8
– cultural text 53, 55, 61
– disappearing 9, 109, 111, 121, 122, 142, 145
– fluidity 8, 54
– frailty / vulnerability 9, 15, 19, 21, 43, 44, 54–56, 61, 142–154
– rise of the 1, 2, 6, 84
– sign receiving system 8
– surface 4, 9, 53, 54, 61
– therapists 9
– without organs 8

body/mind dualism/division 39, 48, 55, 65, 80–82, 85, 86
body pedagogics / pedagogy 1, 13, 14, 15, 91, 95, 98, 101, 104–106
'body projects' 7, 84
body studies 7, 10, 15
body techniques 11, 13–15, 80–93, 95, 97–100, 102, 106, 109, 110, 118, 122, 129–131, 138, 143, 150
– diffusion 80, 87, 91–93
– emergence 85, 91–93
– evolution 92, 93
boredom 28, 34, 35, 99
boxing 86, 88, 97, 135, 138
breasts 57, 62, 67
breath/breathing 14, 37, 46, 71, 95–107

capitalism 4, 5, 7, 15, 25, 30, 33, 34, 151, 153
Cartesian 39, 61, 65, 145
Chicago School of Sociology 12
childbirth 52, 55, 57, 58
children 66, 69, 70, 72, 148, 149, 150, 154
Christianity 7, 20, 23, 34
civilizing processes 27, 93
classical sociology 1, 4, 6, 10, 15
clothes/clothing 38, 68, 73, 75, 96, 149
collective effervescence 4, 6, 41
communities 22, 33, 39, 47, 62, 100, 147
compulsory heterosexuality 7
conflict 1, 11, 12, 14, 33, 37–48
– aggressive impulsivity 41–43, 45
– conflictual party 37, 39, 40, 43–45, 47
– intensity 39, 40, 44, 45
– media 39
– outcome 39
– reactivity 37, 43–45, 47
– systemic location 39
– theory 11, 12, 37, 39, 40, 47, 48
conflict-aversive values 37, 41, 45, 46
conflict-supportive values 45
consciousness 50, 65, 72, 77, 82–84, 90, 112, 118, 120, 127, 129–135, 138, 140, 143–146, 153
– unconscious 71, 72, 77, 88, 122, 130, 134, 143, 144
consumer culture 1, 2, 7, 9
corporeal
– comprehension 134, 135
– mastery 105, 138
– schema 88, 89, 96, 97, 101, 102, 105, 138
counter-culture 7
creativity 4, 5, 9, 152
cultural
– forms 6
– framing of life & death 38
– reproduction 1, 14
– theory, and social, 9, 15, 25
culture 19–35, 41, 45, 51, 53, 54, 56, 65, 72, 74, 76, 84, 96, 97, 99, 105–107, 109–123, 140, 151, 153
– ethical 11
– male 7
– mass 7
– military 95–97, 106
– religious 11, 35
culture/nature dualism/distinction 2, 3, 11, 20, 21, 24
culture/technology dualism/distinction 11, 20, 21, 35
cyborgs 8, 9, 24

dance 12, 71–74, 77, 88–91, 97, 109–123
Darwinism 20, 22, 23
data
– demographic 32
– operational 107
– presentational 107
death 31, 32, 38, 42, 66, 70, 76, 144, 146, 147
death instinct 42
defence 4, 40, 43, 44, 120, 148
diabetes 33, 35
diet 7, 32, 35, 117, 148
disability 6, 54, 55
discourse analysis 57
disenchantment 5, 27
division of labour 5, 25
domestic violence 148, 153
dreaming 135, 136, 138, 143–145, 148, 150
dress/dressing 68, 73, 77, 116, 150
dromology 24

eating disorders 14, 62, 109–123
ecology 7, 9
economic/economy 27, 31, 33, 34, 65
– growth/production 5, 25
– money economy 5
– socio-economic system 5, 33
embodied meaning 89–91, 126–140
emotion management 150
emotions/affects 3, 4, 5, 6, 30, 39, 40, 44, 57, 90, 117, 142, 148–151, 153
– emotion work 6, 150
Enlightenment 8, 20, 27, 29
environmental pollution 33, 34
epistemic agency 12, 50, 52, 54, 58–62
epistemology 8, 50–63
– feminist 8, 50, 52, 56, 58
erotic encounters 4, 5, 66
eternal life 19, 21, 33, 35
ethics 8, 10, 11, 19, 20, 31, 34, 35, 46, 86, 147
– determinism 34
– Protestant 4, 5, 6, 30
– religious 4
– virtue 29
– work 4
Ethiopia 45
ethnocentrism 65, 73
ethnography 14, 21, 66, 74, 77, 91–93, 95, 98, 107, 109, 111–113, 121, 126, 148
ethnomethodology 8, 96
ethology 41, 42, 47
Europe 27, 28, 51, 65, 72, 73
exhaustion/fatigue 6, 69, 74, 97, 104, 110, 121–123, 135, 148
experience
– embodied 52–55, 58, 59, 61, 62, 65, 66, 68, 73, 77, 82, 112, 126–140
– religious/spiritual 27, 31, 90
expressive individualism 30
external environment 7, 9, 11, 19, 38, 39, 41, 42, 45, 83, 85, 90, 95, 131
eye 71, 72, 76, 83, 130, 133, 135, 136, 138, 144

facial expressions 71, 107
farmer/farming 69, 75, 90
feminism 1, 2, 7, 9, 12, 15, 24, 53, 60
feminist body theory 50, 52–56, 61
– postmodern 53–56, 58–60
– poststructuralist 50, 52, 58, 61
feminist health activists 12, 50, 51, 53, 54, 60, 61
fieldwork 12, 13, 21, 65–77, 96, 98
focal awareness 130
food 31, 33, 34, 111, 112, 114, 117, 118

gather/gathering 127–134, 140
gender 53, 66–68
general theory of action 6, 12, 37–39
– action system 9, 47
genes/genetics 2, 11, 20, 22, 30, 31, 33, 34
genital cutting 57
gerontology 32, 33
gift relationship 13
glassblowing 15, 126–140
global warming 33, 34
governmentality 8, 9
Greece/Greek 70, 72, 74, 76, 77, 86
Greek mythology 24
gynaecology 50, 51, 62
Gypsies/Travellers 76, 68, 71

habit 3, 4, 7, 44, 97, 102, 106, 118, 140, 143, 149–151
habitus 29, 86, 97, 106, 131, 132, 137–139
– military 97, 98
head 48, 72, 73, 83, 97
'headnotes' 12, 77
health 1, 6, 10, 12, 19, 34, 50–52, 54, 61–63, 109, 110, 115, 118, 121, 122, 146, 147, 151, 152
– activists 12, 51, 53, 54
– movement 50–52, 61–63
hermeneutics 20, 55
Het Nationale Ballet 112, 114–116, 119
HIV/AIDS 8, 52, 62
Hobbesian 'problem of order' 3
homo duplex 4
hostility level 30, 37, 40, 43
Human Genome Project 8, 31
human rights 21, 153
humanities 1, 2, 75
hunger 5, 115–118, 122
hunter-gatherers 69, 70

Huntington's disease 31
hypnagogic experiences 145, 146
hyperventilating 99–101
hysteria 34

idealism 20, 57, 81, 140
identity 2, 6–9, 29, 65, 66, 68, 70, 73, 91, 119
illness 32, 33, 54, 61, 76, 82, 109, 111, 112, 117, 121
– chronic 33, 55, 110, 119, 121, 122
in vitro fertilization 2, 8
incest taboo 38, 62
inequality 15, 33, 61
information technology 25, 29
injuries 14, 38, 43, 61, 109–123
instincts 11, 41–43, 45, 47, 48, 77, 86
intelligence 3, 39, 81, 83, 85, 88, 118
intentionality 59, 126, 130, 131
intersubjectivity 84, 106, 144, 145
India 25, 65, 69, 70
instruction 4, 71, 83, 100, 104–106, 128, 130, 134, 135, 139
Iran 65, 72
'iron cage' 11, 30
Islam 45

Japan 33, 45, 46

life expectancy/longevity 11, 19, 21, 30–34
living in/as a body 55, 142, 152, 153
London 68, 74
'looking-glass self' 89
lungs 48, 54, 101, 103

Malaysia 65, 66
Malthusian logic 31, 32, 34
martial arts 45, 46, 89, 90, 92, 93
masculine 53, 56, 72
– aggressivity 45, 48
mediation 41, 47, 58, 83, 150
medical
– gaze 12, 51
– intervention 15
– practice 38
– sciences 20, 21, 32, 34, 82
– technology 1, 19, 34, 35
medicine, regenerative 19, 21, 33
menopause 57, 62
menstruation 55, 57, 58, 62
milking cows 69, 70, 75
military 14, 26, 85, 95–107, 148, 152
mimesis 15, 71, 134, 135, 138
mind/body dualism/distinction, see body/mind
modernity 6, 27, 34, 60, 65
moral orders 2, 5, 11, 110, 112
moral righteousness 37, 40, 44, 45
motion/movement 39, 43, 65, 66, 68, 73, 74, 83, 84, 86, 87, 95, 96, 99, 100, 102–105, 107, 111, 113, 119, 122, 130, 133–135, 138, 140
murder 42, 68, 147
music 71, 72, 74, 76, 82, 140

nature/culture dualism/distinction, see culture/nature
nature/nurture dualism/distinction, see culture/nature
neck 48
nervous system 26, 39
New York 25, 110, 120, 126, 127, 140
nomads 70, 72, 73

observant participation 14, 88, 91
occupational culture 109–112, 115, 118–121
organismic dimension 38, 39, 107
– integrity 55, 56
Our Bodies Ourselves 50, 51, 62
outsiders 66, 67, 68, 71, 72

pain 14, 76, 77, 82, 83, 101, 109–123, 147
participant observation 65, 76, 98
perception 82–84, 87, 90, 91, 102, 105, 112, 140, 144
performance 7, 11, 55, 74, 88, 90, 96, 100, 105, 119, 121, 131, 152
phenomenology 9, 22, 29, 50, 52, 57–59, 82, 89, 96, 109, 111, 126, 140, 142, 144
physical capital 7, 25
physical labour 65, 69, 70
pleasure 30, 73, 77, 142, 146, 149, 153
politics of knowledge 50–52, 60, 61
postmodernism 53, 59

post-structuralism 9, 58
posture 37, 46, 68, 71–73, 84, 97, 101, 102, 106, 107, 128, 131, 132
practical knowledge 15, 86–88, 126, 131, 134–140
pranayama 46
pregnancy 57, 63, 67, 68
professionals 11, 14, 48, 62, 63, 98, 110–113, 117, 120–123, 140, 151
psychology 3, 4, 13, 20, 34, 38, 42, 43, 47, 48, 82, 116
puberty 114, 117
pugilistic knowledge 135

qualitative research 13, 87, 92, 93
quantitative research 13, 77, 87, 92, 93, 122, 123

'race' 21–23, 57, 66, 68
racism 52, 68
rape 66, 68
rational choice theory 9
rationalization 5, 27
– rationalized society 6, 86
reactivity 37, 40, 43–45, 47
religion/religious 4, 11, 19–21, 23, 27–31, 65, 76, 89, 90, 97
reproductive technology 19, 21, 31
rigidity 37, 45, 47, 48
– mental 44
– positional 40
risk 12, 15, 66, 70, 76, 77, 109, 110, 115, 118, 121, 142, 147, 149, 151, 153
risk society 34, 142, 143, 151–153
ritual 3, 5, 11, 12, 15, 50, 73, 76, 89, 90, 96, 143, 145, 149, 150
role passage 150
rolling tents 70
running 96, 97, 99–102

sacred 3, 4, 23, 28, 76, 89
science 2, 3, 8, 11, 12, 15, 24, 31, 33, 34, 51, 53, 61, 87, 152
self-help 12, 50, 51, 53, 61, 62
sensation 57, 75, 82, 83, 127, 130, 139, 146
senses 5, 75, 76, 83
sensory learning 65, 96
sensual pleasure 6
sex 38, 42, 66–68, 77
sex/gender dualism/distinction 7, 53
sexual
– exploitation/trafficking 33, 57
– fulfilment 28
– harassment 57
– organs 51, 53
shooting 37, 97, 99, 102–105
shoulders 48, 101, 132, 135
skills 11–15, 39, 68–70, 89, 97, 99, 104, 106, 122, 123, 126–128, 131, 132, 136
sleep 142–154
– danger 15, 142, 146–149, 151, 153
– deprivation 147, 148, 151, 152
– disorders 146, 152
– medicalisation 15, 152
– reversibility 144, 145
– vulnerability 15, 142–154
smell 54, 58, 75, 76, 82–84
social
– actors 3, 4, 10, 22, 98, 104, 106, 107
– and cultural theory 9, 15, 25
– Comte 'social physics' 3
– facts 3, 87, 91, 92
– forms 4–6
– interaction 3, 4, 22, 40, 81, 84, 85, 93, 96, 97, 100, 101, 106, 146
– life 3, 84, 85, 97, 101, 151, 152
– location 52, 57, 58, 61, 62
– movements 1, 50–52, 61–63
– norms 6, 13, 55, 65, 80, 81, 84, 86, 87, 89, 92, 93, 95–97, 113, 119, 123
– order 2
– power 1, 148
– reproduction 14
– sciences 1, 2, 9, 20, 22, 23, 41, 61, 75, 80
– structures 3, 25, 41, 96, 106, 131
socialization 5, 38, 77, 95, 96, 107, 112, 117, 118
society
– industial 1, 3, 7, 29
– patriarchal 7
– post-industrial 1, 25
socio-economic systems 5, 33
sociological imagination 2, 15
sociological tradition 1, 6, 10–12, 15, 30
soil 75
'somatic society' 30, 31

somatics 7, 37–48
somatophobia 53
species being 2, 5, 25, 42
spitting 85
stem cell research 2, 8, 11, 19–23, 31–35
stomach 67, 95–97, 111–113, 119
structure/agency dualism/distinction 2, 11
subject/object dualism/distinction 2
subjectivity 26, 27, 29, 30, 84, 86, 106
subsidiary awareness 130
suicide 5, 34
swimming 86, 87

Tantra 7
Taoism 7
tasting 75, 82, 83, 111
techne 26, 27
techniques of the body, see body techniques
technology 1, 8–11, 19–35, 48, 51, 56, 151
– of the self 28–30
technology/nature dualism/division 20, 23, 24
technological civilization 23, 26, 27
– determinism 25, 26
technoscience 50, 51
theology 20, 28
therapeutic cloning 11, 21, 31
throat 48, 95, 96
time 26, 29, 62, 70, 71, 74, 85, 91, 92, 99, 100, 102, 103, 105–107, 144
tiredness 113, 144, 147, 150
tools 15, 23, 24, 106, 107, 127, 130
tourism 33, 140
training 14, 20, 28, 29, 43, 45, 46, 74, 90, 95–99, 102–105, 109, 111, 113–118, 122, 138
transcendence 52, 53, 55, 114, 144
transgenderism 8
transplant surgery 2, 8, 31, 56
transsexuality 8
tree climbing 70

vagina 51, 62
veil 73
visceral organs 47, 48

war 3, 24, 28, 30, 31, 38, 41, 42
warrior/warriorhood 41, 45
women of colour 58, 61, 63
women's
– corporeality 7, 12, 50–63
– epistemic agency 12, 50, 52, 54, 58–62
– health activism 12, 50, 52–54, 60, 61
– self-help 12, 50, 51, 53, 61, 62
working class 6, 25, 31, 33, 34, 57, 58
worldly instrumental individualism 6
written texts 12, 25, 27, 56, 65, 77, 102, 103, 105

yoga 7, 46
youth subcultures 38, 89, 90

Zen 7
zoology 19